GW00578084

HUGH GRANT

The Unauthorised Biography

Jody Tresidder

To *Pudding*

Extracts taken from *Money* by Martin Amis (Jonathan Cape), *Bengal Nights* by Mircea Eliade (Carcanet Press Ltd), *The Longest Journey* by E. M. Forster (King's College, Cambridge,
and the Society of Authors as the literary representatives of the E. M. Forster Estate), *Rebecca* by Daphne du Maurier (Curtis Brown), and *Brideshead Revisited* by Evelyn Waugh (Peters Fraser and Dunlop) are reproduced by kind permission.

This edition first published in Great Britain in 1997 by
Virgin Books
an imprint of Virgin Publishing Ltd
332 Ladbroke Grove
London W10 5AH

First published in Great Britain in 1996 by Virgin Publishing Ltd

Copyright © Jody Tresidder 1996

The right of Jody Tresidder to be identified as the author of this work has been asserted by her in accordance with the Copyright Designs and Patents Act 1988.

This book is sold subject to the condition that it shall not, by way of trade or otherwise, be lent, resold, hired out or otherwise circulated without the publisher's prior written consent in any form of binding or cover other than that in which it is published and without a similar condition including this condition being imposed upon the subsequent purchaser.

A catalogue record for this book is available from the British Library.

ISBN 0 7535 0069 8

Typeset by TW Typesetting, Plymouth, Devon
Printed and bound by Mackays of Chatham, Chatham, Kent.

ACKNOWLEDGEMENTS

I wish to thank all those who believe as I do, to merrily misquote Christopher Marlowe, that the past is *not* another country (and that the wench, far from dead, is in truth very much alive and eager to chat!). I am indebted to friends and contemporaries too numerous to list here but I appreciate their help and humour enormously. I owe my most grateful thanks to Cathy Meade for help and friendship beyond compare, Alan Ayres, my sisters Megan Tresidder and Sarah Tresidder, Oscar Moore, Fenton Bailey, Randy Barbato and staff at both the British Film Institute and Huntington Public Library, New York. Also Mal Peachey, my editor at Virgin Publishing, for all his advice and tireless support. Finally, above all, I owe my husband David Stewart. For everything.

ILLUSTRATIONS

PROLOGUE

A Year of Living Famously

New York City, 1 March 1994, 10.30 a.m.

It was a bitterly cold, ominously overcast, Tuesday morning; the rush-hour Manhattan madness was just easing into its daily honking, tyre-screeching, curse-bawling, manic rhythm. Everywhere the city's workers slipped and skidded awkwardly around the huge, iceberg-shaped, yellow grit-stained drifts of old snow – thrown up by the snowploughs that had worked almost round the clock throughout New York since January – which lay in ugly waist-high piles in the gutters, even in Manhattan's exclusive Upper East side. Proof – if any was needed – that one of the most vicious East Coast winters in half a century was no respector of prime real estate. Infuriatingly, yet more heavy flurries were forecast for the afternoon as I trudged determinedly along the Upper East side's Park Avenue . . .

At The Regency Hotel, at Park Avenue and 61st Street, one of the best addresses in the district, business was – despite the appalling weather – even more frantic than usual. Tonight, whether it snowed for the seventeenth time this winter or not, was the 36th Grammy Award night and in 1994 it was New York's turn to host the American music industry's annual extravaganza of mutual back-patting, speechifying and partying. (Since 1991 New York and its arch rival showbusiness capital, Los Angeles, have alternated hosting the prestigious show.)

Every fashionable party venue in the city had been

1

booked long in advance by record companies for the post-awards festivities. Arista Records had nabbed the Plaza (with Carly Simon, Aretha Franklin and 1994's most Grammy-garlanded winner-to-be, Whitney Houston, as guests). EMI got the Museum of Modern Art (with Frank Sinatra in tow – making it the most coveted ticket in town). MCA took the perennially hip restaurant, the Four Seasons. Every limo company was fully booked.

Every major hotel was also packed from basement to penthouse. The Regency – a 400-room leviathan and one of *the* swankiest bolt-holes in the city, famously 'cherished by New York's power élite and their compatriots from across both oceans', to quote the smarmily off-putting words of the guidebooks – was no exception. The hotel's winter overnight rates may start at $275 (that's without breakfast), or $675 if you care for a suite – with every bathroom in the building boasting a TV set in addition to essentials like a refrigerator to keep your facial gel at the correct temperature, a phone and matching robes – but tonight the prices could be tripled and still this snootily luxurious retreat would be untroubled by vacancies.

In addition to soaking up the Grammy trade today, the Regency was simultaneously hosting a major multiple film promotion. Dozens of directors, producers, publicists and their stars had been booked to meet both the American and international press to promote their invariably 'sure-fire smash' spring films, via the journalists' glowing articles, to the world's moviegoers.

On 1 March 1994, with Hollywood and the Grammy circus temporarily in town, New York was truly the only place in the world to be seen.

Outside the hotel's snow-capped awnings that morning – seldom less than three or four deep – sleek fleets of highly polished, pearl-grey stretch limos glided, endlessly, back and forth, back and forth, jostling jealously for prime position outside the Regency's main entrance.

The paparazzi lurked in a frozen huddle a not-so-discreet distance from the Regency, waiting to catch a famous face emerging from the limos. The famous faces –

mostly unrecognizable, if highly conspicuous, beneath Russian-style fur hats, dark glasses and voluminous scarves for the undignified two-second dash from their transport to hotel entrance – escaped largely unsnapped by the photographers. Not one paparazzo even bothered to raise a shutter at the slender dark-haired young man in the classically cut English overcoat when he slipped into the Regency that morning.

Inside the hotel, in the luxurious warmth beyond the plump and beaming doormen, the Regency is gorgeously tricked out in America's favourite 'corporate Louis XVI' style, with carpets that tickle your armpits, lots of gold squiggly detail on the mouldings and chandeliers the size of dinghies in the lavatories. The ceilings are all unnecessarily high. You could comfortably fly a kite in the foyer. Waiters dash about in the celebrated 540 Park Restaurant downstairs with platters of low-fat, low-cholesterol eggwhite omelettes in one white-gloved hand and urgent faxes fluttering anxiously from the other. The place quivered with money, glamour and expectation.

As a journalist I was at the Regency that day for the film promotion. My scheduled interview was with the film star Michael (*Batman*) Keaton and the former childstar TV actor-turned-extremely-successful-director, Ron Howard, who had together just made the film *The Paper*. I was also there to set up further interview times with the stars of the latest *Naked Gun* film – including the actress Priscilla Presley – some months before she made the staggering transformation from Elvis's ex-wife into Michael Jackson's mother-in-law. But I'd excluded – simply because of the smallness of his part in the movie – the then utterly unremarkable elder-sportsman-cum-actor who plays one of the cop sidekicks in the *Naked Gun* films, one O.J. Simpson.

I pressed an 'up' button, randomly, on one of the ranks of elevators just beyond the foyer to reach the 'designated' Michael Keaton/Ron Howard suite. The lift doors opened, to disgorge Michael (*Back to the Future*) J. Fox and Paul (*Crocodile Dundee*) Hogan deep in private discussion.

Each was tirelessly promoting *his* 'sure-fire smash' new film to journalists at the Regency that day. Both films would, in fact, flop dismally. Not that I could have cared at that moment. I was merely delighted at how closely Hogan and Fox resembled their screen images. Some stars do look alarmingly different in the flesh from their cinema selves – an observation that once led me, humiliatingly, to start interviewing a woman who answered Susannah York's door in London, under the mistaken impression that she *was* Susannah York enduring an 'off' day. She was, in fact, the star's blameless housekeeper.

The Regency lift doors closed and I rose. They opened again, and a small mob of chattering journalists walked in. They closed, we rose, and they opened again. Hugh Grant strolled into the lift. He flashed a brilliant smile at the journalists – and gracefully accepted a bouquet of compliments from an overexcited American journalist, who declared, gushingly, that she had just adored him in the 'film about weddings'.

'How terribly sweet of you to say so,' murmured Hugh, shooting off another flashbulb series of adorable grins. Then he did a comic double take as he saw me. The full works – eyebrows shooting dramatically to his hairline, his jaw dropping, arms outstretched in a pantomime of disbelief. We were old friends. Hugh seemed oddly tall, taller than I remembered him from the last London party we'd both recently attended (or possibly his height was emphasized by my excited glimpse of Fox and Hogan, neither one exactly a Harlem Globetrotter). He was extremely pale and draped in a large, dark cashmere overcoat from which a white shirt peeped snowily. He was, I noticed instantly, already starting to take on the suspiciously well-groomed look of a superstar. Film superstars are different from the rest of us. They have the patina of really rich people's lawns: weirdly well-tended. When you gaze at a rich person's lawn, at that velvet expanse of rolled, expensively nourished, cherished perfection, you don't generally think, 'How very like *my* lawn.' You softly whistle to yourself, 'I bet it costs *thousands* to keep it

4

looking that good.' So with Hugh in a New York elevator. I wished desperately that I wasn't wearing my mother's early-eighties red winter coat – the one with the *Dynasty* shoulderpads.

Hugh Grant looked like a million dollars. He looked as if it would take three volumes of *Burke's Peerage* merely to explain how he came by his exquisitely sloping upper lip, let alone the drowsy, rainwater-blue eyes, or the silky perfection of his hair. A slightly tired, bruised-below-the-eyes million dollars, perhaps.

But then he had, although I didn't know it at the time, undergone one of the most exhausting and exhaustive pre-release promotional tours ever carried out for a 'small' British film in aid of *Four Weddings and a Funeral*. Two of his other films, *Sirens* and *Bitter Moon*, were also just about to be released in the USA. Hugh Grant was on the cusp of passing into box-office cinema history – though neither of us could have dreamed that in sixteen months' time the name 'Hugh Grant' would be doing daily battle for space in headlines around the world with that of Orenthal James Simpson.

I was very happy – as ever – to see Hugh Grant and kissed him warmly, and we exchanged family gossip. 'What on earth are *you* doing here in Manhattan?' he asked finally, with an air of great interest.

'Oh, I live in New York now – and I'm interviewing the guy who was Batman,' I replied, asking crassly, 'but what are *you* doing here?'

'Oh I'm promoting one or two films I've done,' Hugh replied, modestly.

Then, everything changed. Hugh Grant – in the Regency's peach-and-violet-tinted number four lift – suddenly froze. His good humour evaporated entirely, as did his wonderful looks. His face closed. His charm fled. His upper lip dwindled to a thin, tight, white line. In the space of a heartbeat, Hugh Grant had flown into a terrible, cold temper.

'Actually, I'm not at all sure I should be speaking to you,' he said loudly. 'I gather you've said some fairly unforgivable things behind my back.' I could feel the crowd of fellow journalists stiffen silently in fascinated curiosity behind *my* back. This is one hell of a public way to tick off an old friend, I thought dimly.

'What do you mean?' I asked, genuinely flummoxed and embarrassed.

'A certain someone passed on a conversation you two had about me in a plane to Los Angeles,' snapped Hugh. 'I think you know who I mean. Quite unforgivable.' His voice rose in volume. 'I've just remembered, I really don't think I wish to talk to you *at all*!'

Then he punched a button – and swept furiously out of the lift. I have no idea whether it was actually his floor. I rather hoped it wasn't.

There was an exquisitely embarrassing silence before the titters began. I travelled, crimson-faced, a further ten floors to meet Michael Keaton.

I talked to Hugh, later that same night, when the switchboard operator at the Regency patched me straight through to his $675 suite without blinking. He and Elizabeth Hurley were indeed attending the Grammys that night of 1 March 1994, at the bash thrown by the distributors of *Four Weddings* – the entertainment giants Polygram – at New York's Rainbow Room in the company of celebrities like Grace Jones and U2's Bono. Our talk began – I thought at the time – reasonably civilly. I apologized profusely for any impression I had given to the British journalist William Cash – that 'certain someone', as I had swiftly worked out – that I remotely disliked Hugh.

'Perhaps I'd said I thought you were a bit vain.' I stumbled hopelessly through this part of my apology. 'But it was nothing I wouldn't have teased you about to your face.'

Hugh agreed that Cash was 'a very queer fish', but it was chillingly clear as the conversation faltered and finally died that I'd been bounced from the list of Hugh Grant's friends.

I had indeed, by unfortunate chance, been seated next to Cash on a flight from New York to Los Angeles just before Christmas 1993. He was returning to his flat in LA, while I was on a working trip to interview the white rap singer and Calvin Klein model Marky Mark. It was the first time I had met Cash – and I sincerely hoped later that it would be the last.

Cash was to be, within a few months of our meeting, himself embroiled in a journalism scandal that generated headlines from London to New York, and made him, briefly, the most notorious journalist in Los Angeles. He'd written about how 'the Jews' controlled Hollywood.

He had not been an ideal random plane-journey companion, to put it mildly. The gangly, hyena-voiced Cash had proved enormously and exhaustingly interested in himself. Chapter by chapter, he took me through the book he'd written about working in Los Angeles, *Educating William*. He told me how he had vomited in a famous author's bedroom.

'You haven't *heard* about me vomiting in a famous author's bedroom? Good grief, let me explain!'

Did I know the gossip columnist Taki? I *didn't*? 'Taki was lovely – but some of the company he kept!' Did I know that Cash was, however (by his own much-mentioned admission), a 'very close' friend of Elizabeth Hurley, Hugh's girlfriend? Oh, she was sweet and was, in fact, picking him up at the airport in Los Angeles! (Though later, in what came to feel like an unbearably lengthy coast-to-coast flight, Cash asked if he might share my lift into the city. Perhaps he was concerned that Elizabeth may have forgotten about him. I don't know.) Elizabeth, added Cash, was 'the best-read girl I know'; but he ruined the polished gallantry of his remark by adding, 'Of course, she has all of the *time* in the *world* to read when she's not working.'

Cash had gossiped very freely during that plane journey. Didn't I think, he probed over our complimentary Bloody Marys, that Hugh was gay? 'He must be, mustn't he?' I said I thought not. It *had* always been my impression that Hugh was rather vain, but then, who wouldn't be with those looks of his? I ventured this thought to Cash.

He had then carried his version of our conversation back to Elizabeth in her flat above Sunset Strip in LA, who had passed it on to Hugh, who had brooded on it in London, and had acted upon it in a New York lift.

This was the very start of Hugh Grant's Year of Living Famously.

In March 1994 Hugh Grant was a chap you could reach at his hotel by the splendidly simple device of asking a hotel receptionist to put you through to his room. By July 1995, Hugh Grant was a figure of international scandal, his glamour simultaneously tainted and enhanced by an act of sexist, arrogant stupidity that had become the subject of explanation, analysis and controversy in every household from Tokyo to Taunton.

March 1994 was also the dawn of Hugh's attempts – duplicated by his girlfriend and later business partner Elizabeth Hurley – to divorce himself from former friends; to excise, often on wrong advice and his own skewed instincts, anyone he felt might not be trusted to promote the Hugh Grant 'myth'. At any cost. In other words, to betray his true nature.

Ironically Hugh did not have to worry about a single one of his friends betraying him.

At 1.30 a.m. in Los Angeles, on Tuesday, 27 June 1995, Hugh Grant betrayed himself.

But that snowy, freezing morning, in one of the Regency hotel's elevators, Hugh Grant had already come, I reflected unhappily at the time, a very, very long way from our home-town London suburb of Chiswick.

CHAPTER
ONE

'Man is born unto trouble as the sparks fly upward.'
Book of Job 5:7

Perhaps the gods of mischief were enjoying a little joke on Friday, 9 September 1960. For Hugh John Mungo Grant was born that day into the most sensational and talked-about sex scandal of post-war Britain. As the infant Hugh Grant drew his first breath, society was agog over revelations of a shocking sexual liaison between a shameless member of the English upper classes and a low-life commoner. The story not only provoked an instant storm of outrage and judgement around the globe but became the *chronique scandaleuse* of the decade.

Hugh Grant managed to accomplish his first, and most significant, entrance within 24 hours of the historic decision by the British government to prosecute the publishers of D.H. Lawrence's infamous work, *Lady Chatterley's Lover*. On 8 September 1960 – the eve of Hugh's birth – the British government squared up to Penguin Books: *Lady Chatterley's Lover* was a repulsively obscene piece of fiction, it had been banned for 32 years, and Penguin had blatantly broken the law by putting it back into print.

Rubbish, retorted Penguin Books. *Lady Chatterley's Lover* was art and therefore beyond comparison with 'ordinary' so-called pornography. In one of the most entertaining trials ever staged at the Old Bailey, 35 prominent men and women of letters, including teachers, publishers, editors, moral theologians and critics, paraded before the court to argue that D.H. Lawrence's notoriously explicit novel about an affair between a married aristocrat and her gamekeeper lover was indeed art.

Penguin Books triumphed. The humiliated British government had lost its case.

Thus Hugh Grant's personal debut coincided prophetically with England's most infamous purveyor of 'lewd' sexual conduct, D.H. Lawrence, on trial by the Establishment and, in the process, generating extremely saucy headlines about the British – and their singular problems with the subject of sexual intercourse and class – around the world.

From the drawing-rooms of Belgravia to the editorial pages of the *New York Times*, across the watering holes of Washington to the beer-slopped saloon bars of English pubs, the hot topic on Hugh Grant's birthday in 1960 was sex, collapsing morals and the strangely scandal-prone British. It would not be the only time Lawrence's novel would enter Hugh's life by any means. And thirty-five years later, of course, Hugh Grant, Britain's poshest screen idol, would find himself in an eerily similar scandal with even bigger headlines, an exquisitely embarrassing starring role, and the debate over what is, and what is not, 'lewd' sexual conduct still raging furiously on both sides of the Atlantic.

Plus ça change, indeed!

Hugh Grant's journey from the role of hamster-cheeked schoolboy raised in the prim London suburb of Chiswick to that of a star player on Hollywood's A list has been one of the most unusual – and drama-dogged – transformations imaginable. If chance or mischance, lucky or unlucky accidents of timing, play a larger part in the careers of actors than they do in those of plumbers or accountants, they assume positively scene-stealing roles in Hugh's case.

Hugh would be barely beyond early childhood himself when he saw a lad from his own stuffily academic school achieve that unlikeliest and most glamorous of elevations for an ordinary British schoolboy – to an overnight film star – when his fellow pupil won the most coveted juvenile movie roles of the decade. Just out of his teens and a complete unknown, Hugh would later find his budding acting talents in the guiding hands of one of the greatest Oscar-winning Hollywood directors – and very soon afterwards, would be confidently assuring astounded friends and college tutors that he was on his own smooth way to Hollywood superstardom, and wouldn't have the time to take his final university exams. In reality, Hollywood wasn't quite ready for the untested Hugh Grant then.

Yet the lure of instant, easily won fame, the elusively, horizon-beckoning St Elmo's fire followed by almost all ambitious, naively optimistic young actors, has been a constant, teasing, infuriating companion for Hugh from his earliest days. Time and again, the promise of fame and recognition danced so close to him they must have seemed his absolute birthright. Yet time and again, chance sent them packing. And when Hugh finally achieved international stardom, much later in his extraordinarily uneven career than many had predicted, he rode it like a greenhorn at his first rodeo.

One moment down in the dust, unseated by the sordid revelations about his encounter with a Los Angeles prostitute, the next up again, waving prankishly at the crowds and demanding that the world applaud his apologies and warm to his chutzpah. Yet there lingered a teasing, secret smirk of defiance behind the actor's televised outpourings of remorse after his arrest. There was an unmistakable echo of Iago's tantalizing refusal to reveal the motivation behind *his* actions. 'Demand me nothing: what you know, you know,' Iago had taunted his bewildered accusers. To those who *did* know Hugh Grant, the manner of his fall from grace was not out of character at all.

The charming, likeable, whimsically self-deprecating Hugh had always co-existed with an Englishman who went up a social mountain at Oxford and came down with a chronic case of arrested development. The outwardly confident Hugh walked hand-in-hand with a profoundly distrustful Hugh who had fretted – since adolescence – that people were attracted to his looks, and not to his true personality. A fear, of course, that his new star status reinforced a thousandfold.

The film star the world crudely assumed 'could have had anyone' that night in June 1995 on Sunset Strip was simultaneously a man to whom, immaturely, the titillating *display* of sexual impropriety was as important as the act itself . . .

On 9 September 1960, however, as even the polite citizens of Chiswick debated the *Lady Chatterley* obscenity trial, Hugh J.M. Grant was being welcomed into the world as the last-born and much-wanted second son of James and Fynvola Grant. An intelligent, solidly middle-class and extremely well-matched couple, James and Fynvola would prove as indulgent with their love for their two little boys – Hughie and his older brother Jamie – as they were strict over their behaviour, schoolwork, appearance and manners. From their earliest years, both Grant brothers knew without question that they could rely on unconditional love and support at their modest, suburban West London home – and that they had the highest maternal standards to meet.

In many ways, James and Fynvola Grant gave young Hugh and his brother Jamie – born two years earlier – an upbringing that owed far more to the just departed, steadier-seeming decade of the fifties, than to the swinging, socially mobile sixties. The nurturing, apron-wearing role went to Hugh's mother; the more distant, daily commuting, breadwinning role, to his father, who had been in the army before entering the office carpeting business. But Fynvola's income as a primary school teacher did become important to the family's increasingly rocky finances in the seventies, and friends also describe her, rather than Hugh's father, as providing 'the central stability – the moral backbone' to the family.

The Grants' world was, above all, a safe one, cosy and reassuringly familiar – the family have never moved from their home in Sutton Lane, in the pleasant, leafy West London suburb of Chiswick. Chiswick was not, as Hugh was growing up, an especially fashionable suburb, even if it did have its own claims to fame before its status as the birthplace of Hollywood's hottest newcomer of the nineties. For the most part, Chiswick slumbers quietly on the Oxford-and-Cambridge boat race stretch of the Thames river, an occasionally picturesque, mainly unpretentious, district of Edwardian and Victorian family houses, parks and shops.

Noticeably better preserved than its more raffish upstream neighbour, Hammersmith, Chiswick can boast one unique feature. It is home to England's original Palladian country house. The very first one. Familiar to many generations of local pupils on endless school 'cultural appreciation' outings – including Hugh and Jamie – Chiswick House is a small-scale, composite copy of Italy's famous Palladio villas. Built by the influential arts patron Lord Burlington as a sort of early-eighteenth-century 'show home', Chiswick House sparked the century's greatest architectural craze with every landed family in England stampeding to construct bigger and flashier copies for themselves all over the shires – creating the quintessential English country landscape look of today.

It was, in fact, exactly the creamily posh theme-park look of Britain that the film that would bring Hugh international fame, *Four Weddings*, exploited to the hilt. The distractingly aristocratic-looking adult Hugh Grant may not have been born with anything like a country house to call his own, but at least he could claim he grew up with Britain's original colonnaded mansion practically in his own back yard.

While Chiswick, too, was never exactly Tinseltown-on-Thames (Hugh is almost certainly the suburb's first international screen idol), it had at least once enjoyed a distinctly Bohemian reputation – as a stomping-ground for artists and writers in the nineteenth century. The Pre-Raphaelite artist and poet William Morris once lived on the river, while the Irish playwright and poet W.B. Yeats also lived in Chiswick as a schoolboy – and even attended the Godolphin school, sister school of Latymer, which Hugh would so memorably attend, before it became an all-female, eye-wateringly expensive enclave. (Yeats

13

loathed Godolphin, complaining bitterly of being exposed to 'the rough manners of a cheap school', which probably explains why he isn't mentioned in the Godolphin prospectus today.)

But if not a popularly fashionable area in the sixties, Chiswick – with its villagey, friendly, stolidly respectable air – suited the Grants very well. Their Edwardian terraced house in Sutton Lane overlooks one of the countless, small, pretty patches of preserved parkland that still dot urban London, Turnham Green and where Jamie and Hugh – in the sixties – could roam safely. Or perhaps only comparative safety: Hugh delights in recounting one bizarre memory from his childhood. His mother, he insists, once instructed that he behave extremely politely to a local man accused of murdering his wife – and of then distributing her dismembered body parts about a golf course. Fynvola Grant, he claims, so sternly disapproved of prejudging people, no matter how heinous the accusation, she made it a special point of honour for her sons to greet Chiswick's Dr Crippen with studied civility. When it turned out the man was indeed guilty – 'He'd left her head in the lost luggage department of Waterloo Station,' Hugh told one interviewer – it was, he said cheerfully, 'a seminal experience for me.' However in Sutton Lane, for the most part, the Grants were flanked not by wife-murderers but by harmless hard-working, decent, firmly rooted, middle-class neighbours who were always happy to keep an eye out for the young Grant brothers.

Hugh's parents, his schoolteacher mother and bookish carpet-salesman father had, moreover, a special reason to feel particularly fond of Sutton Lane. Their house was next door to the apartment block – Arlington Park Mansions – famously tenanted by the great novelist E.M. Forster. Forster had fled to Chiswick in 1940, on the advice of friends, to find a safe bolt-hole from the bombs blitzing central London. It would be – quite by charming chance, of course – the film version of E.M. Forster's novel about homosexual love, *Maurice*, that would provide Hugh's first professional big-screen, co-starring role and bring him to the serious attention of the world's critics. For Hugh's parents, who were well aware of the pleasant literary connections of their small corner of Chiswick, it was a delightful coincidence that their film star son had spent his childhood and adolescence following in E.M. Forster's footsteps.

Both Jamie and Hugh had bestowed upon them traditional family names, responsible godparents, a stay-at-home mother with an unshakeable belief in family values, family pride and the virtues of hard work, propriety and loyalty. To outsiders and friends, the Grant family always appeared unusually and enviably close. They were infamous among their relatives for indulging in a quaintly old-fashioned, private family addiction of giving playfully 'silly' names to ordinary things, like 'choccy moos' for hot chocolate drinks.

'It was a pretty wordy household, you know, silly word games, endless daft nicknames for each other, and James [Hugh's father] making horrible puns,' said one old family friend, adding, 'I would say it was a happy family with a great deal of love and a great deal of pride.'

This habit of gleefully giving people nicknames and retaining a fondness for childish banter is one that has persisted with Hugh – to the amusement and, sometimes, annoyance of friends – long into his adulthood. It is also one that was to land him, famously, in hot water just as his acting career was soaring. The staff of a three-star Welsh country hotel in Llanwddyn, Powys, the Lake Vyrnwy, were hurt and dumbfounded to discover that their star guest from the summer of 1994 had turned them into a gallery of comic buffoons in an interview given to the American magazine *GQ* in December that year. Labelling them variously Serial Killer, Fatty Breather – the individual was reportedly suffering from terminal lung disease – and Breathy Giant, Hugh even mocked the food the hotel served him while he was filming on location for *The Englishman Who . . .*, describing one baked vegetable dish as Farmer's Crusty Underpants. The joke, of course, backfired. Hugh emerged less a Nabokovian wit than a

Janus-faced bounder when the hotel revealed how hard it had tried to accommodate the star's requests for an American-made video recorder and late-night meals, even sending on a forgotten pair of his duck-motif green pyjamas. Instead of glorying in his new status as the USA's *GQ* cover star Hugh found himself having to apologize grovellingly to the hotel. Yet it wasn't Hugh's new-found fame, as the hotel's outraged manager complained to the press, that had prompted him to make unkind 'comments about everyday people', it was simply that his audience had grown larger than the recreation grounds of Chiswick. For even at the tender age of seven, childhood friends recall, Hugh had revelled in mimicking 'funny' accents and speech impediments, despite his mother's constant admonishments that it wasn't 'nice'.

Family friends insist there was 'no question' of Hugh's mother going out to work when her sons were young – even though the phenomenon of working mothers was swiftly gaining ground in sixties Britain.

'I don't think [Mrs Grant] would have thought twice about that. James was doing fine at work. She was there for the boys after school and she was a very, very good mother,' says one family friend firmly. 'If anything, she stayed at home with the boys longer than many of the rest of us. There was no question where her priorities were.'

Grant, incidentally, is not an upper-class surname. And, despite repeated assertions to the contrary made on Hugh's behalf as his fame has grown, and as his beautifully modulated voice has helped to capture so many hearts, the Grants of Chiswick, West London, are not an upper-class family. If you define the ever-slippery classification of 'class' in modern Britain in terms of address, social standing, income, choice of children's schools, values and occupation, the Grants are supremely, smack-in-the-middle middle-class. Grant is simply a surname that is far from uncommon in Scotland and which, in all probability, originally comes from the Anglo-Norman 'graund' of 'graunt', meaning tall or large of stature.

Norman nicknames (the basis for many British surnames today) were seldom strikingly imaginative at the best of times. When it came to handing out names, if you weren't a Mr Tall or a Mr Large, you were bound to be a Mr Short or a Mr Thin. Or – very occasionally and quite inexcusably offensively – one might be saddled with a surname like Grayling, meaning Mr Pock-Marked Face. Hugh's unusual middle name – Mungo – is also traditionally Scottish. It is the official byname – or nickname – of the amiable sixth-century Apostle Saint Kentigern, the patron saint of Glasgow.

All things considered, the future international heartthrob and 1995's *succès de scandale* got off lightly with Grant. He was fortunate, too, that, when it came time for him to apply for his Equity card in order to join the compulsory actors' union after university, he was able to do so in his own birth name. Quite frequently, when an actor reaches this step, he'll discover he has no right to what he has always considered to be *his* name because someone else who once played third stranger for one episode of a TV series started using it professionally first. (As one Michael Hugh Johnson found, when he too turned to acting after Oxford. Another actor had beaten him to his name so he dropped the middle name Hugh and pinched the surname York from a new brand of cigarettes.)

It can be very frustrating. But Hugh was lucky. If there were other Hugh Grants out there, he was the first of this élite brotherhood to begin acting professionally. And, of course, it would later prove a useful touch to marketing Hugh's image that another British actor, born Archibald Alec Leach in Bristol in 1904, had had the supreme good sense to seize – quite randomly – on the screen name Cary Grant before *he* popped up as Hollywood's 1940s debonair screen idol.

Hugh's mother, Fynvola – *her* unusual, lyrical name is, of course, as Scottish as haggis – was one of four sisters (née Maclean, a respectable, comfortably off naval family) who obligingly furnished the London Grants with a large number of Scottish cousins to play with over the years.

Friends recall the Grants' family home being regularly overrun by the Scottish relatives at holidays; and Hugh maintains reasonably close friendships with several male cousins to this day – relying on them for unquestioning loyalty, if not for day-to-day advice.

Yet the London Grants were not as financially well-off as many of their relatives. While other branches of the family prospered in business – and sent their sons to Eton – the Chiswick Grants were doomed to remain comparatively poorly off. This would affect Hugh – and his brother – keenly.

The Scottish family background strongly affected Hugh in other ways too. (The slightly sinister motto of that country is: *nemo me impune lacessit*, or no one injures me with impunity.) Indeed, it is partly due to the legacy of spending holidays with their Scottish kin that both Hugh, and his elder brother, James Murray, are accomplished Scottish reelers. Hugh in particular is also a fleet-footed country dancer. Yet their dancing skills were not something that either of the Grant boys especially boasted about when they were young. For various reasons, most middle-class Londoners persist in finding the idea of young men learning formal dance steps – to be performed in nineteenth-century costume of very dubious origin to the skirl and drone of bagpipe music – deeply mirth-provoking.

That's why those who have mastered the art – like Hugh – sensibly indulge in private, on ancestral tartan turf, as it were, and among their own kind, or not at all. Even as a young boy, Hugh was learning to keep these two slightly frictional sides – the traditional Scottish and the streetwise West London – safely separate. As indeed he would later keep other, conflicting, sides of his own personality quietly apart.

As well as having a great many relatives north of the border, which gave them no social cachet whatsoever as they grew up in London, the Grant brothers also had a close branch of the family based in then exotic South Africa, of which both Jamie and Hugh were sweetly and vociferously proud when they were young, as if it did make them appear a touch more glamorous to school-friends.

Hugh's father, James Grant senior was, and is, recalled by Hugh's friends as kind, bookish, highly articulate and gently amusing. A natural charmer by all reports, with a playful sense of humour, he was a man who could also appear vague to a degree verging on eccentricity to Hugh's schoolmates. 'You wouldn't trust him to remember your name, but Hugh's mother always did,' a childhood school-friend of Hugh's recalls. 'He was always very nice, but would look a bit surprised that you were there [at the house] to play with Hugh. But, of course, you didn't really notice anyone's parents unless they were appalling. Hugh's dad was just a bit remote, but quite okay.'

James Grant senior worked, not with what one might call overwhelming enthusiasm, as an executive salesman for the London headquarters of a UK carpet company – selling carpets to new firms and expanding companies just at a time when Britain was lurching towards the recession of the early seventies. It was, unfortunately, one of the least recession-proof businesses in which to be involved – and a disastrous one for anyone less than completely committed. James Grant senior was not. The fact that the business was not successful and strained the family's bank balance cruelly as Hugh was growing up is one of the most enduring and deeply felt influences on the actor today – and indeed on his older brother.

More than anything else, it seems to have informed Hugh's early choice of acting roles, his extreme sensitivity – and reactions – to snobbery based on financial status, his brother's powerful ambitions to succeed as a banker, and their deep shared horror at the prospect of ever finding themselves scraping along in the discreet hell of genteel, middle-class penny-watching.

Yet this was not simple-minded materialism. Hugh wasn't driven to achieve simply to outdo, to out-earn his parents. He and his brother both saw – Hugh perhaps more acutely than Jamie – the chronically disappointing effect of lack of family money on their dreamy, charming father's real passion (his higher calling, as the family regarded it) to paint watercolour landscapes.

Hugh spent his formative years watching his father struggling unhappily in a job he wasn't gifted to perform and did not enjoy – selling carpets – while fantasizing about being able to fulfil artistic ambitions to paint full-time. That was a risk he couldn't afford to take with a family to raise. To lack the money to do what you wished and were almost certainly talented enough to do was a soul-destroying trap of the ghastliest kind, Hugh learnt early. To be doubly trapped, by the responsibilities of a growing family and a mortgage pushing your dream even further out of reach, was – he saw – even crueller. Although Hugh has never commented publicly about the effect of his father's failed ambitions on his own drive to succeed, and to attain absolute, even excessive, financial security for himself, it figures greatly in his personality.

Money was tight enough in the Grant household to acquire a kind of false glamour for Hugh. Although, too, Hugh's own background could not seem more ostensibly different from that of a first-generation immigrant fired with ambitions to make the family fortune, he was only too aware of the sacrifices his parents had made on his behalf and of the perennial scrabbling around for money he saw at home. The round-cheeked, blue-eyed, sharp-as-a-tack and popular little boy many of Hugh's childhood friends remember was also a little boy who would break down in inconsolable, guilty tears if his expensive school blazer got accidentally ripped.

Hugh's mother, Fynvola, or Fyn as she was known to her friends, was, and remains, a respected and much-loved London primary-school teacher, employed at an Asian school near Heathrow Airport. More than that, she is sharp, say friends, opinionated, justly critical, and seemed determined to instil early in her sons the confidence that they were every bit as 'good' as wealthier relations, family money problems notwithstanding. If there is more than a touch of genteel snobbery in this attitude, it is leavened by friends' opinions that she also valued 'self-achievement very highly'.

'She was ambitious for both Jamie and Hughie, of course, but no more, really, than any other good mother,' says one old friend. 'She simply wanted them to achieve their potential as children, which is probably what makes her a very good primary school teacher. She was always there for school events for the boys, very, very supportive. In some ways she had to be extra supportive because [Hugh's father] wasn't quite so involved.'

The obvious place to begin looking for the source of an individual's astonishing good looks is, of course, the parents. Generally this is a poignant dead end. Movie stars' parents are seldom any better-looking than anyone else's parents. In comparison with their gleaming movie-star progeny, in fact, these parents often look far more ordinary than other people's parents.

James and Fyn Grant buck this trend. They were an immensely appealing couple in their own younger years. Hugh's father was blond, rugged, open-faced, bubbly-haired and handsome, and a keen amateur sportsman. His mother was much darker and quietly well put together, delicate in build and very beautifully spoken. Not that either of them, say friends, ever appeared even remotely aware of their own physical charms.

Fynvola Grant, in particular, is remembered as always dressing in a conspicuously unobtrusive manner, if such a style is imaginable. At any rate, very much in the style of a primary school teacher: with extremely neat and well-cared-for skirts and blouses, flat shoes, little make-up, an unchanging hairstyle, no bold colours, a lovely, warm smile. 'A really terrific listener,' says one old friend. 'Tremendously proud of her boys. Oh yes, very bright, with an arch turn of phrase – but no sarcasm.'

Yet the other general rule about very good-looking parents and their children doesn't hold true either in the case of the Grants. When both parents are attractive they seem, all too frequently, to produce markedly peculiar-looking children. Or, even more embarrassing, one absolute stunner and one total dud. By some blessed division of genes, Hugh ended up taking almost entirely after their mother's finest physical qualities and Jamie, their father's.

Hugh inherited their mother's frailer, finer-boned features and very thick, silky hair. 'Even in the shape of his face and in the set of his eyes, you can see his mother quite clearly,' says one old school friend. Jamie, meanwhile, took after their father very closely, inheriting his more robust, square-jawed features. The result was two devastatingly lovely boys.

Jamie Grant was, by common if reluctant consent, the 'golden boy' heart-throb of the school both he and Hugh attended, Latymer School. When Jamie left, Hugh – even more gallingly – instantly took his place and the title. Latymerians were, on the whole, grateful that the Grant parents had called a halt, reproductively speaking, at two boys.

The resemblance between Hugh and his mother is becoming even more pronounced as he matures. Hugh has even taken to grumbling mildly that all he sees *is* his mother when he looks in the mirror. They were also – as mothers and younger sons often are – especially close, and tuned into each other's sharp sense of humour, and remain so today. Friends also recall that, contrary to the assertion that Hugh suddenly emerged at Oxford with an entirely fake posh accent, from their early boyhood both Jamie and Hugh spoke exactly and stubbornly in the ringing cut-glass accents of their parents – and their mother in particular.

'It is true,' says one early-childhood friend, 'that both Jamie and Hugh had more up-market accents than the rest of us, but they *always* had them. They got kidded about the way they talked almost from the first day of school and neither of them cared at all. It wasn't an affectation: they got it from home. Their mother spoke incredibly clearly – almost as if she was making a point of it. Maybe' – this was added with the air of an afterthought – 'it was *because* she was a primary school teacher.' Though many middle-class youngsters do go through standard phases of affecting the rougher accents of classmates in order to bond with them, Jamie and Hugh never did – almost as a point of principle.

The abiding memory of the very young Hughie – he was known by the affectionate diminutive by friends and family alike and began, mildly, to insist on 'Hugh' only at university – is of a normal, naughty, soccer-mad boy, sometimes at the mercy of his strong-willed, older brother, but quick to hold his own in fights.

'Unusually well-mannered? Well, I don't remember that,' laughed one mother whose sons grew up with the Grant brothers. 'He was quite the little vicious shin-kicker – I can still recall the bruises on my sons' legs!'

Yet Hugh is also remembered as an introspective child, in striking contrast to his big brother.

Where Jamie seemed comparatively straightforward and easy, outgoing and affable and loud, Hugh sometimes appeared the reverse. Family friends say, carefully, that Fyn was 'more protective and watchful' of Hughie than she was of Jamie. He was, said one, 'altogether a more complicated package'. He was quieter, more insular and observant. Happy, certainly, but not especially prone to sharing confidences. Like many second children, with a notably confident older sibling, Hugh – say family friends – appeared to mature faster than his brother, locking himself, almost from toddlerhood, into a permanent, breathless race to 'catch up' with Jamie and grumpily resenting that Jamie, through his seniority in age, inevitably got to do everything first.

Although Hugh's extraordinary physical charms would become one of his greatest assets – and millstones – as both an adolescent and as an actor, these were not at all apparent when he was very young. He grew from being noticeably slighter than his sturdier brother into a slope-shouldered, round-faced, almost chipmunk-cheeked lad with a toothy, goofy grin and a vaguely Beatles-inspired haircut.

No one disputes, though, that both boys enjoyed

anything but absolute security at home and an ideal, suburban childhood with friends and schools within easy walking and public transport reach. They were articulate, able and, like most schoolboys, never seen with a book in their hands when a football could do just as well.

They were also – as the offspring of middle-class parents – showered with every intellectual, sporting and artistic encouragement, museum, cinema and pantomime visits, and weekend country walks. Hugh has never referred to his own childhood as anything but well-balanced and happy – if littered with the corpses of countless beloved pets, from goldfish to gerbils.

Still, it is Jamie who is remembered as being confident and upfront, and more obviously personable, while Hugh hung back more shyly. The brothers are also remembered for getting on 'entirely as normal' – bitter physical fights one moment, best friends again the next, and complaining furiously about each other a moment later. There was in later years, however, a fifth, rather less reputable member of the Grant household who was considered, not entirely unkindly, as something of a neighbourhood joke: this was an enormous, overweight ginger tomcat by the name of Wussy (rhymes with pussy), for which both Hugh and Jamie appeared to feel, or perhaps genuinely felt, an enormous affection.

It has to be said that Chiswick was not one of the most swinging parts of London in which to be raised. It was very safe (as long as you avoided the Hogarth roundabout subway after dark), leafy, white, middling prosperous and quite well contented with itself. It was one of the last places near to the centre of London where early closing on Wednesdays or Thursdays persisted, to the convenience of nobody but sniggering local shopkeepers.

Heavy Metal passed Chiswick by. Punk passed Chiswick by. New Romanticism passed Chiswick by. Beatlemania probably passed Chiswick by. It is possibly no coincidence that all these fads also passed Hugh John Mungo Grant by, too.

'Hugh,' says one old friend, 'was one of the least

fad-conscious – apart from football, which *was* an obsession – boys I knew. They didn't watch much television in their house; their parents were old-fashioned about that. Hugh read an awful lot of old boys' annuals and later classics like P.G. Wodehouse, but I can't remember him ever having a thing about this or that pop star.'

Fate, however, lay just around the corner.

TWO

'The school has a fine tradition of excellent dramatic productions, aiming to give everyone the chance to participate in productions both on stage and behind the scenes. Some current pupils are involved in television and films, with several Old Boys making successful careers in this field.'

Latymer Upper School prospectus, 1994

'Look at Winchester. Look at the traditional rivalry between Eton and Harrow. Tradition is of incalculable importance if a school is to have any status.'

The Longest Journey, E.M. Forster

From the day Hugh Grant sidled through the portals of London's Latymer School at the age of eight, his future as an actor was assured. The famous Hugh may often leave the impression that he tumbled into acting by accident as if his choice of career was all vaguely puzzling, but this sits uncomfortably with the fact that Latymer was, beyond doubt, the most conspicuously star-struck, mainstream school in West London.

While the younger pupils at other leading British schools worshipped the senior boys who snatched victory on the cricket or rugger grounds, or were elected to élite sixth-form clubs, like Pop at Eton, or Winchester's Old Croquet Society, Latymer's school heroes were first and foremost those who strutted their stuff on stage. Or more dazzling still, as an impressionably young Hugh witnessed first-hand, rocketed to overnight fame in the movies. Popularity and success in drama were twinned inextricably at Latymer. This – with Latymer's distinctly uneasy image of itself as a 'posh' school and a crucial mentor relationship with a flamboyantly stylish English master – was all to prove a formidable influence on the young Hughie.

Latymer School is in London's Hammersmith district, with its Prep Department for boys up to eleven set in lushly landscaped gardens nearby on Hammersmith Mall and overlooking the broad, grey, timeless ribbon of the Thames.

Latymer was – and remains – an imposing, pompously gabled red-brick Victorian construction surrounded by a rather showy ten-foot-high wall of iron railings and Gothic arches. Catering to the brighter sons of west and south-west London and trading under the gently reassuring school motto *Paulatim ergo certe* – which roughly translates as 'slowly but surely', a rather fitting description of Hugh's early professional career – Latymer was something of a hybrid. Though its boards of governors frequently include a sprinkling of Fellows of Oxford and Cambridge and, on occasion, the odd Nobel prizewinner, its Old Boys do not routinely pop up in later years as ruling members of the British Establishment. Its high achievers are altogether a quirkier crew. This is partly because Latymer is *not* a public school. There are no boarders. No archaic wall games, quaint uniforms, or boys sporting flower-covered straw hats on founders' day, as at Eton.

Yet, in common with the great public schools, it was founded (in 1624) specifically for the education of poor boys. As with the public schools, too, this fine aim fell dramatically by the wayside. Latymer is now in the same bracket, if purely in terms of fees, as many minor public schools, with a term's tuition, plus extras, approaching two thousand pounds sterling. (And, should one wonder out loud what happened to the idea of educating the poor, the school points indignantly to its Governors' Bursaries and Government Assisted Places schemes as if this were precisely what its seventeenth-century benefactor Edward Latymer had in mind all along.)

While Hugh was a pupil, Latymer went through a significant upheaval. It changed from a grammar school into a fully independent school. Or, as its beadily status-conscious pupils saw it, changed from being slightly posh to definitely posh. Hugh took the latter definition to heart. Until his sixteenth year – 1976 – Latymer was a popular, academically demanding, direct-grant grammar, more or less assuring places to clever boys who lived locally, whatever their parents' income. If parents couldn't afford the fees, the local education authority footed the bill.

In 1976, Latymer became independent; that meant *all* parents had to contribute towards the increasingly hefty fees. It was finally in the private sector – yet considered, gallingly, to be not nearly as superior as the loftier St Paul's Boys' School nearby, with which it was now in open competition. On the other hand, Latymer's sporting fixtures were traditionally mainly against comprehensive schools. These, in turn, judged the largely middle-class Latymerians to be extremely posh and stuck-up – with the legend 'Latymerians are pooves' occasionally mysteriously painted on the school's playing-fields (and presumably supplied, as sniggering Latymerians guessed, by less literate comprehensive school opposition). The late sixties and early seventies were a curiously schizophrenic time in the school's history, which seemed to feed the young Hughie's uncertain sense of just who he was.

Posh by some standards, and not by others, Latymer did assuredly aspire to some public school conventions. Instead of Pop (as at Eton), Latymer boasted a series of strictly hierarchical in-school dramatic societies, portentously named for England's medieval drama guilds, which offered its pupils a training in drama that was virtually unparalleled outside stage schools. After graduating from the Prep School drama clubs, the school's youngest lads acted as Apprentices, then later as Journeymen – after the roving bands of actors who travelled from town to town in seventeenth-century Restoration Britain after Charles II had given them back their charters. (These had been removed by the killjoy Oliver Cromwell; it was no accident at academic Latymer that acting also provided the pupils with a lively lesson in history.)

The clubs even had their own vocabulary: members of 'the Pageant' were the stagehands as distinct from actors; and 'the Jantaculum' meant the Friday-night revue shows. Acting with the Apprentices and Journeymen brought Hugh under the wing of the first of a succession of older, male, mentor figures who would have a significant impact on his life. The first was the tall, rake-thin and dashingly elegant Middle School English master, Colin Turner, who died at the age of 56 in 1990.

Drama at Latymer had flourished for decades – the oldest and most senior of the school's societies, the Gild, was established 70 years ago, long before Colin Turner's exuberant rule. But its extraordinary and unusual prominence during Hugh's years was largely thanks to Colin Turner. And although there were other English staff, too, who helped to mould the young Hugh Grant, Colin Turner seems to have made the deepest impression, an impression that runs deeper than Hugh would perhaps like to admit.

Colin Turner was, pupils recall, a master whose famously pungent aftershave fumes often left boys histrionically staggering in his wake along the school's highly polished corridors. Naturally, the urbane English teacher was only too coolly aware of the fact, spinning on his heel to catch a miscreant in mid-comic-stagger and delivering an appropriately flattening quip. Then in his late thirties, Colin Turner was, without question, a wonderful asset to Latymer, the school's very own inspirational, if sharp-tongued, Mr Chips. He was one of those rare masters with instinctive access to the inner lives of young boys, especially those he personally favoured. Even to boys, unlike Hugh, who failed to shine at English, he demonstrated a deft touch. 'He'd approve you reading a Len Deighton thriller as much as any other book,' recalls one pupil fondly.

Colin Turner was also known for his habit of coaxing the most unorthodox opinions about English literature from pupils – then insisting that the boy who agreed with him supply a lively argument in defence. 'Convince me,

29

lad!' he'd demand brightly, as the class sat back in grinning anticipation of one of their own tying himself in knots attempting to outsmart the infinitely more clever Colin Turner. The watchful, intensely competitive Hugh absorbed these lessons well. Colin Turner was an old-style, endlessly enthusiastic master with a much-mimicked ironic wit and the absolute conviction that 'drama has to grow out of what you are doing' and shouldn't be taught as a special subject.

To Colin Turner, the value of drama to very young boys could scarcely be overestimated. He saw it as survival training for the minefield of pubescence, granting lads a focus for emerging energies and aggressions, channelling their boisterous need for self-expression and forcing them to imagine being inside someone else's skin just as their own personalities were coming to the fore. Drama at Latymer under Colin Turner was made a part of, rather than an optional extra to, the compulsory English curriculum; it was an inescapable, central aspect of school life.

Colin Turner was also notorious for unconcealed favouritism. A lifelong bachelor and childless himself, he was openly available to boys of quick wit, agreeable looks and engaging character. To the right boys, Colin Turner was as an avuncular mentor after school hours, creating something of a salon for long flattering chats about the latest London plays, travel and art; and, as the boys rose through the school, he encouraged them to talk about their ambitions and future careers. Colin Turner was also partly responsible for encouraging the acting career of the Old Latymerian and former Royal Shakespeare Company stalwart Alan Rickman, the scene-stealing Sheriff of Nottingham opposite Kevin Costner's Robin Hood in the 1991 film *Prince of Thieves*. The British comedian Mel Smith, whose partner Griff Rhys Jones would later employ Hugh, was another Latymer Old Boy protégé. (The precedent for the cultured, dry-witted bachelor schoolteacher as a mentor to actors is not an unusual one by any means. Richard Burton always gave full credit for his career to the stage-struck bachelor schoolteacher and mentor, Philip

Burton, and another Oxford-educated film star, Michael York, in his autobiography *Accidentally on Purpose*, lays his success firmly at the feet of an influential and wonderfully urbane grammar school bachelor art master, Grahame Drew.)

The lively and attractive Hugh, say friends firmly, was absolutely a Colin Turner favourite. More than that, they recall, Hugh sought to style himself on Colin Turner, who was, unquestionably, among Latymer's 'posher' masters, one of a handful of senior staff who gave the school its air of having more in common with a public school than was strictly justified.

If Turner, with his arch vocabulary and mannerisms, sometimes gave the impression that he fancied he was employed at the fictional Greyfriars of the *Magnet* comic fame rather than a boys' school on Hammersmith's main shopping street, Hugh took his cue accordingly. As he progressed through the school, Hugh, too, delighted in affecting an arcane vocabulary – 'spiffing' and 'don't be so beastly!' – and twitting his peers as if he, too, was a Greyfriars character. It was an affectation that both amused and sometimes wearied his friends. There are even echoes in some of Hugh's fruitier utterances to journalists – 'I quite like people to be charming, to be stylish; I don't really care if it *means* anything, it's enough in itself' – that uncannily recall Colin Turner's own stagy, aphoristic delivery.

At Latymer, the young Hughie also gained an early lesson about the glamour of acting. It was a madly excited and envious nine-year-old Hugh Grant who, say friends, saw a fellow Latymerian scooped up by the movies. In 1970, the talented, broodingly pretty Dominic Guard hit the jackpot of juvenile roles when he won the title part in the film, *The Go-Between*.

The overnight transformation of Dominic from just another drama-clubbing, chubby-faced Latymer schoolboy into big-screen child star in the achingly romantic adaptation of L.P. Hartley's Edwardian tale swept the corridors of Latymer with an epidemic of longing. Everyone wanted to be Dominic Guard up there on the screen alongside the established British luminaries Julie Christie and Alan Bates. (As they all did all over again five years later when Dominic went on to co-star in the smash Australian movie, *Picnic at Hanging Rock*.)

For the time being, however, Hugh had to content himself with being a star of the Journeymen, where the emphasis was mainly on 'fun' acting. In the weekly club meetings the younger boys threw themselves into improvizations, debates, games and sketches. Hugh's quick wits and physical agility rapidly made him a prominent Journeyman, winning him a leading and memorably knockabout part – as Nagis the Dwarf in the Lower School play. Yet another Colin Turner protégé, a promising lad named Simon Kunz, was in the chorus of this play and would also pursue a successful professional acting career. (Simon Kunz appears in *Four Weddings*, playing one of the victims of Hugh's character's social gaffes.) Hugh also excelled at the Journeymen debates, thriving under intense peer pressure to be as cutting and funny as possible in an atmosphere that was not unlike a very short-trousered House of Commons.

In addition to the 'fun' acting, Hugh and his mates also gained valuable early training in the classic stage techniques. They were schooled in standard relaxation exercises – lying in giggling and farting heaps on the classroom floor while trying valiantly to concentrate on 'nothing' – and taking part in music, movement and mime exercises.

Yet, even though masters openly encouraged boys to audition for juvenile roles in West End productions (Hugh didn't manage to get any parts), the school maintained a strong contempt for 'stage schools'. The reason for this was Latymer's proximity to West London's Corona private drama school. Though there was little if any formal contact between the two schools, pupils did bump into one another at Ravenscourt Park, which was a mere 100 metres from Latymer's gates. Ravenscourt Park, then a sooty strip of bushes, tennis courts and narrow dog-fouled cycling paths, was also the nearest tube station for both Latymer and Corona, and pupils from the latter were all too easily identifiable. They not only wore egg-yolk-yellow socks and algae-green blazers, but could often be observed ostentatiously tap-dancing to loudly hummed Broadway tunes on the station platform. Hugh and his friends despised the Corona pupils both as appalling show-offs and for their assumed sin of pretentiousness.

The boys' school was every bit as stage-struck as Corona of course, but the idea of nakedly proclaiming your ambition to be a star by enrolling full-time at a special drama school and wearing showy custard-and-pea-coloured uniforms was anathema to Latymerians. Latymerians were naturally only too aware that Corona couldn't boast any pupil to compare to the legendary Dominic Guard. Braver boys would occasionally taunt Corona pupils with this fact, deriving enormous satisfaction from watching them run away in fright.

With Colin Turner's frequently expressed creed that drama should come out of what you are already doing – and not be taught separately – also drummed into him, Hugh had powerful reasons indeed for later rejecting the option of drama school.

THREE

'The star of the show was undoubtedly Hughie Grant . . .'
Hugh's first school rave review, 1975

'Hugh Grant . . . overdid the moustache and dumbness – this was too crude a lover . . .'
Hugh's last not-so-rave school review, 1978

'I was at school with him. You wouldn't believe it, but in those days people used to say he was a little bitch; just a few unkind boys who knew him well. Everyone in pop liked him, of course, and all the masters. I expect it was really that they were jealous of him. He never seemed to get into trouble.'

Anthony Blanche on the character of Sebastian Flyte, Brideshead Revisited

As an academically diligent pupil, who excelled at English, represented the school on the *Top of the Form* quiz show, played rugby and cricket with commendable zeal and was fast gaining a reputation for his acting skills, Hugh enjoyed a charmed and protected position at Latymer.

'It was all kings and courtiers with Hugh and his friends, the further they went up the school, with Hugh as king,' says one contemporary.

Many of his fellow pupils, though, have far less-golden memories of the school. Bullying was perennially a serious problem and the lot of boys who didn't remotely enjoy acting was a miserable one. The masters, too, were the usual uneven mix of the quick and the half-dead, the competent, the dyspeptic and the downright peculiar who remain frozen in the memories of their former day pupils as caricatures whom they imagined vanishing into thin air the moment the last bell of the day was rung, and being resurrected in time for morning assembly. For pupils, too, who weren't 'in' with the posh masters, as Hugh always was, Latymer could be an unforgivingly cliquey school. Many were grateful, for that reason, that Latymer wasn't a boarding school and that home was a mere bus ride away at the end of the day.

Hugh's charmed position, however, did not make him immune from teasing. He was ragged mercilessly by his own set for his girlishly pretty features.

'I think you could safely say,' says one of his old friends cheerfully, 'that this was one of the sole topics of conversation at Latymer!'

He was also a victim of the typically tyrannical snobbery of British boys' schools, where an individual's status is partly defined by his father's occupation, and was taunted for 'having a dad who did something in carpets'.

'It was unforgivable, really,' says one contemporary. 'But we all knew basically what everyone's father did and Hugh *did* act very posh and sure of himself.'

Hugh, however, learnt fast to give as good as he got. 'Hugh Grant was famous for vicious and witty put-downs. The fighting, among his set, was pretty much verbal and Hugh was as sharp as a knife ... We even called him Mr Perfect because he was so fussy about his appearance!'

Though Hugh couldn't deny his emerging, angelic good looks, he sweated valiantly to establish a compensating reputation as a macho demon on the playing-field. A real killer, very fast and very competitive, say friends. School match reports regularly chronicle Hugh's skills in rugby, especially when he graduated to the second and then first XV: 'Hughie Grant showed his great skill as a kicker, and the robust Guy Bensley [a close chum both at Latymer and Oxford, and afterwards] used the hard parts of his body to good effect.' This is a tongue-in-cheek reference to a Latymer rugby coach's notorious pre-match pep talks to 'hit them with your hard parts, lads', which Hugh, ever the connoisseur of wickedly suggestive remarks, loved to mimic in the changing-rooms afterwards. And he offset ribbings about being Colin Turner's 'pet' by performing unerringly accurate imitations of that much-admired master's distinctive gait and voice.

Having an older, extremely popular brother at the same school was only rarely a double-edged sword. Jamie, naturally, got to join senior school clubs before he did, a constant thorn in Hugh's side, and was also, as a sixth-former, permitted to wear the stylishly battered tweed or corduroy hacking jackets – then very much in vogue – to school while Hugh was still stuck in school uniform. On the whole, however, Jamie's accomplishments at Latymer, and his hugely envied success with the prettiest Godolphin girls, acted as a spur to Hugh's own fiercely competitive nature.

Jamie was also a keen member of the drama societies, and continued to act, though sporadically, at university. At Latymer, Jamie effortlessly grabbed the leading roles thanks to his handsome, open good looks and air of relaxed confidence. Perhaps too much relaxed confidence at times: in contrast to the worrier Hugh, Jamie was famously lackadaisical, his fellow actors from Latymer recall, about learning his lines on time, optimistically trusting that they'd 'come all right on the night'. Jamie won a highly flattering school magazine write-up for his acting in T.S. Eliot's *Murder in the Cathedral*, in which he was noted as being 'full of shining devotion after his beautiful speech [following] the murder'. He was also made deputy head boy and won a place at Worcester College, Oxford.

Hugh, however, was coming up behind him fast. He submitted to the indignities of wearing a frock on stage, as one of the Von Trapp daughters, Birgitta, in a boys-only production of *The Sound of Music*, though he hated the inevitable teasing this prompted.

'It was the sort of thing that gets you labelled a complete queer at fourteen,' one old friend of Hugh's explained. Hugh, also, hadn't wanted the part at all precisely because, as he rightly suspected, it would make him a target for ceaseless mockery – but he wasn't given a choice. If he wanted to appear in the school's play, it was as Birgitta or nothing, and Hugh desperately wanted to act.

Hugh's beautifully modulated, clear-pitched, schoolboy voice also made him an obvious choice for delivering special readings at assembly. Edward Pilkington, another contemporary, now a senior *Guardian* journalist, remembers 'the entire school eating out of the palm of his hand at a special assembly when he recited from T.S. Eliot's [*The Hollow Men*]. It was when he came to the lines, "This is the way the world ends/This is the way the world ends/This is the way the world ends/Not with a bang but a whimper." You could have heard a pin drop. It was absolutely brilliantly done. They aren't particularly easy lines to say without sounding like a stuck record, but he was in total control of them and us.'

Though he acted in almost all the interschool productions, including the football-terraces play *Zigger Zagger* and Arnold Wesker's gritty drama of sausages, egos and chips on shoulders behind the scenes in a restaurant, *The Kitchen*, Hugh rapidly became frustrated with the Journeymen. He was aware that they were regarded as the 'babies' of the school's drama hierarchy and itched to break into real acting – alongside the Godolphin girls – with the Gild. His chance came sooner than he expected.

In 1975 the lower fifth year of the school – Hugh's year – were permitted to stage their own play. This was a first in Latymer's history – usually several school years united for drama productions with the younger boys relegated to supporting roles. Young Hughie was about to be given the first of a series of extraordinary lucky breaks that would characterize his later career, since casting was to be done uniquely from his year alone without any distracting competition from more senior pupils. What is also extraordinarily prescient about the leading role he landed – and something of a poke in the eye for future film directors who would take years to focus on Hugh's real forte – is that the school's entirely amateur drama department instantly detected in the young Hugh his unique talent. For comedy.

There was no question about it. Everyone – classmates and teachers alike – agreed. Hugh was disgracefully funny.

'Hugh was always an incredibly good pupil, always wanting to be top of the class, and he was a favourite with the teachers,' recalls one friend. 'He enjoyed that. Hugh definitely liked being very well-regarded. But one way he made himself very popular with the rest of us – without breaking any rules – was mimicking the masters. He was spot on at voices and accents and very, very funny.'

Before his astonishing physical beauty became the most immediately arresting thing about him, Hugh's genuine comic talent made him stand out.

Ironically, almost twenty years later, a trio of world-class movie directors – the Polish-born, French-naturalized Roman Polanski, Australia's John Duigan and Britain's Mike Newell – would all be warmly congratulating them-selves and each other on having 'discovered' this talent in the adult Hugh.

Hugh's debut leading-man role in his lower fifth year was in the light comedy – much beloved by school drama departments, if virtually nobody else – *The Italian Straw Hat*. It remains the only one of around 150 farces from the tireless quill of the nineteenth-century French dramatist Eugene Labiche to have survived the stern test of time. And, despite being held up by the French philosopher Henri Bergson as perfectly illustrating his theory of com-edy, it has survived pretty shakily at that.

The jaded jokes sending up middle-class pretentions, the round-and-round-the-stage farcical pursuits, the manic stuffing of surplus parlour maids into handy cupboards and the weakly risqué humour were so old they probably elicited groans at the play's première in 1851.

Nevertheless, as far as school drama teachers are con-cerned, such drawbacks are heavily outweighed by other considerations. The number of parts the play offers is practically limitless. You can never have too many servants colliding with the scenery in a farce. Nor will unscripted mistakes be horribly obvious. Hooberman junior can take a dive from the stage and still return home a hero.

Also, most importantly, *The Italian Straw Hat* is highly unlikely to offend anyone's mother on parents' night.

As one of the leading players, Hugh outshone everyone else by miles. Though only in his fifteenth year, Hugh revealed that he had a far more professional attitude towards acting than any other member of the cast. This international heart-throb-in-the-making had done something no one else had.

Hugh had somehow – very coolly – managed to see a professional production of *The Italian Straw Hat*. This is an extraordinary accomplishment in itself. *The Italian Straw Hat* is not *Hamlet*. It has been filmed just once (by René Clair in 1927). Professional productions of the farce are exceptionally thin on the ground. In New York Orson Welles put on a horrible version in 1936, retitled *Horse Eats Hat*, which, not surprisingly, bombed. In 1957 it bobbed up again very briefly on both sides of the Atlantic, to be greeted by strained politeness at the Arts Theatre, Ipswich, but critically machine-gunned across the Atlantic at Manhattan's Fourth Street Theater ('It ain't funny' snarled the *New York Times* theatre correspondent, who vastly preferred the notorious new British play that had just opened at the Lyceum, John Osborne's *Look Back in Anger*).

But, as the resourceful Hugh told the school magazine in a post-production interview that is fascinating for revealing how seriously he was already taking his future profession, the 'professional production [of this play] was technically perfect: none of the screens fell over, none of the curtains fell down, none of the sound-effects went on too long. In that way it was a bit boring, it was a bit flat – too perfect ... the bloke who played Ashil wasn't anything like as good as Chris Law [the fellow lower-fifth-former who played this part] anyway.'

Even in the lower fifth, Hugh's technique for handling interviews is already startlingly poised: a charmingly batty analysis of the dullness of perfection, an admission of relishing when things go wrong and an adroit angling of the spotlight away from himself and on to someone else –

with a self-deprecating shrug. Elsewhere in the article Hugh complains mildly that there was insufficient re-hearsal time allowed for the actors and that the first-night audience for the play was more relaxed than the second night's. Again, he was quite the seasoned pro. No one else quoted or reviewed in the Latymerian magazine sounds even remotely as self-assured as the young Hugh Grant.

As the 'bloke who played Fadinard', Hugh was unfor-gettable. There is a note of genuine awe about the extent of his revealed talent in the Latymerian magazine notice – a review that goes far beyond the usual 'a splendid effort all round, both in front of the curtain and behind it, so let's not give anyone a big head now, shall we?' formula for school play reviews.

While stolidly congratulating everyone who *did* manage to get through his or her part without fainting, and including the deflating comment about one young actress that 'she had obviously put a considerable amount of work into the part' (no mention, perhaps mercifully, of the fruits of all this labour), the reviewer writes, 'The idea of producing a play solely for a particular year within the school has, to the best of my knowledge, never been attempted before, and when the year happens to be the lower fifth, a relatively inexperienced year when it comes to acting, I doubt whether many people had very much confidence in the success of the production. To be quite honest, I went to see the play on its second night fearing the worst. I expected to see an exceptional play [a permis-sible overstatement] spoilt by sub-standard acting, from a young cast who had only rehearsed for a matter of a few weeks. In many ways I couldn't have been more wrong: the production was of a very high standard, with a number of exceptional performances from a cast who all acted admirably well ... However the star of the show was undoubtedly Hughie Grant with a marvellous performance ... He was totally confident and moved and delivered his lines with a great deal of flair. It was a very large and difficult part for someone so young, but he tackled it brilliantly and overall his performance was superb.'

Perhaps the only other British screen actor who can beat Hugh in terms of approaching a school play with such dogged early perfectionism is Alec Guinness when he was cast as the messenger in *Macbeth*. The messenger is a part usually given, in school productions, to small boys whose enthusiasm is not matched by any discernible theatrical skill. The schoolboy Alec Guinness timed the scene immediately preceding his entrance, withdrew to the far end of his school playing-fields, started running at top speed, re-entered the school hall with his lungs bursting and flung himself on the stage – on cue to the second – to make his speech in a state matching the physical collapse of a messenger hot off the battlefields. It brought down the house.

Not only did Hugh bring down the house at Latymer with his star turn, but at last he got to act with girls. The play was an unusually popular production within the lower fifth because it involved girls from the Godolphin School – a whole year early. Normally the two schools acted together only from the upper-fifth year, when pupils could finally join the Gild – the school's most senior drama club as well as the schools' joint film society.

Their early inclusion was especially welcomed, not just for the obvious reasons but because they liberated the boys – particularly those who, like Hugh, were obviously pretty – from having to take on female roles. Here is the young Grant, again in the same priceless school magazine interview, summing up his feelings about the Godolphin girls' involvement. The interview also reveals a striking similarity, down to Hugh's mirth-provoking *double entendres*, to the interviews he would be giving – exactly twenty years on – with the American chat show kings Jay Leno, Larry King and David Letterman in the wake of his downfall with a prostitute.

'At first it was a bit silly – [the girls] just sat in a corner, but in the end, certainly by the cast party, it was very different.' (The interviewer notes here that the other boys present during the classroom interview explode with laughter at the mention of the cast party – Hugh had spent much of it in a passionate clinch with an attractive Godolphin girl, to the deep envy of friends who had no success at all in this area.) 'There's nothing like a play for bringing people together and I think that's one of the most important things about it. We only have three weeks but during that time you get to know people better. You feel you're creating something together.' There was more rib-ald laughter, notes the writer, at Hugh's suggestive choice of 'creating something together'.

Hugh insists, though, that the presence of the girls was 'just an extra – but a very nice extra', and certainly wasn't his sole reason for acting. The interviewer notes here that an unidentified classmate interjects, 'Hughie Grant makes a very nice girl'; to which Hugh responds with a comically affronted, 'I don't do that by choice you (expletive deleted)!'

On the cusp of adolescence, young Hughie found himself both envied and admired as the 'star' of the lower fifth's play. His first fans outside the school were already appearing, friends recall, in the shape of other boys' adoring mothers, who were quick to lavish praise on the unrivalled star of *The Italian Straw Hat* – often to the intense envy of their own sons! Hugh lapped up the attention. He was justifiably proud of his rave review. No longer just Jamie's pretty little brother – or Grunt Minor, as he was dubbed by some of the older boys, with Jamie, naturally, tagged Grunt Major or 'Jammy' Grunt – Hugh was emerging as a school character in his own right. It was a heady and defining time for the schoolboy actor and he could hardly bear the wait to join the Gild proper – even campaigning, unsuccessfully, for lower-fifth boys to be officially admitted to its glittering ranks.

Though Hugh's early performance in *The Italian Straw Hat* remains the most memorable and inspired of his school career, he nevertheless continued to pile up the parts, both comic and serious, Shakespearian and contem-porary, good and ghastly, at a breakneck rate during his senior years at Latymer. He appeared in a Godolphin sixth-form production of *A Midsummer Night's Dream*, which gave him his first experience of acting in a real theatre. The comedy was staged at the Cockpit, a professional theatre in West London, which local schools were occasionally awarded the privilege of using. 'Hugh took it all *terribly* seriously,' recalls one of the Godolphin drama society regulars. 'I remember watching him do a read-through for *Look Back in Anger* – for which he wasn't ideally suited and really *fussing* about getting the pace exactly right.' Hugh was even able to act in a play with Jamie in the spring term of 1976 when Latymer made *Romeo and Juliet* the official Godolphin-and-Latymer school play.

From the moment the choice of play was announced, there was never any genuine doubt over the role of Romeo: Jamie Grant. As an exuberant school magazine article about the whole production put it: 'Mr Owens [Chris Owens, the play's producer and director, was head of Latymer Upper's English Department], with a sharp eye for type-casting, placed Mark "rebel" Bottomley as the tough-talking, hard-fighting Tybalt, Charlie Graham as the amiable but rather ineffectual Benvolio, Jonathan Tafler as the gay (but ever so bitter) Mercutio and, of course, Jamie Grant as our hero, the love-smitten golden boy.'

Graham, Grant and Bottomley were – both on stage and off – Latymer's sixth-form cult figures. Bright, macho, rowdy and swaggeringly self-confident, they were, above all, the school's cocks of the walk. The author of this article was Mercutio himself – Jonathan Tafler, yet another stage-struck Latymerian who would go on to a professional acting career and whose father, Sidney Tafler, had been a notable Ealing Studios comedy actor.

As Romeo, Jamie got the privilege of wearing a doublet that had originally been made for a much younger Colin Turner when Hugh's mentor had once played Mercutio; and the school magazine article cheerfully notes that the amply-padded Jamie in rehearsal 'spent several happy minutes running around the School butting people in the stomach and saying "James Caan, Rollerball!" as if this were some sort of reasonable explanation.'

The production was an enormous popular success with parents, and the school magazine commented, a little archly, 'Hughie Grant (what a talented clan these Grants are!) as ever impressed, though his part was but a small one.' Behind the scenes of *Romeo and Juliet*, the gossip was all about Romeo Jamie Grant's romance, not with his Juliet, but with the genuinely gifted Godolphin actress who played Juliet's nurse, Tracey Scoffield.

Hugh would play the soldier lover of the same Tracey Scoffield, then his brother's ex-girlfriend, eighteen months later in a joint Godolphin and Latymer production of Bertolt Brecht's *The Caucasian Chalk Circle*.

At school, despite the distractions of acting, Hugh was a star pupil academically. He was determined to follow his older brother to Oxford – in the event outdoing Jamie by winning a scholarship to New College. The paragon schoolboy Hugh was a tireless contributor to the school magazine, submitting highly romanticized reports of cricket matches to its pages:

> Late afternoon, mid-summer. Looking very much rounder, the sun is edging its way down behind the plane trees on the distant boundary. The heat haze has lifted, and from the blue shadows of a mighty ash the second eleven watches an ungainly opponent fumble his fielding. 'Bovine', remarks Edwards, 'appertaining to a cow'. Radice nods. Kee giggles. Lipwick settles deeper into the striped canvas of his deck-chair.

This, by the way, is extraordinarily reminiscent of the precociously well-read Hugh's beloved E.M. Forster. It strongly recalls the opening chapter of *The Longest Journey* with a generous dash of Billy Bunter's Greyfriars, complete with the introduction of a character like Hurree Jamset Ram Singh – one of Bunter's chums.

'Only Chaterjee, who is still muttering fond oaths

against the umpire, seems unmoved,' wrote Hugh, who concludes his fanciful report with what appears to be a slyly coded reference to drinking at one of the Thameside pubs such as the Dove – haunted by technically under-age sixth-form Latymerians and possibly one of Hugh's favourites: 'Later, content in the knowledge that out of nine games they have only lost once, the second eleven will sit watching the sun finally disappear beyond the irridescent trail it has struck along the Thames.'

In his final and A-level year at Latymer, Hugh even interviewed his mentor Colin Turner for the school magazine on the sacred topic of teaching drama. Hugh asked, 'What does drama provide in a school?' The English master's soberly considered reply was, 'Most boys will say that drama is some sort of relaxation, but I think they come to realize it can be hard and exhausting work. Drama is paradoxically closer to [physical education] than any other subject because both train people to have good coordination and to work as a team. They learn to depend on each other and to accept each other's ideas and give good reasons for doing so.'

Later in the interview Hugh, who displayed at Latymer a sweetly priggish pride in handing in his homework precisely on time and reaping consistent top marks, asks, 'No one would deny that during the week of [a school play's] performance the academic workrate of those concerned drops alarmingly. How would you justify this?'

Colin Turner, his upper lip almost certainly quivering above a grin, makes his response: 'One can't really justify it. One can only say that it happens. I've not yet met anybody who has become so involved in a major production that his work has gone completely to pot.

'It is interesting to note,' the teacher continues, 'that the people who perhaps win our highest academic successes in the school are those who have been involved very actively in sport or drama or music.'

In December 1978, Hugh learnt that his name would be joining those tricked out in gold on the Latymer honours boards. He won a scholarship – the highest award possible at Oxbridge entrance – to read English. His old English master would have been perfectly aware that Hugh was widely regarded as one of the school's Oxbridge certainties at this point. There is a certain amount of cosy mutual reassurance in the exchange.

And how, Hugh asks, would drama be taught in Colin Turner's ideal school?

'Drama would be taught – and this sounds very much like we've reached perfection – very much as it is taught here at Latymer. It must be rooted in the teaching of English: I don't agree with special people being brought in to "do drama" ... Drama has got to grow out of what you are doing.'

Hugh was acutely aware, throughout his senior years at Latymer, that he wasn't without his enemies. His habit of affecting public-school airs genuinely infuriated some contemporaries. They found his preference for referring to boys who didn't meet his high standards of wit and intelligence as 'oiky drones' less than endearing. Hugh was also very pushy when it came to the plum acting roles – a point he appears to acknowledge in his next question to Colin Turner.

'It is often said that the school's true acting ability is never fully realized because the casting has become centred on a clique of type-casts and favourites. Do you think this is a valid criticism?'

The short answer was 'no'. Colin Turner pointed out that, at any time, up to a fifth of the entire school was involved in acting, 'and I don't think this number can really be called a clique'.

In the same issue of the school magazine, Hugh confirms his own status as the Gild's star player with yet another article based on a gentle interrogation of a group of fourth-formers – coincidentally including the young Simon Kunz who would appear sixteen years later in *Four Weddings* – about what they hoped to get from acting. It was entitled 'An Interview With Members Of The Fourth Form On Drama In The School'. They respond, artlessly spouting the unofficial Latymer creed, 'It's a status symbol ...

One of the big things is that there's an audience out there that has come to see you – or the play, anyway. The praise you get for doing it is one of the things that makes it enjoyable.'

One of Hugh's last major acting roles at Latymer was not the unalloyed success he wished. In Brecht's *The Caucasian Chalk Circle* he was hopelessly outclassed by his brother's former girlfriend, Tracey Scoffield, who defied all predictions by eschewing a stage career after Oxford for a job as a literary agent and is now the partner of one of Britain's leading novelists, Hanif Kureshi. The chief defect of Godolphin's and Latymer's 1977 (and over-ambitious) production of this highly stylized drama was that only a few of the enormous cast had bothered to read the entire play. As a member of the cast, actually with sixteen lines – one of a number of spare peasants, limping matrons and sundry others who auditioned only with a view of cosying up to Hugh Grant – I had only the dimmest idea of what Brecht was on about. Though Tracey Scoffield's leading performance as the wise peasant girl Grusha was judged one of the most mature and moving by a Godolphin girl in years, Hugh – in the role of her lover – was badly bruised in a conspicuously tough but fair school magazine review by the Latymer English master Chris Owens.

Hugh was, of course, a seasoned Gild actor by now, no longer a lower-fifth neophyte, and this weighed heavily against him. 'The most difficult part in any way,' wrote Chris Owens, 'is that of Simon Chachava, the soldier lover. He's too simple, too likeable, too stolid by half. Hugh Grant acted well and enlisted our sympathy, but overdid the moustache and dumbness – this was too crude a lover for Grusha; when he played the part straighter in the last scene he was altogether more convincing.'

The review ended on the generous, if strained, note: 'Brecht entertains but demands from his audience concentration and thought. This was clear from the opening moments of the play and the cast, and hence directors, rarely let us off the hook.' The play, a little overambitiously perhaps, was also put on at the nearby River-side Theatre for a memorably difficult Sunday afternoon audience – mainly parents and distractingly noisy young children. Again, Hugh had the privilege of appearing in a real theatre even before he left school. He was not, however, the only member of the cast who would survive the chaotic experience of *The Caucasian Chalk Circle* to go on to greater things. Playing the role of the governor's wife – and earning a glowing review for her efforts – was a strikingly talented and energetic red-headed Godolphin girl, Samantha Bond. She later became a protégé of the highly respected stage and television actress Dame Judi Dench and won brilliant notices opposite Ken Branagh as a member of his Renaissance Theatre Company, which he formed in 1987.

Though Hugh would later develop a pose of absolute indifference to his contemporaries' stage careers, claiming that 'nobody goes to the theatre anymore', he couldn't ignore Samantha Bond's rise. In 1989 the actress was the star of the widely praised, four-million-pounds-sterling, Anglo-Japanese period drama series, *The Ginger Tree*. More importantly, she was the younger sister of one of Hugh's closest Latymer and Oxford University friends, a gifted and – like Hugh – heroically good looking lad, Matthew Bond. And as everyone at star-conscious Latymer knew perfectly well, the siblings' handsome actor father, Philip Bond, had been a British heart-throb himself as the seaman Albert Fraser in one of the most successful British television series of all time, *The Onedin Line*.

At Latymer, as at Oxford and afterwards, fame never appeared something terribly remote to Hugh Grant. It flickered, constantly, all around him.

FOUR

'Come, let us go, while we are in our prime;
And take the harmless folly of our time.'
                                    Robert Herrick

Off stage, at Latymer, Hugh was also scoring notable successes. With girls, girls, girls and more girls.

Though his older brother's near legendary status as a school heart-throb was hard to dent – Jamie had cut a swathe through the cream of the sixth form at Godolphin at one time or other – Hugh rose to the challenge with gusto. In the late seventies in West London, in an area bordered roughly by the Great West Road, Gunnersbury Avenue, the Vale, Acton and the first bit of the Goldhawk Road, if you were female, sixteen or over, comely rather than otherwise, a pupil at one of a tiny handful of select day schools (Godolphin or St Paul's Girls') and were prepared to be frisky in mixed company, the chances were that you could grab your own piece of paradise.

Paradise, at that particular period, was one Hugh John Mungo Grant. Hugh wasn't merely a good-looker among a bunch of other good-looking chaps at school. All middle-class boys' schools have a quotient of clean-jawed heartbreakers and Latymer was no exception, even running to a few, like Hugh, who learnt early how much easier it was to beguile, rather than to bully, favours from girls. But by the time he reached the upper fifth, Hugh was edging, Roman nose first, into another class altogether.

Godolphin girls began to confide casually in each other that they didn't find Hugh all *that* desirable purely in order to measure up the competition. At lunchtime, Ravenscourt Park – roughly midway between the two schools – doubled as the unofficial trysting ground of Godolphinae and

Latymerians. That is, a few minutes after the last bell of the morning, two gender-specific herds of pupils would converge on the thin, sour grass, puff terrifying numbers of Number Six cigarettes and the bushes would shake and giggle. A rapid, if ginger, retreat around the dog-fouled cycle paths would be beaten back to the schools a few minutes before the afternoon bells. And exactly the same ritual would be enacted 24 hours later. If Hugh Grant showed up in the lunchtime pack – with his delicate bemused fawn looks and funny wisecracks – the following day there would be roughly twice the number of Godolphin girls wafting optimistically around Ravenscourt Park.

Latymerians, seething with testosterone and piqued by quite understandable resentment, swore on their grandmothers' graves to Godolphin girls that Hughie was, absolutely, irreversibly, totally gay. 'Can't you tell just by *looking* at him?' they'd beg plaintively. 'Everyone at Latymer knows that about Hughie. It's just you Godolphin girls who have it all wrong. He practically got up in front of the whole school and *announced* it just the other day,' they'd insist. Godolphin girls paid not the slightest notice.

First, because the lad who was making the accusation was invariably, at the very same moment, sighing great big hot and hopeful cheese-and-onion-crisp-flavoured sighs at the Old Ship or the Dove pub on the Thames, while blocking one's view of Hugh lounging gorgeously in his trademark white collarless shirt and fawn corduroy drainpipe jeans at the bar and talking up a storm about football.

Secondly, the other detail that scuppered the Hughie-is-gay theory was that Hugh did not bolt into the night every time a pretty girl winked at him at a party. On the contrary, he was a wildly athletic joiner-in of the spare-room (ostensibly for coats) sessions at West London parties, where he and his girlfriend of the moment would start off kissing on the quivering summit of a pyramid of other people's parkas, only to set off a slithering Polyester-assisted landslide and ending up wedged together between the side of the bed and the wall, being showered, not unpleasantly, with old bus tickets and a small fortune in small change.

Yet, if a girl pointed out this flaw in the reckoning to her cheese-and-onion-breathed Latymerian pub wooer, he'd grumble that he hadn't invested in a half of lager and half a packet of crisps to sit round all evening discussing Hughie bloody Grant's undeniable homosexuality!

By the time Hugh reached the lower sixth, in 1976–77, he had lost the final remnants of his old, slightly hamster-cheeked look. His voice had deepened impressively, his naturally lean frame was filling out, he had shot up in height. Hugh's masculine beauty was, sometimes, almost too much to behold.

From the age of sixteen, Hugh had the sort of timelessly classical profile that might turn up – Zelig-like – on a silver sestertius unearthed on a Welsh smallholding, or in a sepia pasteboard portrait of someone's precious boy lost at Ypres. Lavender-rinsed old ladies would twinkle and grow pretty when he passed. Young teenage girls would giggle openly on the street, stick their noses in the air, trip over the kerb and look back furtively only to see him vanish round a corner, leaving a faint Cheshire grin.

Hugh also bent the normal rituals and rules of courtship between young adult males and females of the same age terribly out of shape. In social anthropologists' parlance he was 'a non-recurring phenomenon'. Girls mature much earlier than young men and will usually, with a disdainful snort, quickly throw back into the pool specimens of the wrong age even if their looks are right. Godolphin girls matured even earlier than average. With kohl-black Cleopatra eyes, Vidal Sassoon *coupes sauvages* and pouts honed to perfection on a succession of blithely impervious French mistresses, they were an army of thin-limbed viragos, embarking often on personal A-level courses in anorexia nervosa and bulimia nervosa, as well as French, German, Spanish, history, biology and special English.

One infamous glossy magazine article at the time de-scribed Godolphin girls as 'hardened Londoners who try hard to acquire the offhand attitude to life by dropping Camus quotes and sniffing smack' – a gross libel that appalled the school's governors but was gleefully pinned up in the sixth-form common-room. In theory, Hugh should not have been of much interest to girls of his own age. So much for theory. He was of the greatest interest.

Mallary Gelb, one of Hugh's brightest and prettiest Godolphin girlfriends from this time – who also went on to study at Oxford and who enjoyed, as a BBC Radio One news reporter, having a score of listeners' babies named in honour of her unusual first name – recalls honestly, 'I was *desperate* to go out with him. That I do genuinely remember. I must have known him from the Gild [the Friday-evening acting club] but I can't say my interest was in the plays; it was definitely Hughie. But as far as I can recall, *everyone* wanted to go out with him. He was, by far, the most beautiful boy around and I can still remember this lovely intense feeling of excitement when we first danced and kissed at a party.

'It's ridiculous what sticks in your memory but I was going to a fancy dress party in Barnes, and I think I knew he'd be there. I wore this wonderful pair of old Land Girl army jodphurs . . . I just remember Hughie then as being extremely charming to me, and that it made me very happy to be with him – even though I got kicked out of some silly girls' gang at Godolphin because of jealousy.

'My overwhelming memory is of having enormous fun. Perhaps this was the age we were but with other boyfriends from more or less the same time my memories aren't nearly so nice – they're quite bitter. I can only assume that the relationship ended very nicely with Hugh. It was a typical, lovely teenage romance.'

One Old Latymerian (now in leisure services marketing and clearly still not recovered from the shattering experience of being forced to share his formative years with Hugh Grant) complains loudly to this day, 'It was pathetic the way the girls all flung themselves at Hugh – he didn't have to do anything at all. He was also such a bastard – in schoolboy terms – always dropping one girl for another and getting away with it.'

Yet it was not quite true that Hugh courted without some scripted effort. He had a number of approaches to females that were well-rehearsed and quite staggeringly successful. Among them were: 'My girlfriend doesn't understand me' (delivered wistfully, with a brave smile); and 'Do you have the foggiest what D.H. Lawrence is going on about? I don't!' (delivered on a light note of challenge, and with a handy copy of *Lady Chatterley's Lover* thrust warmly into his jacket pocket).

And, the best of the lot and a world classic of its kind, if probably lifted from one of his beloved Ealing Studios films, was 'God, you're clever as well as beautiful; I think I shall kiss you' (delivered firmly).

One former and, again, ravishingly pretty, girlfriend of Hugh's – who is now married and working in financial publishing – says, 'I think I can honestly say that he was far and away the most lovely boy I ever went out with: he was sexy, a fantastic kisser, and very funny. Looking back, you might say he knew exactly which buttons to push. At the time it didn't feel like that at all.

'I simply remember him very, very fondly. I also don't know why other boys didn't use the "clever-as-well-as-beautiful line". It was a killer. This sounds awfully corny but – even at that age – Hugh made you feel special, and that's not something other boys of seventeen could do.'

Another girlfriend recalls, 'Hugh was wily too. I remember he always had the perfect, polite excuse if he couldn't meet you on a Friday night – his Scottish cousins! He would be obliged to join in some family event, to which you couldn't possibly object. Then maybe you heard afterwards he'd been spotted at a party in Putney instead! Or he wouldn't be able to see you on a Saturday because he had to do gardening – helping out friends of his parents. I used to think him very noble. He had the most lovely manners. He'd use phrases like "I think you are going to break my heart" – which you'd hug to yourself for weeks.'

For the record – which will probably label me the Alan Clark of adolescence – I fell for Hugh on 18 February 1977, and was still chronicling his movements and *bons mots* at parties and drama meetings a full year later. Love does many strange things. In my case I secured a tiny speaking part as somebody's elderly sister-in-law in that chaotic production of *The Caucasian Chalk Circle* in March 1977, simply because Hugh was co-starring. I spent most rehearsals furtively scrubbing the crayonned age lines off my face, to the irritation of the make-up people, just in case Hugh sauntered by.

I wasn't the only member of the production mad about Hugh. There was one 'shouting woman', a 'peasant girl by the bridge' and at least two 'sundry musicians' in *The Caucasian Chalk Circle* whose eager interest in school dramatics was exclusively inspired by Hugh. One of these, Tess Hoare, later an artist, and one of a legion of Hugh Grant's girlfriends, quite by coincidence provided the gorgeously painted waistcoats for *Four Weddings*.

Acting, though, made me ill with worry. I began to wonder whether Bertolt Brecht wasn't too high a price to pay for love. Wisely, I have resisted venturing on stage since. By 21 May 1977, I was a lost cause, recording in my diary (in a mixture of French, Italian and some sort of numbers-for-letters code which is difficult to decipher) that, at a party attended by Hugh, I spent all evening acting 'very low strung since Hughie put the problems he had with his girlfriend down to her being very high strung.'

How I behaved in a low-strung manner, I really don't know. But Hugh was worth it. He resembled a flesh-and-blood embodiment of the famous 1915 portrait of Rupert Brooke in the frontispiece of the poet's collected works (a standard teenage girls' bedside text along with a translation of *Bonjour Tristesse*). He charmed mothers all over west London with his lovely manners and spotless shirts – at a time when other lads were affecting weekend Mohicans and Sid Vicious sneers.

'Hugh never went through a punk thing – he rather disdained all that,' said one close Latymer friend. 'As a prefect he'd actually tick off younger boys for looking "too radical" or "too greasy". His style was more classic:

white shirts and drainpipe trousers and incredibly square, lace-up desert boots!'

I was, personally, enchanted by the 'high-strung' girl-friend come-on technique. A high-strung girlfriend was clearly a terrible burden. And how clever to call his girlfriend 'high-strung' instead of 'a complete cow'. How wonderfully challenging she sounded and how sensitive of Hugh to be alert to her jangling inner chords!

By 23 May 1977, I was a lovesick fool for Hughie. On 27 May, I had fallen out of love with Hughie and in love with an impossibly beautiful Royal Shakespeare Company actor named Clive Arrindell after seeing him in *Love's Labours Lost* at the Regent's Park Open Theatre with my best friend, Isabella. Mr Arrindell squeezed me in the interval because he took me for the producer's daughter. Isabella was of course, I noted, gratifyingly envious.

On 30 May I was back in love with Hughie, since Mr Arrindell hadn't seen fit to reply to my letter of proposal by return of post. It is fascinating how ill memory serves the facts sometimes. It has always been my self-serving impression that I graciously gave in to Hugh's affectionate overtures after a seemly period of playing it cool.

On 30 May, however, I record, to my intense embarrassment, 'Unfortunately the boy [Hugh] will not be at Georgina E[. . .]'s party at which I had intended to seduce him. So I will have to contain myself and hold on until I have another opportunity.'

Seemly period of playing it cool, indeed!

On 17 June I noted victory in the matter of Hugh Grant. The following day I was, a little prematurely, practising my new signature over and over again as Mrs Hugh Grant. I also practised his signature. I don't know why. Perhaps I intended to forge his big film-star cheques one day.

By 24 June our relationship had progressed to the point where I casually recorded that we spent that evening's date 'talking about perversions for some time'. Things were certainly going swimmingly.

On 21 July after a month of Hughmania entries, I make a rapturous diary announcement that Hugh claimed his nose 'tinged green' at the thought of my 'getting off' with French chaps during my looming summer holiday in France. Note Hugh's very precise shading; a nose tinging green is not as jealous as a nose that *is* green, and it's nothing like as pigmentally extreme as a green-eyed monster. I should have read the writing on the nose.

By early September I was back in Chiswick after my French experience wondering if Hughie would bother phoning me. The casual use of 'bother' is undermined by the fact that, in recording this single word, my Biro had drilled through three pages in my diary.

On Friday, 23 September, I met Hugh and friends at the Old Ship pub in Hammersmith. 'At about 7 p.m.,' I record, 'the Grunt rose to his large feet, mumbled something about a drinks dinner he was forced to attend, told me he would ring later and shuffled off.' Hugh, true to his promise, later phoned me while I was babysitting. I was wallowing in the TV adaptation of H.E. Bates's *Love for Lydia*, starring the luscious actress Mel Martin, who looked, in a shining, black, bobbed wig, I thought jealously, awfully like Mallary Gelb.

'I don't think it's working,' Hugh told me over the phone as Mel Martin skated prettily round and round a pond. For one surreal moment, I thought he meant the television reception. I was about to tell him it was working absolutely fine, meaning the television, not the relationship. Then I twigged. Mel Martin skated on in a circle. I went numb. My life was finished. The phone went dead. I lunged for a handy thesaurus and recorded – in one great burst of fury – 68 unflattering adjectives, both single and compound, about Hugh Grant. It is certain that I didn't have a dictionary with me, since I describe Hugh in rather confused terms: 'crass, pretentious, Amazon-chinned, desert-shoed, skinny, over-sexed . . . puritanical, cowardly, mastadonic, atavistic, bovine, cretinous . . . splay-footed, fallen-arched, ferret-like, feral . . .' I was hopelessly in love.

And yet it was worth every tear afterwards.

The high point of going out with Hugh Grant always

began at the top of Turnham Green Terrace at its junction with Chiswick High Road. This is where we would part. Or begin to part. Much of the point of spending the evening with Hugh was parting. Typically, we would have passed the evening at a Thameside pub discussing D.H. Lawrence's *The Rainbow* and *Lady Chatterley's Lover*. Hugh was extraordinarily keen on discussing Lawrence.

'I don't know what the fellow's getting at, do you?' he'd ask. 'Well, er,' I'd blurt, not having read *The Rainbow*, but pretty clued up about what Lawrence was generally getting at, 'it's probably about, you know, sex as usual.'

Hugh would grin, slowly, heart-stoppingly, his long firm chin nuzzling my neck and creeping a hard cricket-muscled arm around me. 'Crikey, do you think so? You're much cleverer than I am, aren't you?' And off we would dance, into the darker recesses of Lawrence's prose, with Hugh reciting ripe chunks of the works from memory.

How extraordinary that over sixty years after the book was published it was still being displayed as a sexual trump card by English schoolboys. How even more extraordinary that schoolgirls still fell for it every time!

Sometimes we went barn-dancing, a pastime much encouraged by middle-class West London parents who could think of no healthier way of sublimating whatever it was you had to sublimate at seventeen than when you barndanced. Up and down some low-ceilinged public building we charged, under the eyes of a beetle-browed, beady-eyed adult 'caller' in shorts, sometimes joining arms to form 'baskets', sometimes canoning against a flimsy partition wall and hoping your face wasn't too red and sweaty. Hugh's perfect porcelain countenance never was. He was a terrific barn-dancer too. Outside the barn-dancing building, teenagers who managed to escape the monitoring gaze of the caller by slipping out through a side door, threw themselves into barnyard antics. Sometimes we sloped off to Notting Hill Gate garden parties and made the shrubbery vibrate.

But, on the whole, we met only so that later we could say goodbye very, very slowly. Preferably in the warm, damp, summer's evening darkness of one of the shaggy municipal horse chestnut trees that lined Chiswick High Road. From the pub or a party to this junction, Hugh wheeled his bicycle, at a very leisurely pace, with one fist firmly clamped at the apex of the machine's handlebars, just behind the removable dynamo lamp, while the other rested lightly – not at all clammily – upon my shoulder.

Together, Hugh, the bike and I formed an oddly handicapped three-legged race. Sometimes I would pause to remove a great wet, green horse chestnut leaf that had swooped down and then clung, batlike, to my face. We always walked in this fashion with the bicycle between us rather than on Hugh's kerb-facing side. I can still remember the pain as the bike's viciously free-spinning pedals slammed time and again into my shins.

Then, at the junction, we would stop and shuffle backwards into the recessed forecourt of a small garden machinery shop. There was a pause as Hughie would responsibly chain his bike to the lamppost. I would furtively test my breath against the palm of my hand. Then we would gingerly approach each other across that small, yet suddenly endless, void of pavement, arms stretched apart, as if participating in a mime about two people meeting, each carrying a cumbersomely large and rectangular sheet of glass.

An hour or so later, carrying the warm, hard imprint of Hugh Grant all over me in reverse impression, I would skip dreamily home, on freshly dew-dampened pavements beneath a canopy of smiling stars.

Slightly less satisfying were evenings that concluded not in a park or Chiswick High Road but in the Grant family kitchen, with Mrs Grant fussing helpfully over cups of tea. And one was seized with the burning, guilty conviction that Hugh's mother could read one's mind. She *knew* it had taken an hour and twenty minutes to cover the last 50 yards to the front door. Oh God, she *must*!

Hugh has caricatured himself in interviews as a kind of Woody Allenish nitwit when it came to his teenage romance techniques (Woody Allen was one of his early film idols), 'half strangling' one girlfriend in a cinema in an attempt at an intimate clinch, he has claimed. But girl-friends' memories serve him more kindly. Hugh had an air of playful sophistication that was at odds with his years. He was physically a late developer and therefore still boyishly and, thankfully, smoothly hairless while his fellows were sprouting coarse, off-putting thickets in all the oddest places.

He gave girlfriends innocent, though waggishly suggestive, birthday presents – yellow plastic bath ducks and feet-shaped sponges. Hugh, in his final sixth-form year at Latymer, was a heartbreaker bar none. He was responsible for more tear-dampened pillows from Kew Gardens to Parson's Green than probably even Jamie.

'Hughie was simply irresistible,' says one very bright Godolphin girlfriend, a Cambridge graduate who is now in law. 'Intensely passionate but also a terrifically good gossip. He made absolutely no pretence about having had loads of girlfriends but gave a wonderful impression that you were, at last, someone special. He could lift your spirits just by looking at you. I remember him as surprisingly sentimental, too, talking about his *feelings*, which was certainly not what other boys did. I remember being introduced to his mother – and then I was dropped. Instead of being mad – although I was very hurt – I felt grateful he had gone out with me at all!'

Perhaps only one memory intrudes upon Hugh's shiny reputation as the effortlessly charming, effortlessly girl-hopping bounder of the 'Remove'. It concerns my joint eighteenth-birthday party before many of us took A-levels and Oxbridge.

The party, planned as an elegant affair, collapsed in local infamy when it was crashed by a crowd of drunken Chelsea punks. I observed Hugh, trembling, white-faced with anger, furiously – impotently – scrubbing with hand-fuls of damp paper napkins at the green globs of guacamole that clung to his tweed jacket, hurled by some lout. Hugh had – bravely, it must be said – called the interloper something rude, some polysyllabic insult that dripped with sarcasm. For once, his clever words hadn't been enough. Life had lobbed back an ugly missile of creamed avocado. It was the only time I'd seen Hugh look anything less than perfectly, socially, at ease. And he looked as if it pierced him to the marrow.

CHAPTER

FIVE

*'Undergraduates owe their happiness chiefly to the
fact that they are no longer at school ... The
nonsense which was knocked out of them at school
is all put gently back at Oxford or Cambridge.'*

Max Beerbohm, Mote in the Middle Distance

*'But oh, beamish nephew, beware of the day,
If your Snark be a Boojum! For then
You will softly and suddenly vanish away,
And never be met with again!'*

Lewis Carroll, The Baker's Tale
*(the inspiration for the name of one of the societies
Hugh belonged to at Oxford, the Boojums)*

To all outward appearances Hugh Grant slipped into his
new life at Oxford with the ease of a bather into a
blood-temperature pool. He had passed an idyllic summer
in a manner most appropriate to a young gentleman about
to go 'up' to university, wandering in E.M. Forster's
beloved Toscana region of Italy, in the hills between
Florence and Siena. (The writer had, in fact, made *his* first
'grand tour' of the same area almost 80 years earlier and
with his mother for company, after graduating from Cambridge, not before.) For his pilgrimage in Forster's
footsteps, Hugh chose to be accompanied by a young lady
rather closer to his own age, a lively, curvacious, period-
ically platinum-blonde-haired girl from Godolphin, who
discreetly describes their Italian retreat as 'a most poetic
and sensual time'.

Together they read, swam, sketched and walked, and
bathed in lakes while staying as paying guests at a charming country villa. Hugh had worked doggedly for his

Oxford entrance and felt he deserved a lull before university life – even if it was a lull on a tight budget, which made the notoriously scruffy European youth hostels a thrifty and not especially stylish necessity while later travelling on his own and without the curvacious Miss M.

From the very start of his first Michaelmas full term in October 1979, Hugh felt entirely in his element. Oxford was hardly unknown country to Latymerians. His brother Jamie had, of course, preceded him – but to a different college. Two of his closest Latymerian mates, Guy Bensley and Matthew Bond, were starting their Oxford first years, too, and there were also other Latymerians spread throughout the three undergraduate years at the university. Hugh was finally, through his own efforts, a pukka member of one of the grandest, most fashionable and most stylishly ivy-clad of all this ancient university's ancient institutions, New College. It fitted him perfectly.

If Hugh had ever felt that Latymer was somewhat ersatz, the same could never be said of New College, which was so popular with day-trippers it became one of the first colleges in either Oxford or Cambridge to charge tourists an admission fee (20p) merely for the privilege of entering the main quad in the early 1980s. This was thought shockingly élitist – an attempt to create a gulf between town and gown – though all the other popular colleges would swiftly and shamelessly follow suit. But Hugh – and the trippers – were right to be drawn to New College. It remains one of the most splendid and romantic colleges, a dreamy, heavenly place with famously vaulted cloisters that seem, in the hush of early winter mornings, to echo with the ghostly footfalls of generation upon distant generation of chilled undergraduates scurrying on their way to lectures – the same stone cloisters that, cool as caves in the heat of the summer, enclose a square of the softest and most vividly emerald grass in all of Oxford. Never one to miss a chance to pose against an elegant backdrop, Hugh and his friends from the college's drinking society the Boojums Society, named nonsensically from the Lewis Carroll lines quoted above, would throw an elegant drinks party at the cloisters in the summer of his second year.

New College also boasted extravagant ancient gardens that might have been grown from clippings pinched from Eden, a remnant of the old city wall from the time of Henry III and one of the finest dining-halls in the entire university with its pleated, early-sixteenth-century – and evocatively named – linenfold panelling. Among many other distinguished names, it was also alma mater to another once very famous Hugh – Gaitskell, the Labour politician – as well as Tony Benn (ditto), the writer John Fowles, and the cricketer Brian Johnston.

By happy chance, New College was founded in 1379, a tidy six centuries in advance of Hugh's arrival. (It was named New College because it *was* new, of course, when it was established after Merton, University, Oriel, Balliol et al.) The year 1979 marked a host of sexcentenary celebrations including a grand ball featuring scantily clad females mud wrestling, among other attractions, and splendid celebratory formal dinners. It was a dazzlingly memorable year to arrive at New College, with Margaret Thatcher newly in power and the British media beginning to celebrate the return of the 'bright young things' to Oxford.

As the then editor of the *Tatler* and an Oxford graduate herself, Tina Brown, commented jubilantly in the *Sunday Times* in 1981, 'What has changed in Oxford is that it's fashionable again to be rich and smart ... in the Sixties and the Seventies the rich and smart went on existing but were rather more on the defensive.'

Because of Oxford's arcane academic dress codes, the scholar Hugh was very visibly a member of the college's élite when he first caught the appreciative eye of many of his fellow students. Scholars were not only awarded the best rooms in college – and Hugh had a lovely set overlooking the quad – but they, and the aptly named Exhibitioners, were required to wear, on formal occasions, rather glamorous shin-length, academic gowns to mark their superior status. But the vast majority of undergraduates – commoners – were forced to endure extremely unflattering hip-length commoners' gowns, a bit like badly shrunken Batman capes, on the same occasions. Scholars could in fact substantially reduce the frequency with which they wore their impressive robes by not opting for formal evening meals. Hugh, however, was very proud of his gown. 'We had,' said one friend, 'a joke about whether he even took it off for bed!'

And he was, friends recall, an unforgettable sight, habitually crossing New College's magnificent front quad at dusk, his floppy haired and pouting angel profile set off a treat by the bible-black academic robes that billowed dramatically behind him: a well-thumbed, second-hand, biliously yellow-jacketed copy of Henry Sweet's 1876 *An Anglo-Saxon Reader* seemingly permanently in one hand, the other tugging at the gown, which threatened constantly to slip from one white-shirted shoulder.

'When I first saw Hugh,' says one male contemporary (who is now happily married and employed in a responsible position for the government, yet can effortlessly transform himself back into a gibberingly jealous callow youth at the memory), 'he was standing in his gown one late afternoon that first term, talking to three girls at once beside the porter's lodge. One was a very pretty redhead from Surrey that everyone in the college was dying to get to know better. I remember coming to a halt and standing quite still for a moment, feeling very cold, looking at Hugh, and then looking at the three girls looking at him, and telling myself, "Bloody hell, you're in serious trouble, if there are dozens more here who look like him!"

'To my considerable relief no one else was remotely as good-looking as Hugh. That is, the rest were good-looking in the very normal way.'

To many of Hugh Grant's contemporaries at Oxford, there appeared to be three distinct Hughs at the university. There was Hugh the First, the bright, hard-working, witty Hugh who played rugby and tennis with his Latymer mates and sank pints at the university's main student pub, the King's Arms. Then there was Hugh the Second. The scholar aesthete, who dabbled in watercolours at the weekend and sloped about with his pockets bulging with obscure European novels. And, finally, there was Hugh the Third, the Great Pretender, the Piers Gaveston Society 'pet' who spouted quotations from Huysmans's classic novel of decadence, *Against Nature*, and who was chosen as a symbol of Oxford's *jeunesse dorée* for the film *Privileged*.

By the end of his first term, however, Hugh was sufficiently confident about college life to co-host a traditional New College tea party, with one of his new chums, an admiring fellow New College English undergraduate with whom he would remain in contact for many years after university, Tim Whitby. Perhaps, in retrospect, there is something a little precious at the sight of strapping eighteen- and nineteen-year-old fellows serving their friends with oblong, crustless egg-and-cress and cucumber sandwiches and Earl Grey tea (or a very dubious punch if you preferred), from crested college crockery in rather naffly furnished college bedsitting-rooms on a gloomy December Friday, as if it was in the middle of the Henley Regatta.

When, in fact, the very next day, most were due to return home to their 'real' lives for the Christmas vacation with bin-liners heaving with dirty clothes, rather more noticeably florid accents than the ones they'd arrived with, and carefully prepared, emotionally loaded speeches about the unforeseen overdraft situation.

Certainly there would have been one or two mothers, had they observed their own hale offspring daintily nibbling and sipping in such a refined manner, who would have fainted clean away in shock.

Yet Hugh seemed born to the part of Oxbridge host. Dressed in a tweed jacket he darted about proffering plates and cups at his party with a dottily agonized 'I don't think these are *too* disgusting – *please* say you don't mind'; and entertaining friends with stories of his 'terrible Italian confessions' – anecdotes of romantic encounters with foreign girls. Yet he failed to become ridiculous. There was, until he fell in with one of the richest and smartest

Oxford sets, the amused edge to Hugh, the side that slyly winked and whispered, 'You're not taking this *too* seriously are you?'

One Old Etonian, who knew Hugh well at Oxford, says, 'We were all acting, we were all trying on new personalities to see if they fitted. The aesthete one week, the academic the next. Here were all the OEs [Old Etonians], pretending in their first term that they hadn't been to Eton, because, of course, it wasn't the slightest bit cool for a while. It was quite the reverse. And here was Hugh, acting like he had been to Eton. It was all pretty confusing!'

It was thanks to his scholarship status, and a quickly gained reputation for rapid-fire wit, that Hugh was almost immediately referred to as one of the 'brilliant' set at the university, though, it must be said, there were a fair number of such folk about. The whole point of being at Oxford, not that anyone ever acknowledged that there *was* a point, was that one was surely surrounded by extraordinarily brilliant people the whole time. This had the effect of creating some dizzyingly circular conversations.

'Have you met Hugh Grant yet?'

'*God*, yes. You know he's quite brilliant.'

'Absolutely. Sarah told me.'

'God, *her*! I've heard she's incredibly brilliant too.'

'Oh, she is! Though Fenton says she thinks you're brilliant.'

'Me? What about Fenton? If anyone's brilliant, he is.'

'Yes, that's what Hugh Grant was saying.'

Though it is frequently the self-deprecating claim of Oxford graduates like Hugh that 'a newt' would be more than capable of completing a degree course at the university, this is not quite the case. His English tutors included Professor Anne Barton, now at Cambridge University, a world-class authority on Shakespeare and an exacting intellectual guide, who remembers Hugh as being tremendously entertaining as well as a thoroughly conscientious student.

The tutorial system at Oxford requires undergraduates to attend weekly meetings with a tutor in very small groups – sometimes even one-to-one – to discuss the term's authors and to present essays. When you are one-to-one with a tutor, it is hard to melt into the background. Because the Oxford academic terms are up to four weeks shorter than those at other universities, New College instituted termly 'collections', that is, mini-exams or timed essays to make sure holiday reading projects weren't entirely ignored. A newt, basically, would be rumbled fairly quickly.

At the end of the summer (Trinity) term of his first year, Hugh sat his Honour Moderations, a mandatory set of six exams for all students of English, covering their first year's work, including the dreaded compulsory Old English translation. Hugh Grant is probably, with the exception of another University College graduate, Michael York, the only Hollywood star familiar with Byrhtnoth's crime of 'ofermod' in the Old English poem, *The Battle of Maldon*.

Thus on Friday, 27 June 1980, at 9.30 a.m., Hugh Grant was reduced to an anonymous 'candidate number' to wrestle for three hours with brain-teasers such as – to quote from the terrifying paper – 'Symbolism, Imagism, Expressionism, Fauvism, Cubism, Futurism, Vorticism, Constructivism, Serialism, Dadaism, Surrealism, Structuralism ... Why has the twentieth century been *par excellence* the age of -isms?' Or, 'In what ways has the "Celtic fringe" altered the appearance of modern literature?'

That same day, at 2.30 in the afternoon, Hugh was back at his examination desk, attempting to choose between making sense of Samuel Beckett on the art of Matisse (well-nigh impossible), and commenting on the relationship between the Bible and the study of English literature. Perhaps, though – an intriguing thought – the future Los Angeles vice cop's detainee might have been stimulated to pass comment on a passage from John Henry Newman in which a true English gentleman is defined as 'one who never inflicts pain'.

In any event, Hugh did well enough in Mods to retain his scholarship status. He had also, setting a pattern that would continue – with the occasional interruption for a blonde – for the next fifteen years, found himself a dark, glamorous, exotically beautiful and feisty girlfriend.

SIX

'*It is better to be beautiful than good. But it is better to be good than to be ugly.*'

Oscar Wilde,
The Soul of a Man Under Socialism

When the eponymous character Zuleika Dobson came up to Oxford in Max Beerbohm's frothy fantasy novel of 1911 – still a favourite read of 1980s undergraduates, and adored by Hugh – she had one singular advantage over every other female in the university. Which was rather the point of the whole book.

Zuleika Dobson was actually a looker.

(No, a *looker*.)

As Beerbohm wrote, in sorrow more than mirth, 'Beauty and the lust for learning have yet to be allied.'

Elegantly expressed, it was nevertheless a gross collective libel about Oxford ladies (and Oxford men too) that took root and flourished for the next fifty years. Even as late as the sixties it was still the norm for a young college blood in search of a girl to escort to the May Balls to be found either sniffing round the city's numerous secretarial establishments, or importing some chap's sister from London if he desired someone sans moustache and kipper feet. It was not unknown, *in extremis*, for a man to borrow a foreign-language student – and pray she'd keep her mouth shut for the evening. Naturally this was all in the days before the majority of colleges had gone – like boiled sweets – mixed, and had therefore as much to do with the comparatively tiny numbers of women at the university as it had with the unkindly exaggerated lack of physical charms among those pioneers.

But, by the early seventies and ever after, the myth of

the Oxford harpy was over. As the numbers of women at the university multiplied it became obvious that Oxford was bulging with hordes of staggeringly pretty – as well as formidably bright – female undergraduates. Hugh did not exactly suffer while studying. The *Tatler* magazine then was smartly off the blocks to start celebrating Oxford's new belles. Out went all the two-O-level Carolines from the counties posing with their heads cocked to one side while curry-combing their horses, and in came full-page portraits of adorable creamy-skinned things called Ginny, peering from beneath clouds of bright red hair and above captions explaining that 'Ginny is studying Politics, Philosophy and Economics at Wadham College, works for Elite Models during the long vacations and hopes to join the Federal Trade Commission in Washington after graduation. Ginny has been styled by . . .'

The wails from the cruelly abandoned secretarial colleges have been keen ever since. It was enough to make them all fall, ceremonially, on the sharp ends of their Biros.

And yet the future Hollywood superstar Hugh would act, gratifyingly, far from immune to the 100 w.p.m. charms of one of their kind.

For at Oxford University Hugh gave up his former 'snogathon' existence in favour of one serious girlfriend, one acting girlfriend – and several mistresses.

His serious girlfriend was Mary Glanville, an outstanding-looking young woman even by the standards of Oxford's new model army. His acting girlfriend was the stunning Victoria Studd. And the mistresses included academic work, parties, the Piers Gaveston Society, parties, tennis, painting and parties. Usually, but not always, in that order.

Mary Glanville was a ravishingly pretty, green-eyed, raven-haired, half-Russian, modern languages undergraduate, who was the toast of the Gaveston Society. Oxford's beauties at the time tended to fall into two camps: the pre-Raphaelite nymphs with curtains of hair, sleepy eyes and high, round bosoms; and the rail-thin, sharp-as-tacks blondes who were always being photographed at parties with their mouths wide open. Mary was one of the former, Victoria one of the latter.

Mary is described by one friend who acted with her in her first year as 'almost immediately, one of the most glamorous girls in the university. Mary was not the most beautiful but she was incredibly pretty and very stylish and exotic. She was very groomed-looking. This was at a time when most of the rest of us looked as if we still got our mothers to buy our underwear. Which, of course, most of us did.'

Another (male) friend recalls, 'Mary was a poppet, but she had an extraordinary temper. She could act very temperamentally one minute at a party – the big shouting scene; very Russian, I suppose – then go back to the smiles the next. She was great fun to have around and a very good match for Hughie, a *femme fatale* with a serious side. There was a black-and-red dress she wore which seems to have coloured my entire memory of Oxford.'

Mary Glanville and Hugh Grant had more than their extreme good looks in common. Mary – her mother was Russian, her father English – had seriously considered drama school instead of university because of her interest in acting. She had accepted her Oxford place largely on the advice of her parents rather than her own instincts. 'I felt that they probably knew me better than I did at the time,' she says now.

Mary, like Hugh, had also attended one of London's better single-sex schools – Mary Datchelor's in South London – which also placed special emphasis on the arts, and music in particular. At Oxford Mary read French and Italian at the then women-only Somerville College (where Margaret Thatcher had been a student, as had Indira Ghandi, Shirley Williams and Iris Murdoch).

Her choice of Somerville – where, like Hugh, she spent her first two years living in college rooms before moving out into private rented accommodation in the city for the final year – was deliberate. 'I'd always had single-sex education and it suited me. I preferred to create my own environment rather than join one that had been created by someone else. Anyway, Somerville was lovely, full of eccentrics,' she says generously.

Mary and Hugh met early in their first year at Oxford, on the standard introductory tour given to freshers of the Oxford Union building. The Union is the university's early-nineteenth-century debating society. Becoming President of the Union is almost obligatory for undergraduates who intend to pursue a career in politics, particularly Conservative politics. It is Mary's impression that neither she nor Hugh – whose interest in politics has always been extremely slight – summoned the strength to visit the Union a second time during their three years at Oxford, except to attend Gaveston parties.

The two became firm friends before they became lovers – which is not wholly typical of university relationships. They played tennis, with each other and with two of Hugh's closest Latymer mates (and later close friends of Mary's, too): the charmingly urbane Matthew Bond (who was at Wadham College) and the amiable and very funny Guy Bensley (at University College).

It was only gradually that they transformed their relationship into something more intimate. 'I really didn't fancy him at first – I just liked him enormously. We used to sit and talk and talk until five in the morning and then we'd go back to our respective rooms. This went on for ages. Then I suppose there just came a moment at five a.m. one day when I felt, "Gracious, this is ridiculous",' says Mary delicately.

At Oxford, as at any other university in the country, there was no special or discernible overall pattern to sexual relations between undergraduates. There was simply lots of it, going on everywhere, against a more gloriously honeysuckle-scented and cloistered background than anywhere else imaginable in Britain; and Mary and Hugh were, in this respect, the norm. At Oxford, as was rarely the case with one's woefully unliberated parents at home, the placement of a medium-sized wastepaper bin outside one's bedroom door, and a legible note pleading,

'Please do not disturb', generally produced just that effect the next morning. On the occasions when it did not, the consequences were not generally too severe.

If a couple were surprised *à deux* before breakfast in a female undergraduate's college room, the 'scout', or college cleaner, would usually hiss, 'Ooh, it's that little baggage in number four again!' before slamming shut the door and rattling around in a handy mop cupboard until the door was heard to open and close a second time and male footsteps pattered down the hall. If it was a man's room in which the warm bodies were discovered, the door would be more gently shut after a fleeting wink had been exchanged with the male occupant. This was 1980, after all, not 1990.

Together Mary and Hugh also evolved into one of the most relentless partygoing couples of their year. Yet Hugh, at least, remained as scrupulous about fulfilling his academic obligations as he had been at Latymer.

'He was very conscientious about his work while I was the opposite,' confirms Mary. 'There was never any question that he might not finish some work, or skip something, or miss doing something. There was no way he would even have turned in an essay late. He even got at me for not being conscientious enough. It's true, I wasn't.

'Nigella Lawson [daughter of the former Chancellor of the Exchequer, Nigel, now Lord Lawson, a former Godolphin girl and a leading light of the university party scene] was my tutorial partner for a while and she was also terribly conscientious. I remember at one point feeling genuinely worried and going to the head of my faculty and saying that I really didn't think I was going to get my degree at all. He told me that the really unfair thing about Oxford was that there were some people who spent all their time in libraries and some people who did the exact opposite and in the end everyone gets a second.'

The faculty head's words were prophetic. Both Mary and Hugh, despite their noticeably different approaches to academia, received respectable second-class degrees.

But unexpectedly, while Mary became heavily involved

in student drama at Oxford, Hugh – perhaps oddly at first – did the exact opposite. The stage-struck Hughie of Latymer Upper had entirely vanished.

At Oxford – as at most universities – the opportunities for acting are legion. If you wished to act, however minimal your talents, there was no excuse at all for not doing so.

In addition to the prestigious shows staged by the official – and self-impressed – university society (the Oxford University Dramatic Society, or OUDS, of which Richard Burton was a starring player) and the major independent groups (the Experimental Theatre Company), there are dozens of independent and college-based societies and clubs all friskily competing with one another for actors, reviews and audiences.

And, should you not rate any of *them*, you merely went ahead and established your own company. If you had fancied a night out at the threatre in Oxford on Thursday, 17 May 1981, in the summer of Hugh's second year, for example, you were – in theory at least – marvellously spoilt for choice with *Once a Catholic* at the New Theatre, *Titus Alone* at the Playhouse, *Sisters* by David Storey at the Newman Rooms, *Orpheus Descending* at Somerville, *Erik Satie – A Velvet Gentleman* at Oxford Polytechnic and *A History of the Devil* and *A Dangerous World* at the Newman Rooms.

Mary wasted little time in getting involved in Oxford as an actress. She appeared in Somerville's freshers' play (which marched off with top honours at the annual university-wide first-term 'Cuppers' competition) and averaged a couple of productions a term for her first two years. This was about the maximum permitted before tutors started knitting their brows and muttering thinly about how Oxford is *meant* to be a university and *not* a provincial offshoot of RADA. Mary's Nurse in the Playhouse production of *Romeo and Juliet* (February, 1981) was one of the biggest hits of the year – and so popular with both gown *and* town audiences that it helped the play make an almost unheard of £900 profit. Mary's performance '. . . with her flapping arms and scolding totter, risked upstaging the rest of the cast by its hilarity,' noted the university magazine *Isis* approvingly.

Mary still remembers that role with affection. 'It was one of the few times I wasn't cast on my looks or my voice.' Mary Glanville's voice is foghorn-deep and as husky as a coconut. Her looks made her obvious casting as, say, a Prohibition era calypso Cleopatra. 'I think people were surprised I could be funny,' she notes drily. 'I also wanted to make people *cry* when I found Juliet dead; it was sheer manipulation!'

In the cloistered world of acting at Oxford it is only mildly surprising to find Mallary Gelb, one of Hugh's ex-girlfriends from London and now up at Lady Margaret Hall, working as stage manager on a production of *Candide* in which Mary appeared. Or to discover that Victoria Studd, who would play Hugh's girlfriend in the film *Privileged*, designed the costume Mary wore as Helen in *Troilus and Cressida*. Or that one strikingly handsome blond actor Nick Hutchison, who has a small part in Hugh's 1995 movie *Restoration*, not only played Achilles in that same Oxford production of *Troilus and Cressida* with Mary Glanville, but was also an undergraduate with Jamie Grant at Worcester College, and played opposite Hugh's older brother as an upper-class twit in a production of *Le Misanthrope*.

(Today Nick Hutchison – who turned down a lead role in Hugh's first film *Privileged* – has a production company, Aquinas, with the actress Joanne Pearce and Tim McInnerny, who shot to TV fame in *Blackadder*, which was written, of course, by the *Four Weddings* author Richard Curtis. The Old Boy network grinds merrily on!)

In sharp contrast to his schooldays, however, Hugh was mostly content to remain on the audience's side of the curtain while at Oxford. He was happy to attend Mary's performances. Friends remember him 'gurgling helplessly with laughter' during a woefully under-rehearsed production at Somerville of Oscar Wilde's *An Ideal Husband*. But this was never, says Mary, a source of friction between them.

'I can't remember my acting ever causing any problems,' she says simply. 'Though if we *had* both been acting, I think it would have been terrible for us, *terribly* competitive!' Hugh has said that he shied away from university acting because it was 'too cliquey' for his tastes. This is certainly a very familiar complaint about drama at Oxford and one that has been aired almost annually since OUDS was established in 1885.

It was widely agreed that the cliquey nature of OUDS had really become a little too cute when, at one point in 1981, its president, treasurer and co-opted member all shared one house.

Nevertheless, Hugh did become a member of the Piers Gaveston Society – which is, to say the least, considerably more cliquey than OUDS. He had also been part of the golden inner circle of the Gild at Latymer, without noticeably suffering from claustrophobia.

The truth was that Hugh was rather shrewder about his career than he sometimes gives himself credit for. He *had* joined OUDS in his first year, in a production of *Twelfth Night*. The play had toured northern France – it was a famously stressful tour because of organizational problems with one or two minor, if noisy, 'nervous breakdowns' among youthful cast members – in the early spring of 1980, with members of the cast staying with obliging host families. Perhaps even now there is a family in Caunes or Rouen – two of the cities toured – tremulously waking up to the tremendous realization that they once gave duvet space to Ooog – as he's known throughout France – *le star* of *Quatre Marriages et Une Enterrement* et *Quelques Minutes sur Sunset Boulevard*.

Hugh played the servant Fabian, a character with a mere few dozen not amazingly funny lines ('A fustian riddle!' being typical). And, although Shakespearian servants are indeed notorious scene-stealers, in *Twelfth Night*, it is another servant named Feste to whom that honour usually falls. In short, Hugh's part was not an easy one in which to shine.

Those who saw the 1980 *Twelfth Night* remember

chiefly a stunningly elegiac production, with a beautifully effective Viola (Jenny Waldman) and a super Olivia (Linda Brandon, who died early in 1992).

Fabian is dimly recalled as a stiffish and unhappy-looking, though very good-looking, fellow. Playing seventh fiddle as one of the most minor characters did not suit Hugh at all. He had already spent ten years at Latymer climbing from chorus parts to starring role. The idea of beginning this race from the bottom all over again and being marked as a drama 'hack' – one of dozens of undergraduates cosying up to untested directors – was, he decided, too yawny for words. Though a majority of the *Twelfth Night* cast did doggedly press on with acting, appearing in numerous OUDS and college productions and cutting their teeth as demon directors, Hugh's contempt for the official Oxford acting scene was all too evident. He was already discovering that another side of Oxford existed, which permitted dressing up in costume and playing roles without the fag of learning dozens of lines. And, besides his academic work, there was Mary – and so many *parties*!

'We had,' says Mary, very fondly, 'an absolutely wonderful and frivolous time together at parties. I felt like I could act my age for the first time in my life. We had no responsibilities at all. I was also very aware that it was a temporary stage I was passing through, that it was all going to end after three years and that it wasn't terribly real.'

They made an unforgettably handsome, sleekly dark-headed pair, flitting, hands clasped, in the damp blue dusk of Oxford's summer evenings, from college to yellow-lit college, across the Broad and the High Street, along the Cornmarket, the Turl or down St Giles' for cocktails at the city's popular palm-potted – and far from cheap – restaurant, Brown's. They looked – many remember with pangs of envy – like Hollywood's idea of a genetically boosted Oxford undergraduate couple.

Hugh was sometimes in formal evening wear, usually with his trademark, open-at-the-neck, white shirt and the same unchanging *Four Weddings* haircut – romantically overlong at the front, with a regulation national-service-length trim at the back. Mary was slim as a whip, but not in the least boyishly built, all flashing green eyes, four-inch heels and a vividly scarlet mouth, always stunning in black – though this was not purely an affectation, but grew out of economic necessity.

'Because I bought all my clothes from Lawrence Corner [a cheap but very trendy army and navy surplus store in London] and everything there was black. I suppose student poverty can sometimes give you a kind of glamour,' she says in amusement now.

Friends and contemporaries remember the Glanville–Grant relationship as intoxicatingly rowdy, foreshadowing his similarly temperamental liaison with Elizabeth Hurley – particularly when measured against the rather beige Laura Ashley standards of the period.

'They were a time bomb. Mary was very beautiful and Hugh was very beautiful and they'd sort of shake up parties because you'd never know which one was going to erupt first,' recalls one friend. 'Though Mary was sweet, and rather kind, I think, underneath.'

'It was volatile, yes,' agrees Mary. 'It certainly felt pretty dramatic at the time. We would have an argument and he would go off one way and I would go off in another, then I would unexpectedly turn up at a party where he was and I'd bellow "*Hughie!*" across the room ... I think we slightly played up to it all. It wasn't Burton and Taylor by any means but I am very fiery by nature. We were not the quintessential Oxford couple – I suppose you could say we were one of the few dark-haired versions of the "Oxford couple". Somehow Oxford was a terribly *blond* society then and Hugh and I weren't. We had a certain reputation as a "public couple". In a way, being with Hugh was like having a safe mate. I was much too shy to turn up to things on my own. It was lovely having this partnership.'

Although Mary is uneasy about discussing why the way she and Hugh looked should have made a difference to their social life as students at England's most élitist university, she concedes, 'It's a lot easier at Oxford – as it is in life – if your looks are right. It makes things smoother, it gives you a foot in the door. If people find you attractive, they want you to be with them – as a million boring career and management studies have shown.

'In a bizarre sort of way Hugh, especially, was cultivated by various social sets. It was as if they chose him, adopted him I suppose. There were certain social queens who decided who was acceptable and who wasn't, and they decided Hugh was. But I wasn't aware that Hugh was ever at all concerned about his looks. That was other people's concern and Hugh was very, very pragmatic about it. He completely had his feet on the ground. I remember thinking his family was also very pragmatic and down-to-earth. No matter how much flattery he received, or how much attention he got, he stayed bemused by it rather than anything else.'

The flattery – and attention – did establish Hugh very firmly as one of the university's leading heart-throbs in residence. It was not always a position he relished since it came rather as if he'd been suddenly appointed ambassador to some vaguely hostile but dependent republic, trailing all the more difficult diplomatic burdens of office.

Such as trying to be perfectly charming while dampening down unwanted or unsolicited sexual advances, which arrived in numbing numbers from both men and women.

'Mostly it was all a joke, sometimes it was really off,' says one close friend of both Hugh and Mary from Oxford. 'There were one or two men who would go round saying openly, "I just must have that boy, I insist," as if Hughie had nothing to do with it. Mind you, Hughie could be a brilliant actor when he wasn't in a play; he could out-camp the best of them at Oxford.'

Other friends weren't always convinced by Hugh's role-playing skills, however. What appeared as a mercurial, enchantingly flash personality to some was regarded as oily and also slightly threatening by others.

'I never understood Hughie's game at Oxford at all,' says a slightly younger fellow Latymerian. 'I'd see him and he would ask, in a very searching way, how I was doing and how he had been thinking about me and how intelligent I was. It was as if he was throwing himself on my mercy! Then afterwards, you'd wonder if he'd been laughing at you. As if he'd been saying to himself, "How much praise will this very stupid person take from me?" It was a very unsettling feeling. I hated it.'

Though Hugh infrequently publicly exercised his skills as an actor while at Oxford, he did so often – to the genuine delight of Mary and other friends – in private. Mary says, 'I always thought Hugh incredibly funny. He got away with murder sending up people's mannerisms and openly aping people. I used to think of it as a Bruce Forsyth sense of humour. Hugh attacked people by mimicking them quite openly, right in front of them. He derived a lot of humour from people's looks. He was always very conscious and aware of the shape of people's bodies, their walks and voices.

'Hugh's sense of humour is like the old cliché – you know, telling someone to fuck off in a foreign language they can't understand and in such a polite way the deadliness is completely unobserved. I also used to make Hugh read to me because I loved it so much. I'd make him read anything and everything. I always had to ask him, of course. He'd never offer – or just start declaiming out of the blue! He just had an extraordinarily beautiful voice, very modulated, with a wonderful delivery. Someone said he had a voice like crystal, and that is exactly the sound: it is so incredibly clear.

'There are certain voices that you could listen to endlessly, and Hugh has one of them. His looks may be thought of as very special but, compared to his voice, they really come way down the line. His was very special.'

Yet it was Hugh's face – 'his shining Parsifal profile', as one later friend of the actor's put it admiringly – that gained him admittance to the various lofty social sets that 'cultivated' him. The most important of these – in terms of both social status and its effect on his personality – being undoubtedly the Piers Gaveston Society.

SEVEN

'I think it was some time in my second year [at Oxford] that the slippery-slidy slope began. There was a sort of posh set that I wasn't in, being a grammar-school boy, but I rather fancied being in it. So I used to gate-crash with a friend called Daggenhurst [spelling corrected]. He was a total fraud. His real name is Karamanos and he's a Greek ... But we used to gate-crash a lot of parties and rub shoulders with the nobs, snog them a bit and go home again. I think they slightly despised me. Deep down I don't think I was posh enough for them.'

Hugh Grant,
quoted in the Sunday Times, UK, 1994

'I'm afraid I was Mr Dull at Oxford.'

Hugh Grant,
quoted in Premiere magazine, 1994

Hugh prefers to keep quiet, or express no more than the odd tantalizingly vague reference to his membership of the gay-themed Piers Gaveston Society at Oxford – the exclusive and riotous all-male undergraduate club to which he was tremendously partial for the better part of his three student years.

It is hard to blame him. A sense of discretion, sometimes approaching Masonic paranoia, has always been a byword of the Piers Gaveston Society for obvious reasons. The less known for sure about members' rumoured debauched antics, the more thrillingly glamorous they appear. A certain caution serves also to protect the youthful reputations of its wilder acolytes. Gaveston parties were rarely held twice at the same Oxford location – not simply to provide a change of scene, but because even Oxford's famously long-suffering catering staff baulked at clearing up for a second time this rowdy lot's inevitable debris of vomit, discarded knickers and smashed glasses.

Discretion, too, usefully cloaks the fact that the homo-erotic façade of the society was largely a pretence. The idea of Hugh and his overwhelmingly heterosexual fellow Gaveston cronies winking at each other in camp fancy dress while tipsily mouthing the motto, 'In him! Up him! Through him!' – a toast to the society's inspiration, King Edward II's favourite, Piers Gaveston – is not an especially edifying one in the climate of the 1990s.

But, as one former Gaveston friend of Hugh's warned, there is a danger of breaking the butterfly upon the wheel. The Piers Gaveston was a dining society devoted to hedonism. It wore its snobbery on its sleeve. It was made up of almost exclusively upper-middle-class, public-school-educated – mainly white – young men, some barely out of their teens (although Hugh attended Gaveston reunions well into his late twenties), who were hell-bent on enjoying three carefree years of university life at a time when Oxford heaved with similar societies. It gave not a damn about soaring unemployment levels, then approaching two million in London alone, in an England on the brink of recession. And this was no freakish accident of the period. The spectre of the 1981 *Brideshead Revisited* television series had a levitating effect on the affectations of the university's social élite.

Evelyn Waugh reappraised his own novel about *la belle vie* at Oxford in the 1920s as a 'panegyric preached over an empty coffin', when he trimmed some of the excesses of the original for later editions. Nevertheless, the giddily romantic television adaptation had wheeled the gilded corpse back into public view. Richer students were galvanized into the self-conscious activity of *proving* that their Oxford did not compare wanly to Waugh's fictional version. Snobbery and exhibitionism were raised into stylish virtues. *Elan* – the spirit with which you conducted yourself – was everything. Fancy dress and dining clubs multiplied like bacteria throughout the headily social hot-house atmosphere of the wealthier colleges.

At the Vile Bodies Club, named after another of Waugh's works, teddy-bear-toting undergraduates attended dinners dressed up as Waugh characters and skipped off pointedly to Calais for May Day celebrations rather than gathering for the charming tradition of dawn choristers at Magdalen Tower – which was, of course, open to the *hoi polloi* of Oxford, thus no longer remotely counting as stylish. Keats Society meetings – which Hugh also attended – had precious little to do with the poet and everything to do with drinking, stylish eating and, if one struck lucky, athletic sexual couplings with willing female guests beneath dining-room tables while the lads cheered on. The innocent name was, as members were only too merrily aware, enormously useful when booking function rooms.

'But remember, this *was* fifteen years ago – it was all pre-AIDS and it was all before Olivia Channon too,' one cohort of Hugh's cautioned. Olivia Channon was, tragically, the 22-year-old who became a symbol of the *Brideshead* hangover's darker side. The undergraduate daughter of Britain's then Trade and Industry Secretary Paul Channon – the MP for Oxford while Hugh was a student – Olivia Channon died after drinking and taking drugs at a post-Finals party in Christ Church College, Oxford, in June 1986 – four years after Hugh's graduation. Her death profoundly shook the university authorities out of a curiously *laissez faire* attitude towards drink and drugs among its young scholars and it temporarily sobered the rich, fast student set. The body of the once so privileged young Olivia Channon was found in the rooms of Count Gottfried von Bismarck, great-great-grandson of Germany's Iron Chancellor.

But back in the early 1980s the main aim of the rich, fast Gaveston set was to have unfettered fun – in great style – while cocking a cheeky snook at the longer-established Oxford societies: the Bullingdon Club, for instance, which held its own point-to-point meetings, and was founded, as members seldom failed to mention, in

1880; and the Grid Iron, which became, a few years after Hugh's time at Oxford, the club of choice of the disgraced fraudster Darius Guppy, was founded in 1884. By comparison, the Piers Gaveston Society was a brazen stripling, formed only in 1976 by a group of decadent-minded students including, coincidentally, Mary Glanville's older sister, Helen.

Mary says, 'I actually believe it was *more* outrageous in their days. They were genuine hedonists! By the time I became involved there was a fixed determination, the *affectation* to behave outrageously – but it was still great fun.'

Benazir Bhutto, as its founding members are prone to boasting, used to attend the earliest Gaveston drinks parties in the days when she was President of the Oxford Union. Mercifully this didn't appear to impede her subsequent career as Prime Minister of Pakistan and the first female leader of a Muslim nation.

As every English school pupil knows, the deposed King Edward II was killed in 1327 by the ramming of a red-hot poker up his backside, which served the twin purpose of leaving no easily visible scorch marks and symbolizing his murderers' disgust for his supposed homosexuality.

Fifteen years earlier, Edward's favourite, the stylishly arrogant Gascon knight Piers Gaveston, was believed to have met his end, so to speak, in the same fashion. The students took Gaveston as their hero, and gleefully incorporated some of the known facts about him into society lore – how he scandalously turned up at Edward's coronation all in purple and dripping with pearls, for example, and loved to give nobles rude nicknames, and then beat them in duels.

Gaveston officials were given lubricious quasi-historical titles: the Poker was the most senior, followed by Master of Debaucheries, Warden of the Closet, Keeper of the Plumes, Secretary to the Anals and Dispenser. On one occasion, when a Gaveston official studying modern languages was required to spend the mandatory year abroad, he was given the courtesy title Queen In Exile – a witty nod to Edward II's estranged wife Isabella, who plotted against her husband and his favourites after fleeing, fed up, to the French court in 1325.

Each member had a Minion or a Catamite who was supposed to take over the title of his 'master' when the latter graduated from university. In reality, this didn't always happen. Some members dropped out because they couldn't afford the fees; others because they fell out with each other. There was, past members confirm, a vicious amount of squabbling for position among officials. Hugh was variously a Minion and Keeper of the Plumes.

New members were selected on the unabashedly élitist basis of 'looks, money and election'. Elections were held in secret by a cabal of officials – that is, a bunch of giggling former public schoolboys debating whether a candidate's Harrow background counted as 'posh' enough to warrant admission. Or whether, in another case, the chap's old family connections with a liquor company might usefully provide the Society with cheap, but quality, booze. They did, and he was in.

Those judged to fulfil the criteria satisfactorily would discover an engraved Gaveston card, bearing the happy news, slipped anonymously into their room.

'I remember,' says one, 'the sheer excitement of finding the note between the pages of T.S. Eliot's *Sweeney Agonistes*. It was *appalling* how much it mattered to me, how I felt I finally belonged.'

Swiftly following the acceptance note came a bill for around seventy pounds sterling. To undergraduates like Hugh, who lacked the cushion of a trust fund or indulgently wealthy parents, the membership fee represented a painful chunk of a term's grant. Nevertheless, the investment meant he could now cavort with his new 'posh' Gaveston friends on their level. And Hugh, prettier than all of them, wittier than most, and dazzled by their easy certainty that the world was their private oyster, was an enthusiastic convert.

One, to whom he remained close after university, was the floridly affable Geordie Greig. Greig was a rare Gaveston member from St Peter's College – which wasn't remotely considered a 'posh' college, but he more than made up for this breach by hailing from an impeccably well-connected family. His sister, Laura Lonsdale, was a childhood friend of the Princess of Wales and her flatmate and, later, a lady-in-waiting.

Though by no means an academic dazzler at Oxford, Geordie Greig went on to carve out an impressive career in journalism as the *Sunday Times* New York correspondent, even interviewing his old Gaveston friend, Hugh, for a highly flattering profile about his acting career (which made no mention of the Gaveston link).

Hugh's closest Gaveston chum, however, was the high-spirited, aggressively charming, public-school-educated Danny Daggenhurst, whom he unkindly outed to the *Sunday Times* as a 'total fraud' for being, in reality, 'a Greek named Karamanos'.

This typically sly dig of Hugh's refers to the decision by Daggenhurst's parents – his father Tassis Karamanos was a Greek diplomat – made a long-buried two decades ago, to bestow thoroughly English names on both their adolescent sons to help them, one assumes, to oil their passage into English society.

Hugh's friend, born Athon Karamanos, son of Tassis and Persa and grandson of the splendidly assonant Athanasios Alexopoulos, re-emerged at the age of fourteen at his top-ranking British public school as Richard Geoffrey Daggenhurst – but was known to everyone at Oxford as Danny. His older brother by eleven months, born Henry Tassis Karamanos, was transformed into Henry Godfrey Daggenhurst. The olive-skinned, raven-haired brothers were already established at Winchester as Karamanos major and minor when the highly unusual 1975 name-change was officially announced. As a result they weathered, say contemporaries, a small storm of sniggers and snobbish comments about 'hiding' their ethnic roots. The arcane complexities of schoolboy Wykehamists' snobbery could virtually be taught as a separate curriculum subject and any lad even slightly different from the majority of his peers could be, and was, a legitimate target for teasing.

Nevertheless, it was rare in the school for pupils from non-standard-British backgrounds to go to the trouble of assuming new identities – with surnames that sounded suspiciously like a cross between a town in Essex and a pukka British military college. But both, too, were insulated from the worst barbs. The Daggenhursts were admired as quite outstandingly brainy, which counts for a great deal at Winchester. They were members of College, Winchester's *crème-de-la-crème*, scholars-only house, for which special exams, stiffer even than the school's notoriously exacting entrance exam, must be passed.

'College' boys had a near-mythical status among the rest of the school's commoners for owning freakishly high IQs. Henry, in particular, was an outstanding sportsman to boot, representing the school in tennis, boxing and fencing. A Wykehamist – or so ran the rule after the initial titters had died away – ragged one of the Daggenhurst/Karamanos brothers on the subject of their new English monikers only at his peril!

Hugh rapidly allied himself instinctively with the only other Gaveston member who might, by virtue of his different background, be considered an outsider. Precociously bright, and something of a dandy, the darkly good-looking Daggenhurst was just seventeen when he won at exhibition to read law at New College, and he was every bit Hugh's intellectual equal. Hugh also found his friend's physical vanity highly amusing. Daggenhurst boxed for the university and was enormously proud of his splendid physique, invariably being one of the first to strip off at parties or pose in the buff for official Gaveston pictures. Yet it was Daggenhurst's Greek side – his tender Achilles' heel – that never failed to intrigue and tickle Hugh.

He took a particular delight in Daggenhurst's grumbling about one of the New College 'scouts' – a matron employed to tidy the undergraduates' rooms. It seemed, to the sensitized Daggenhurst, that the woman always put an unusually heavy emphasis on the word 'home' when she remarked to him at the close of each term that she expected he would be looking forward to 'getting *home* for the holidays'. She seemed to imply that home could not have been, as it *was* in Daggenhurst's case, an extremely smart address in London SW1, but somewhere very hot, foreign and probably not terribly *nice*. Hugh found this genteel racism and his friend's impotent annoyance absolutely hysterical. The two became inseparable.

For a brand-new club among so many already flourishing at Oxford, the Gaveston Society took root and thrived remarkably quickly. Part of its appeal was that, unlike the right-wing Bullingdon (the Bully) or the Oxford Assassins, it had absolutely no political axe to grind. It simply hymned decadence. By the time Hugh and Daggenhurst joined, the society had its own Latin motto, which was written as '*Sane non memini me audisse unum alterum ita dilixisse*' – a version of 'certainly I never saw anybody who was so much delighted by another man' – which some members believe may have been lifted from the sixteenth-century chronicles of Raphael Holinshed.

The Gaveston Society also had its own distinctive crest. This was a shield surmounted by three fleurons and bearing the silhouette of an erect penis, with testicular sac attached, slanting, Tower-of-Pisa-like, from the top left to the bottom right of the shield. Or a rampant phallus from the sinister chief to the dexter base, to put it in the appropriate formal heraldic terms. Members could flaunt the shield on Gaveston bow-ties, in a curiously nasty shade of air-stewardess blue with the emblem in venous purple stitching. These were most certainly *not* supplied by the university's official outfitters. The Society had the ties made up privately in London.

Some members, including Hugh, occasionally sported the penis shield on their bare chests – carefully painted in waterproof theatrical make-up at Gaveston bashes. Cross-dressing at parties was standard – though Hugh favoured fancy dress of a more playfully muscular fashion: tight breeches and leopard-skin togas and manfully torso-baring, short-sleeved leather jackets. Like many Gavestons, Hugh discovered an alternative decorative function for that useful, if pedestrian, item of Oxford student life: the bicycle-chain lock. Despite the genuine risk of one's unlocked bicycle being stolen while one was partying, the chains lent an air of fetishism when worn around the neck – or when attached to a cuff around one's girlfriend's wrist.

Some Gaveston members assuredly went the whole hog in terms of dressing up, lashing on the mascara and draping themselves in shimmering homemade lurex togas, naturally looking absolutely *le dernier mot* in divine decadence when inspected by the dim rays of a 40-watt college-room bulb; but losing a certain *je ne sais quoi* when the pins gave out at the back halfway through the evening and the make-up started to run.

'We'd start out looking like our sisters and end looking like our mothers and *very* much the worse for wear,' lamented one friend of Hugh's sorrowfully. But seldom Hugh. He was always more Pan (as in J.M. Barrie's *Peter Pan* rather than the dark god of the sensual earth as praised by Hugh's beloved E.M. Forster), choosing delightful, often rented, theatrical costumes that made him appear charmingly puckish rather than racily kinky. Even his kohl eyeliner, friends recall, was seldom, if ever, smudged.

Within the Gaveston set, Hugh would refer to his girlfriend by her surname adding the tag 'minor', as if she were a younger lad at public school. He, too, thoroughly enjoyed the antics of the 'Gaveston Girls' or 'Pussy Posses' – pretty, uninhibited younger girls from Oxford's secretarial colleges and polytechnics or friends of friends from London who were happily herded along to liven up Gaveston parties and who could be relied upon to show up in micro-mini rubber skirts and suspenders – in short, tricked out like fantasy hookers. And all too frequently living up to their costumes' image, too, after quaffing many vodka cocktails.

Memories remain sharp of an exceptionally energetic

and charming Gaveston chum of Hugh's who managed to score, often with a Gaveston girl, at every party the Society threw. When asked at one party by his suspicious regular girlfriend to explain fresh mud stains on his trousers – he had in fact been pleasuring a Gaveston girl in a flower-bed nearby – he solemnly confessed he *had* been overcome by a powerful urge outdoors that would explain the mud stains. He had, said this dreadful youth, been praying!

To Hugh, who had been brought up to 'respect' girls, the Gaveston-girl phenomenon was an eye-opener. Here were young men, his own age, with the confidence, the swaggering assurance of an upper-middle-class public-school upbringing, to import giggling gangs of females to their 'naughty' society, fill them full of drink and persuade them to behave outrageously, then to send them home on the morning train full of coffee and aspirin, with a squeeze of thanks for being 'such jolly good sports'.

And the girls didn't seem to *mind*. They came with obliging frequency in a fragrant Friday exodus from London, flashing long legs in tiny skirts, and willing to flash a lot more for the privilege of being admitted to the 'damnably magical' inner enclave of Oxford's élite. For a grammar-school boy, who had only rarely been away from home until university and had never boarded, the Gaveston Society offered Hugh intoxicatingly titillating entertainment.

Gaveston parties were thrown – complete with embossed formal invitation cards – in 'honour' of obscure historical or literary figures who might possibly, quite spuriously, be suspected of homosexual liaison. Rude puns about dicks, penal codes, Roman camp and the like were warmly encouraged as descriptions of 'dress codes'.

Hugh, brought up in a family to whom wordplay was second nature and from a school that rated wit highly, found this part reassuringly familiar. As a Minion of the Society Hugh invited select friends to celebrate 'The Morrow of the Feast of S.S. Barlaam & Josaphat' with dress code 'Uranus' at Oxford's lovely Rhodes House (Barlaam being a hermit who converted Josaphat, an Indian prince, according to a popular Christian work of the Middle Ages, which makes no reference to anything but a strictly spiritual relationship between the two men). As Keeper of the Plumes, Hugh asked friends to join the Society 'on the Morrow of the Feast of St Walbuger' for a party at New College's Red Rooms (dress code 'Imperial Leather'), where a cabaret group crooned Grace Jones's 'Warm Leatherette'. Hugh looked divine in skin-tight white breeches, knee-length suede boots and a mini-jacket with gold epaulettes. Other parties were held at the Macmillan and Gladstone Rooms at the Oxford Union and Oxford City Hall. Often accompanied to Gaveston events by Mary Glanville, and later by other pretty undergraduates, Hugh, according to contemporaries, certainly *did* indulge in damp displays of French kissing with fellow male Gavestonians.

'He was a very nice kisser too,' says one stoutly, 'if you liked that sort of thing, which personally I didn't. But if you had to do it, then rather Hugh Grant than some of the others!'

But it was all for show. The Gaveston Society thrived on the spurious *semblance* of sexual naughtiness, of disguising straight sex in ribbons, ruffles, chains, gold spray paint and presenting its gilded image to a *Brideshead*-bedazzled university generation. It was a lesson Hugh absorbed deeply. A Gaveston member who produced a camera at a dinner could guarantee a sudden energetically exhibitionist flurry of lowered trousers, male snogging and scenes of spanking and pouting. Afterwards, it would be back to drinking and snogging with female guests (or decidedly not, for the tiny minority of out-of-the-closet gay Gavestons).

Members were, naturally, encouraged to boast about their sex lives, but on this Hugh did not quite get the rules straight. He rather overdid an anecdote about a highly charged bondage session with an experimentally minded girlfriend. So much so, that it got back by pub gossip to the girl in question, who was understandably incensed that

Hugh had betrayed their intimacy to quite so many people – a foreshadow of a few of the problems Hugh would experience in 1995. Worse, perhaps, was that half the university appeared to know the embarrassing nature of the substance Hugh had asked the girl to lick from his body: henna hair cream.

For the most part, Hugh and Daggenhurst used the Gaveston's links to other societies, like the Kay-Whyte Club – named (almost) after a brand of lubricant jelly, KY – and the Keats Society, to party to their hearts' content in the company of the university's self-appointed élite, and with Hugh's looks, as ever, his passport to social mobility.

But, though Hugh loved to drink and snog girls – and boys – in front of revellers and found the mania for dressing up that convulsed the Oxford party scene a handy outlet for his own frustrated acting ambitions, he did not touch drugs. Hard and soft drugs, from opium to cocaine to cannabis and benzedrine, were a routine feature of Oxford society, but Hugh declared himself 'much too frightened' of becoming addicted to dabble. He also chickened out of one of the Gaveston 'special outings' with slightly more convincing than usual homo-erotic overtones. A 'special outing' other members felt themselves, perversely perhaps, honour-bound to endure. This was a notorious jaunt to London to enact a semi-nude display of oiled wrestling for the entertainment of an 'appreciative and older civil service type' gent at his quarters off Marylebone Road.

'Horribly embarrassing! We all had to get frightfully drunk to do it. You know, really steel ourselves,' says one ex-Gaveston 'Poker', now a sober-suited, married legal professional. 'It was,' says another who took part, very cheerfully, 'a major cringe-maker. But I recall a sort of sense of pride afterwards simply for having done something so undeniably sordid.'

Hugh has referred to his giddy Gaveston partying as part of some 'serious social mountaineering' he undertook at university. What was also undeniable is the effect it all had on his personality. Playing up his 'posh' side became

The author in 1977, the year she went out with a youthful Hugh Grant

Above Hughie Grant and Oxford's undergraduate club
The Boojums request the pleasure of the author's company

Right The flamboyant members of the Piers Gaveston Society
flaunt themselves in the spring of 1982; Hugh Grant is in the
middle row, far left

Left Hugh bringing home the bacon as Lord Adrian in *Privileged*, his first film role, 1982

Right A very English trio: Hugh Grant, Rupert Graves and James Wilby in Merchant-Ivory's *Maurice* in 1987

Below As the 'soggily self-deluding Clive Durham' with his wife (Phoebe Nicholls) in *Maurice*

Above Hugh Grant (Chopin) and Julian Sands (Liszt) sharpen their piano skills in *Impromptu*, 1989 – 'the worst wig film of his career'

Left With Emmanuelle Seigner in Polanski's *Bitter Moon*, the film that finally ignited Hugh's career in 1992

Right As the dapper Cardinal in *The Remains of the Day*, also starring Anthony Hopkins and Emma Thompson, 1993

Left As the best man (*Four Weddings and a Funeral*, 1994) . . .

. . . and clergyman (*Sirens*, 1994)

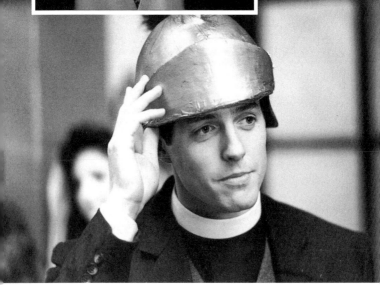

a full-time pursuit. To friends outside the Gaveston circle, Hugh increasingly presented himself as a public-school parody. His vocabulary became absurdly peppered with odd bits of slang that sounded wearyingly like crumbs picked up from too many public-school dinners. He was so much in character as the Gaveston's beautiful grammar-school pet, he seemed at a loss to pick up the old self-mocking Hughie.

Hugh became notorious for camply propositioning other undergraduates' straight boyfriends at non-Gaveston parties, awarding them babyishly diminutive nicknames.

'Hugh made a point of trailing his sexual ambiguity – which was entirely fake – behind him in clouds of glory,' said one Old Etonian Oxford friend. 'He constantly demanded reactions, which could be insufferably tiring.'

Yet his self-possession with the Gaveston crowd was not so complete that he could ignore rumblings that some of his public-school 'friends' thought him both 'insincere' and 'smarmy'.

Hugh once, probably from a mixture of insane cheek and a genuine desire to see if he could pull it off as an actor, claimed to a younger Old Etonian at Oxford, one he had never met before, that he had been schooled at Eton himself. 'No you haven't!' the boy snapped back scornfully. There was no mysterious intuition on the younger student's part: he had merely fired one or two basic if shrewdly worded questions about Eton. Hugh badly fudged the answers. Witnesses to this exchange insist there was no question of Hugh's trying to turn it into a delightful joke. It was simply hugely embarrassing.

The charges of insincerity from some of the Gaveston crowd were well-founded. Hugh regaled college and Latymerian friends with indiscreet stories about some fruitier Gaveston friends which, though funny, sat uneasily with his continued and enthusiastic membership of the society. He seemed to regard himself as genuinely upper-class as a result of social osmosis – yet bitched about his new friends' assumptions of superiority. At heart Hugh was bitterly envious of their supreme confidence. His

Gaveston chums – from Eton and Winchester, and (occasionally) Harrow and Marlborough – seemed, so effortlessly, to be sure of their place in the world.

Beautiful Hugh was their equal only by indulgence. If he'd been a pimpled and plain, yet witty, Latymerian, it is inconceivable he would have been admitted to their ranks – unlike a dreary but socially well-connected old Etonian with the invincible ego produced by that school. Hugh's looks were everything and that, as Hugh knew, was an entirely superficial reckoning. Many of the Gaveston crowd's fathers were socially prominent too: philosophers, economists, diplomats, politicians and peers – none of them unhappy Hammersmith office carpet salesmen. The outrageous snobbery of early 1980s Oxford was a bindweed around Hugh – yet, at the same time, many of the Gaveston crew were genuinely charming, gentle, likeable smiling boys individually. As a pack they brayed and posed and egged each other on to excess while defending their often brutishly hooray behaviour as a last stab at 'harmless' larks before taking up responsible positions in society.

This wasn't an entirely spurious defence. Many did go on to become prominent in the British judiciary or to take up careers in diplomacy and politics. Hugh didn't have this justification. Nor did he quite have the electric force of personality that Richard Burton had owned, when he, too, found himself taken up, after his brief career at Oxford, by a posh Oxford set when he joined his RAF squadron. The proudly working-class Burton was given a joky public-school background and nicknamed Burton of Blundles to justify his inclusion among the officer set and that was that. Hugh might have saved himself a lot of heartache and criticism if only he'd done the same.

Yet Hugh's pose as a beautiful upper-class hooray did bring him to the rapt attention of someone at Oxford – another outsider – who was about to change the course of the actor's life.

EIGHT

*'I watched the film in a near empty cinema in
London practically hiding behind the seat with
shame!'*
One of Hugh's fellow actors in Privileged

Hugh seldom refers to the 'little student film', *Privileged*,
which set his career rolling without a studied wince of
embarrassment.

Privileged, Hugh says bluntly, though 'rather a success',
was also 'the most humourless and pretentious thing you
have ever seen,' and he condemns his own performance in
the movie as appalling. The rare few members of the
public who sat stupefied through *Privileged* – a 90-minute
muddle about effete students putting on a melodramatic
play at Oxford University, and awarded a deservedly
fleeting release in the UK in 1982 and New York in 1983
– will heartily endorse Hugh's harsh opinion.

But the movie *is* nonetheless quite remarkable.

Privileged not only gave the unknown Hugh Grant his
first shot at commercial stardom, but also the personal
guidance of a veteran, Oscar-winning Hollywood director.
In addition the film incubated the talents of a truly
startling number of future international big-screen names.
And, perhaps most importantly, the 'little student film'
presented the then uncommitted and highly impression-
able young undergraduate actor with a dazzling notion.

It convinced him that fame and the promise of a
Hollywood future were prizes that fall ripely into your lap
– if you happen to be blessed with the right face.

When Hugh was in his second year at New College,
dividing his time between his books and his Gaveston pals

and carefully keeping his distance from the university's snootily cliquey acting élite, his path crossed with an older American student, Mike Hoffman.

In 1981 Michael Hoffman, who was born in Boise, Idaho, was some 3,000 miles from home studying at Oxford University, courtesy of the glamorous exit visa of a Rhodes Scholarship. Like a certain Bill Clinton just a dozen years earlier, Hoffman had won one of the 20 plum Rhodes Scholarships annually awarded to bring to Oxford outstanding overseas students from the former British Colonies and Germany. Such scholarships are traditionally awarded to students who are judged not only to be academically gifted, but also to exhibit outgoing, live-wire personalities thought likely to enrich Oxford University life. This was a promise the young Mike Hoffman would fulfil with unique panache.

The compact, wiry, ginger-headed Hoffman was a quintessentially happy Yank at Oxford.

Formidably energetic and a self-confessed film and drama fanatic, Hoffman made no secret of his long-nurtured ambition to become a movie director himself. By all accounts, he was instantly smitten by the ancient charms of the university town and deeply – perhaps a little naively – entranced with its quirkily olde-world traditions.

Hoffman, viewing the city with an outsider's eyes, was genuinely tantalized by the sight of a generation of young Englishmen who seemed compelled to re-create Evelyn Waugh's fictional Oxford for their own amusement. It was a subject he referred to over and again in conversation. Didn't Oxford, he asked friends in amazed delight, with its students on perpetual parade in their photogenic, archaic black caps and gowns, its champagne punting scenes and its soaring architecture, resemble nothing so much as a permanent film set of itself?

Like many American 'Rhodies', as the overseas scholars were known, Mike Hoffman threw himself into this bizarre new world of English privilege with a cheerful gusto. And, unlike many of his more laid-back British contemporaries at the university, he appeared determined not to waste a minute of his Oxford experience.

Almost overnight, and by sheer force of personality, Hoffman became a landmark Oxford 'character' himself. With a camera slung permanently around his neck, and his seventies-style sideburns bristling, he roamed every quad-rangled and cloistered cranny of the city, beadily observing the rituals of the Union Debating Society, the drama and dining societies, and the self-consciously 'intel-lectual' clubs that mushroomed in college rooms with a view to setting the world to rights through weekly late-night chats over numerous bottles of college wine.

'He seemed to be literally everywhere,' says one former friend fondly. 'You'd start to say to someone you knew, "You must meet this extraordinary American," and they'd say, "Oh, you mean Mike Hoffman? Yes, as a matter of fact he crashed my drinks party last week!"'

Hoffman is recalled by everyone who knew him as unstoppably talkative, friendly and enquiring, bouncing from pub to party to library with his distinctive half-trot gait and flapping scarves and chatting up a storm about his ambition to direct a 'ten-minute' film while at Oxford. Mike Hoffman was, contemporaries agree, the sort of infectiously extrovert American who seemed to know everyone and 'who you couldn't slap down even if you wanted to'. He was an early example of the compulsive 'networker', blithely unafraid of approaching acquaintan-ces of acquaintances – or even senior academics – to demand help in making his film.

Hoffman's Rhodes Scholarship gave him a place at Oriel College, an exquisitely tranquil huddle of medieval build-ings tucked behind the city's High Street, a college that provided many Gaveston members – which also, most fortuitously, presented him with a conduit to one of Britain's most celebrated and successful film directors, the Oxford-educated John Schlesinger. It was simply a con-nection waiting to happen.

By 1981, when he was 55, Schlesinger's status as a leading Hollywood film maker had long been secured. He had won – among numerous other honours – a Best Director Academy Award for *Midnight Cowboy* (1969),

Best Director Oscar nominations for *Darling* (1965) and *Sunday, Bloody Sunday* (1971) and the distinction of having directed Laurence Olivier's last Oscar-nominated film performance in *Marathon Man* (1979).

That a director of Schlesinger's undoubted success should stoop to overseeing – as 'consulting director' – a tiny student film production being mooted at his old university, by an untried 23-year-old American Rhodes Scholar no less, is not the mystery it first seems.

After dining one night with senior masters at Oriel – and talking, as usual, of little else but his desire to make a movie – Mike Hoffman locked in to the oldest and most valuable network of them all: the Oxford Old Boys' Network. According to students who helped make *Privileged*, it was the then Provost of Oriel, Sir Michael Swann, who graciously offered to put the irrepressible young American in touch with Balliol College old boy John Schlesinger 'just to see what might happen'. In 1981, too, Schlesinger had reason for feeling particularly affectionate towards his former university – it was the year he was finally awarded an Honorary Fellowship from Balliol for his extraordinary services to film.

As luck, again, would have it, Schlesinger also had a special, very personal reason for looking favourably upon Mike Hoffman. For, before graduating to direct British feature films and later storming the Hollywood ranks, the callow 22-year-old Schlesinger had, while still at Oxford, precociously directed *his* first movie.

The famously likeable and perfectionist Hollywood director read Mike Hoffman's final proposal to shoot what became Hugh Grant's big-screen debut, with what must have seemed a spine-tingling sense of *déjà vu*.

Here was a mere student, an amateur with stars in his eyes and lashings of chutzpah, who planned to raise the finances personally to form a film company to produce an outlandishly ambitious melodrama starring Oxford University students and featuring doomed lovers and a shockingly bloody tragedy. Hoffman's 'ten-minute film' had along the way radically ballooned into a full-blown drama. Hoffman, he further learnt, also hoped to cut costs to the bone by using local people and scrounging help with costumes and sets. It was all, of course, hopelessly pie in the sky.

Yet back in 1948, the unknown but feverishly ambitious and resourceful student Schlesinger had pulled off precisely the same audacious stunt.

With a $400 loan from his grandmother, the undergraduate Schlesinger formed a film company, Mount Pleasant Productions, and shot a mini-melodrama *Black Legend*, about a tragically doomed love affair, starring fellow Oxford students and shot in two weeks with sets begged from a local Oxford wood mill, food donated by his parents and the completed film cut on the family dining-room table. Hoffman's 1981 film, Schlesinger read, would also feature a production of the bloody seventeenth-century dramatic tragedy *The Duchess of Malfi*. Schlesinger's 1948 *Black Legend* debut effort had been based on a bloody seventeenth-century lovers' tragedy, too.

Moreover, Schlesinger had the warmest memories of *his* final year at Oxford, when he toured the USA with a band of university actors in a scheme generously sponsored by the American National Theater Association.

The august Hollywood director got back to the irrepressible young Yank at Oriel College. Yes, he would indeed be available as 'consulting director' for Hoffman's student film. When would they start?

By the time Mike Hoffman and an American fellowship student friend, Rick Stevenson, were ready to begin filming *Privileged* in the autumn term of 1981, there was scarcely an undergraduate in any of the university's drama or arts circles who wasn't abuzz with excitement about the production in progress. Schlesinger's name lent unique glamour to the project – as did, to a significant extent, the fact that it was being helmed by two brashly confident Americans who seemed to know the ropes of film-making.

Over pints of beer in the city's pubs and endless cups of tea and toasted bacon sandwiches in the covered market, Stevenson and Hoffman assembled their production team, persuading a dazzlingly talented Oxford music student, Rachel Portman, to write the film's score and neatly skirting another issue of expensive music royalty payments by engaging one of the university's most popular amateur bands, Kudos Points, to perform their own music for the film's party scenes.

With generous advice from the British Film Institute, the script went through rewrite after tortuous rewrite. Hoffman meanwhile, dashed around Oxford personally auditioning, it appeared, almost every undergraduate with even the remotest connection to acting, including stage hands and wardrobe mistresses. This, in itself, was an unorthodox casting method, since it had been assumed that Hoffman would surely rely on the proven pool of talent at the university's main drama societies for his 'stars'.

But Hoffman was looking for 'faces' of privilege, for beautifully photogenic young people to illustrate the Oxford he observed as an American. They might be anywhere. Hoffman's scattergun approach to casting, as it turned out, proved remarkably prescient.

Hoffman, many contemporaries remember with mostly good-humoured exasperation, also entertained few qualms about grandly promising a 'major role' to any number of attractive actresses – or even non-actresses – only for them to find that, after the next rewrite, the part had all but vanished. Even Mallary Gelb, Hugh's ex-girlfriend from Godolphin, found herself being hotly pursued by Hoffman for a speaking part, which she wisely turned down on the reasonable grounds that she simply couldn't act!

Hoffman, however, absolutely refused to take no for an answer from Hugh Grant after seeing him – along with dozens of other tried and untried talents – audition.

As the script for *Privileged*, co-written by Hoffman and another student, Rupert Walters, inched closer to its final rewrite – with its central theme of the hollow inner lives often lived by beautiful, pampered young people dominating the plot – Hoffman instinctively and obsessively grasped that Hugh's stunningly aristocratic looks were essential to the film. Hoffman also shrewdly persuaded members of the Piers Gaveston Society simply to play themselves on screen for one scene of *Privileged* 'debauchery'. They prepared for this ordeal by fuelling themselves with disgusting cocktails of lemonade and blue curacao liqueur.

Contemporaries recall Hoffman raving to them – his eyes shining – about 'discovering' Hugh and demanding to know if there could possibly exist a more beautiful male undergraduate in the whole of England.

Hoffman himself has since candidly described his first reaction to meeting the shockingly handsome young Hughie as 'just flat-out envy. Myself, I was three years older and already sort of balding.' And the young director, like millions of fellow Americans and fans the world over in years to come, was also thoroughly disarmed by Hugh's ironic British wit. He found himself especially tickled by the actor's cheery protestations of horror that playing the part of a 'weak aristocrat' in *Privileged* would make him look like 'the biggest twit in the university'.

Although Hugh did nurse reservations both about Hoffman's abilities as a neophyte director – and the potential humiliation of exposing his own limited acting talents to the permanency of film – these were ultimately swept away both by the sheer excitement of the project and Hoffman's bombardment of flattery. Hugh was also aware that landing the role – a pivotal one in the film – was a rather neat put-down to the lofty OUDS crowd.

'Hughie didn't crow about getting the part. He complained about being practically badgered into taking it – which suited him very well,' one friend observed drily.

Privileged was made for just £30,000, its pauper's budget raised largely by the film's cast and crew selling 'share options' to indulgent family members and friends and by agreeing to work free themselves in return for sharing in a net-profits scheme. Hoffman and the film's producer, Rick Stevenson – who had, at least, some previous experience of film-making after shooting, by his own admission, 'a rather poor documentary in

Washington for the US Congress' during a summer vacation – also organized blatantly commercial pay-to-attend dinners at Oxford's Rhodes Hall to boost funds. Local hairdressers were cajoled into promising to work free.

Later, local townsfolk would obligingly volunteer as extras, standing around all day in the chilling rain of an early Oxford autumn in return for the chance of a split second of celluloid immortality – and one cup of soup.

And the remarkable, trimly white-bearded, John Schlesinger came up trumps. The great director patiently coached Hugh and fellow actors through intensive private rehearsal sessions away from the cameras in the famed gardens of Oriel College, lengthy away-from-camera rehearsals being a standard Schlesinger technique with even top Hollywood actors. Crucially, he persuaded film colleagues to offer bargain-price technical services to Hoffman and Stevenson. To his everlasting credit, the exemplary Schlesinger deferred graciously to Hoffman's instincts about his film in every respect. He offered only his expertise, never his interference. Filming *Privileged* was not remotely a collaborative effort. It was Hoffman's film entirely.

By September 1981, Hoffman and Stevenson had their final cast assembled. The tiny budget allowed them the indulgence of hiring just one professional, the actress Diane Katis, in the lead role as a student beauty. Almost all other parts went to student – and Oxford secretarial school – unknowns: 'Hughie' Grant, as the morally feckless young toff, Lord Adrian; a broodingly handsome Rob Woolley (Lincoln College), as the amoral 'privileged' student of the film's title (chosen after catching Hoffman's eye playing a Shakespearian buffoon in a college production of *Love's Labours Lost*); the vivacious Oxford secretarial college pupil Victoria Studd as a vacant love interest. And there were smaller roles played by the university's two leading female actresses, Imogen Stubbs (Exeter College) and Jenny Waldman (St Anne's College), and by James Wilby (a ruggedly good-looking blond import out of Durham University and RADA).

Many of the cast recall the 35-day shoot as galloping, heart-racing chaos with the novelty of seeing themselves in the rushes of the film adding to their nervousness of being in front of a movie camera for the first time. Hugh – though disciplined and watchful on set – moaned comically to friends that he felt one scene, in which he had to stagger through sunlight-dappled countryside beneath the weight of an obviously puny dead deer on his shoulders, smacked horribly, in the rushes, of a Monty Python sketch.

A third of the way through filming Hoffman and Stevenson did some urgent mathematics, and discovered they were shooting twice as many scenes as they needed for a 90-minute film – and had to chop out vital bits of an already highly convoluted plot. On another occasion, a lorry load of manure arrived at Corpus Christi just as Hoffman, who couldn't afford to lose the shot, was filming a romantic view of the college gates. But the delivery men calmly insisted on dumping it in full view of the rolling cameras. Student extras also caused continuity nightmares by eagerly arriving to be costumed and made up for party scenes in the morning and drifting away, bored, at lunch-time before filming was completed.

Yet, if Hugh joked laconically about his role away from the cameras, he was, according to cast members, an especially diligent and attentive pupil of John Schlesinger during key scene rehearsals. And, away from his friends, he was as exhilarated as everyone connected with the film about its commercial prospects. The two sides to Hugh Grant – the charming self-deprecating jester and the sharply focused, deeply pragmatic opportunist – were already beginning, quietly, to co-exist.

Victoria Studd, a striking, bright blonde who had studied stage design at the Bristol Old Vic Theatre School before signing up at an Oxford secretarial school was cast in *Privileged* – initially to her total astonishment – as Hugh's rich, fickle and dizzy girlfriend, Lucy. She had hoped only to assist on the film's design or costumes, but was auditioned on a sudden, urgent whim and landed a principal role. Victoria vividly remembers how Hoffman exuberantly described her co-star.

'Mike said, "You'll be playing opposite Hughie Grant in the film – do you know him?" I said I didn't. I had been involved doing stage design for the university's dramatic society, but I hadn't met Hugh. Mike grinned and said, "Oh, he's *devastatingly* good-looking, just *wait* until you see him; you're really going to fall for him!" I remember thinking, "Please don't let me fancy him too much, or I'll just go to jelly!"

'In fact when I first saw him, I thought, "He's too good-looking for me, thank God!" He really was the most beautiful boy – so beautiful it was scarey. Hugh was really, really charming the whole time we filmed. He was very gracious, never put himself forward and very disciplined. If you can believe it, in the film I had to abandon him for someone else – I don't know how I could,' she laughs now.

'For all of us, it was such an exciting time. We felt so youthfully hopeful and enthusiastic about the film. And to have John *Schlesinger* directing us in theatre workshops in Oriel's gardens! It was so exhilarating to be directed by him. I think we would have done anything to make the film work.'

The fact that, ultimately, *Privileged* didn't remotely work was not due to any lack of goodwill shown to the film. Oxford University authorities were unusually flexible in allowing Hoffman free rein to shoot around the city, closing streets on request and waiving all location fees – except in one instance, when a charge of £20 was levied for filming from one of the university's older church towers. The producer, Rick Stevenson, was much mollified, however, to learn that it had cost Michael Cimino – as the director of the epic movie *Heaven's Gate*, which was partly shot in Oxford and famously drove Hollywood's United Artists Studio to bankruptcy and liquidation – £3,000 for exactly the same church-tower shot just the previous year.

The BBC bought a three-hour rough cut of *Privileged*

for £20,000 – pushing it almost into the black before it was even released. (At the last minute, the film's original working title, *Chameleon*, was changed to *Privileged*. *Chameleon*, it was wisely decided, sounded too much like a nature documentary.)

Hugh's face, to his delight, appeared on the original promotional posters, looking – with his pale, brooding features and wind-riffled hair – like Heathcliff with an Oxon BA Hons. The poster in fact, with its strapline 'In the city of dreams . . . in a class of their own', was one of the film's better points.

Privileged didn't work because the acting was self-conscious, uncertain and unconvincing. Hugh, in particular – though he photographed beautifully – spoke his lines in the lah-did-dah splutter of a footman raising sniggers in the servants' hall by mimicking his master. Ironically, in view of his naturally patrician looks, he came over not so much a lord, as a suspiciously pretty end-of-pier fraud.

The film was – quite rightly – pronounced dead on arrival at the box office following its very limited release in both London in 1982 and New York the following year. The plot – which no longer made sense after the last minute cuts – revolved around a student production of *The Duchess of Malfi*, a rapist at large in the modern city of Oxford, the myth of the nature of 'privilege' and the truth about 'privilege', and had the tragic events of Webster's complicated play echoing, counterpointing, complementing and occasionally throwing into ironic light the 'real' lives of the student actors in the play. There was also a stern moral message, which stubbornly stalked the main action, like a small but annoyingly persistent Salvation Army brass band.

It is not at all surprising that *Privileged* flopped commercially. Reviewing the film on 8 April 1983, the *New York Times* movie critic, Vincent Canby, struggled valiantly to be kind. Hughie he singled out for playing 'a decadant young peer who seems to have read an awful lot of early Evelyn Waugh', before swiping briefly at the 'incoherence' of the screenplay and declaring the film a 'prettily precocious but overwrought undergraduate melodrama'.

What gives *Privileged* its enduring resonance, however, is that the young and inexperienced Mike Hoffman had the gut instincts to bring together, for the first time, so many future famous names. Though few, if any, of his extras were ever heard from again, the actors with speaking parts would triumph.

James Wilby, who once described his character in *Privileged* as 'a real wet-behind-the-ears, pain-in-the-arse [type]' went on from strength to strength, appearing in successive Merchant–Ivory hits: *Maurice* (with Hugh), *A Room with a View*, and *Howards End*. He also established himself as a leading romantic British stage and TV actor.

Within four years of her small role in *Privileged*, the radiantly talented and beautiful Imogen Stubbs was hailed as the 'new young star of the Royal Shakespeare Company' by Britain's exacting *Sunday Times* theatre critic, John Peter, for performances in the plays *The Two Noble Kinsmen* and *The Rover*. Her career has continued to soar, with leading London West End stage roles, French, English and American movies including *Nanou*, *Eric the Viking* and *Fellow Traveller*, and the starring role in the hit British 1994 female-private-eye television series, *Anna Lee*.

Victoria Studd, who never acted again after *Privileged*, also became a household name in British television in the nineties – as a popular travel show presenter. (In the autumn of 1994, Victoria married Edward Bonham Carter – brother of the *A Room with a View* star, Helena Bonham Carter.)

Rachel Portman, the shy, crop-haired Oxford music undergraduate who wrote the score, has become one of Britain's best-regarded composers for film and television, whose numerous credits include the music for Hugh Grant's 1994 film, *Sirens*.

Both Rob Woolley and Diane Katis also continued their acting careers, he in British repertory theatre, she in British television. Jenny Waldman, though she gave up acting, continued to work in theatre and is now Director of Art Centre Projects at London's prestigious South Bank Centre.

Kudos Points, the Oxford pop band featured in *Privileged*, did release a record – but broke up after its members left Oxford. However the group's saxophone-player, Charlie Mole, is now a highly sought-after pop composer – he recently worked with Kylie Minogue – and continued to play football with Hugh Grant right up until the star's breakthrough role in *Four Weddings*.

And Mike Hoffman more than fulfilled his promise. The Oxford Film Foundation he established to make *Privileged* still exists to nurture succeeding generations of university film talent. Hoffman also realized his dream of becoming a professional film director. He went on to make the comedies *Restless Natives* (1985), with Rick Stevenson producing; *Sisters* (1988 – US title: *Some Girls*), written by his *Privileged* co-writer Rupert Walters; and the gritty smalltown drama *Promised Land* (1988). To date, Hoffman's biggest commercial hit has been *Soapdish* (USA 1991/UK 1992), a delightful piece of comic lunacy about the world of American daytime television, starring Sally Field.

Yet it would be thirteen years after the making of *Privileged* before the puckish red-head from Boise, Idaho, reunited professionally with the devastatingly beautiful young actor from Chiswick, West London. Not until the period farce *Restoration*, made in 1994, did three of the *Privileged* alumni work together again with Hoffman, as director, Hugh Grant as actor and Rupert Walters as screenwriter.

Back in 1981, *Privileged*, still in the can, was brought to the beady attentions of London's leading casting agents as a result of vigorous campaigning by Hoffman. It helped, of course, that 'posh themes' were very much in vogue. Half the world was humming the heart-swelling Vangelis theme music to the 1981 Oxbridge-based movie *Chariots of Fire*, while the director Charles Sturridge's long-awaited

TV adaptation of Evelyn Waugh's benchmark Oxbridge novel *Brideshead Revisited* was on the eve of broadcast. Sturridge, with marvellous generosity, endorsed *Privileged* as 'one of the most honest and accurate portrayals of Oxford life I have seen on film'. Anything – no matter how third-rate – to do with lissom young men in crumpled off-white linen at Oxford was bound to create frissons of excitement among casting agents.

And, within days of the arrival of one of London's top casting directors in Oxford to meet the cast of *Privileged*, an amazing rumour ripped around the university.

Hughie Grant – Gaveston leading light and scholar of New College – was, even before his debut film's release, in the running for the lead role in *Greystoke – The Legend of Tarzan, Lord of the Apes*.

CHAPTER

NINE

*'I'm terribly sorry – I may not be able to take my
Finals. It seems they want me to go off and become a
movie star . . .'*
Hugh Grant, to New College tutors, 1982

Only since becoming Hollywood's hottest new star has
Hugh Grant revealed how jejune over-confidence gave him
the peculiar impression, in his final year at Oxford, that he
had landed the lead role in the movie *Greystoke: The
Legend of Tarzan, Lord of the Apes.*

To interviewers the world over, he offers the same
fetchingly abashed grin and roughly the same version of the
strange tale: that it all came as a jolly rude shock to discover
that just because he had auditioned for the role of Tarzan, it
didn't automatically mean the part was his. He merrily adds
that he even posted an amateur snapshot of himself, taken
by a friend in New College gardens, showing him stripped
to the waist in his tennis shorts, smothered in baby-oil and
glowering manfully in an attempt to sway the opinion of
casting agents that he possessed just the body for the job.

It's a lovely story – but it is not true. Hugh Grant never
auditioned for the role of Tarzan at all. He only – rather
more genuinely embarrassingly – *thought* he did.

By the end of 1981 and beginning of 1982, Hugh's
ambitions were finally turning towards an acting career –
and no one could blame him for that. As the editing of
Privileged continued, Mike Hoffman's excited assurances
to Hugh that the young actor's exquisite face was *made*
for film were ringing delightfully in his ears. The BBC's
immediate interest in the film was a further enormous
boost to his confidence.

And intriguingly, right through Hugh's time at Oxford, Hollywood had never really seemed all that distant. Even in his first year at the university, Hugh had by chance witnessed firsthand all the excitement and razzmatazz glitz of the Hollywood circus sweeping into town – to his very own college, no less, for location filming for Michael Cimino's period epic *Heaven's Gate*.

Cimino had not, in fact, originally intended filming in Oxford. It was only after he was refused permission to film at Harvard University that the infamously extravagant director promptly threw budget cautions to the winds and transferred his international cast, including the American (and a former Oxford Rhodes scholar himself) Kris Kristofferson and Britain's John Hurt to Oxford. Hugh's New College and the stunning seventeenth-century Christopher-Wren-designed Sheldonian Theatre just down the road had been selected as acceptable stand-ins for the American university.

In April 1980, at the start of the Trinity Term, dozens of Hugh's friends and contemporaries at New College found themselves in the enviable position of topping up their grants to the tune of £15 a day, and getting deliciously catered meals, in return for parading as extras in lavish nineteenth-century costumes (a not inconsiderable sum, which would then have paid for six return coach trips to London). It seemed marvellously easy money for little work and the chance to rub shoulders with Hollywood's élite.

Now in his third and final year, with *Privileged* in the promising limbo of post-production and its fatal critical drubbing still months away, Hugh once again saw Hollywood come knocking, in the shape of the doyenne of London's casting agents Patsy Pollock. Ms Pollock, as every young male actor in Oxford swiftly learnt, was scouting for the Old Etonian director Hugh Hudson, and Hugh Hudson – as the public was perfectly well informed, thanks to a blizzard of hype – was hunting for a new Tarzan.

Hudson's debut movie had been the wildly successful

winner of four Academy Awards, *Chariots of Fire* (1981), about the 1924 Olympics and featuring legions of wonderfully noble-profiled young men in baggy shorts legging around timelessly sunlit, old stone quads in Cambridge. For his next movie, Hudson intended to retell the original Edgar Rice Burroughs story of how Tarzan, the baby son of shipwrecked British aristocrats, was raised by the apes and then returned to upper-crust society, with the emphasis on the upper-crust aspect.

It is likely that Hudson felt his project was not unduly threatened by the recent 1981 remake, *Tarzan the Ape Man*, in which the emphasis had been almost entirely on the upper-*chest* aspects of Bo Derek as Jane.

Hudson was then the boy wonder, the darling of the British film business, and it was taken for granted that the 'new Tarzan' would be assured of stardom. So, with a carefully orchestrated ballyhoo, highly reminiscent of the search for *Gone with the Wind*'s Scarlett O'Hara, and a gust of genuine excitement too, the race to find the ultimate vine-swinger for *Greystoke* was on. The actor Rupert Everett – educated at the Catholic public-school establishment of Ampleforth – became England's great white Tarzan hope for a while. (Everett's then flavour-of-the-month status stemmed from a starring role in yet another early-1980s, posh-themed smash hit, the spies-at-public-school play, *Another Country*.) Also tipped as top Tarzan favourite was every single male member of the Bolshoi Ballet; the redoubtable Patsy Pollock flew to Amsterdam to check them out personally.

Then Ms Pollock swept into Oxford, with Hugh and his *Privileged* co-star Rob Woolley, as well as a handful of other gorgeous young university actors, on yet another list of possibles. But, amazingly, what never seemed to occur to the understandably swollen headed young Hugh (or to the handsome Rob Woolley, who obligingly provided Hugh Hudson's London office with a fetching Polaroid of himself in his underwear) was that there was a whole *film* to cast, not just the lead role.

Hugh was only ever briefly under consideration for the

part of the 'young Lord Esher' – which was later rewritten for a much older actor, and played by James Fox in the final film. (Nine years after *Greystoke*'s release, Hugh would get to meet the actor who 'stole' his role when he played the godson of James Fox's Nazi apologist Lord Darlington in *The Remains of the Day*.)

It was for the part of a young English lord in one of the high-society segments of the film that Hugh was invited to London, and later Shepperton Studios, for camera tests and workshops. As Pollock confirms, 'Yes, I know, Hugh *did* seem to think he was going to be Tarzan and told all his friends and tutors – which is a hilarious story. But he was never going to play Tarzan. Though I did,' she adds warmly, 'find him brilliantly witty and self-effacing.'

Yet Hugh returned from Shepperton to confide to his stunned family, friends and tutors, absolutely seriously, they recall, that he was afraid that taking his Finals was likely to be out of the question because 'it seems they want me to go off and become a movie star' and play Tarzan. Stylishly nonchalant, apologetic, even, about this extraordinary stroke of fortune – as he misunderstood it – Hugh nevertheless had the glint of triumph in his eye. He had gone, so he thought, from a tiny student film to being mentioned in the same breath as Britain's most fashionable movie director Hugh Hudson, and it was all so easy. No 'ugly thrusting' – a much-savoured university expression of Hugh's to describe contemporaries he judged to be tiresomely ambitious – had been necessary.

To his credit, though, Hugh good-naturedly endured the astounded splutters his Tarzan 'role' created around Oxford. Inevitably, the mere mention of Tarzan creates a mental image of the very well-nourished and credibly monosyllabic Johnny Weissmuller. The moment one thought of Hugh saying 'me Tarzan, you Jane', you could hear him interrupting himself with 'Look, I'm terribly sorry, but the jungle's had the most deplorable effect on my grammar.' It was, in a word, unthinkable.

And as the weeks wore on, humiliatingly, with no word from Hugh Hudson about loin-cloth fittings, Hugh Grant accepted the inevitable. Yes, playing Tarzan *was* unthinkable. And he hadn't gained the Lord Esher role either. Getting *into* the movies was never as painless as it looked *in* the movies. He'd been a fool to believe what he'd chosen to hear from the London casting agents. Hugh became as withdrawn and tongue-tied on the subject of *Greystoke* as he'd previously been amusingly loquacious.

Hugh Hudson went on to 'discover' his Tarzan in the sultry quarter-French actor Christopher Lambert – who did indeed find himself fast-tracked to international stardom as a result. As Pollock says, in her beautifully theatrical, gravelly voice, 'Tarzan is such a *difficult* part – we don't breed Tarzans in this country: we're a nation of Hamlets.'

But quite by coincidence, *Greystoke* – released to very mixed reviews in 1984 – taught an equally uncomfortable lesson about the fickle promises of Hollywood to another aspiring star. She was a fashion model trying to make the perilous leap to film acting, and who hoped desperately that her debut role opposite Christopher Lambert in the film would give her the credibility she lacked. Instead, she found herself publicly hosed with humiliation.

A torrent of leaks from the production confirmed that her *Greystoke* screen voice was deemed to be totally unacceptable and had to be dubbed over by another much older actress – Glenn Close. This model-turned-actress recovered – after some heartache – and would later pop up in Hugh Grant's romantic smash hit of the nineties, *Four Weddings and a Funeral*. Her name was Andie Mac-Dowell.

Hugh was left – after the *Greystoke* débâcle – scrambling to make up his studies and coping with living 'out' of college for his final year at the university. From September 1981 to June 1982, Hugh exchanged the sequestered comforts of his handsome front-quad set of rooms at New College for a shared house with his closest college mate and Gaveston chum Danny Daggenhurst. Finding reasonable and affordable rented accommodation in the city of

Oxford, as opposed to squalid and cramped basement dungeons with running walls, can be a nightmare. Hugh and Daggenhurst were extremely fortunate to be able to move – thanks to contacts – into an airy, unusually roomy Edwardian house in the city's Stanley Road, a short bicycle ride from the town centre. The house was owned by the mother of another Gaveston chum from Magdalen College.

Though Hugh's friends remember him steadfastly revising for his Final exams – putting in hours of study at the university's libraries and returning home, pale and drained, long after dusk, only to return to his books in his room – the giddily sought-after First Class Honours Oxford degree eluded him. Nor did he 'narrowly miss' a First, as William Cash – the close friend of his future girlfriend Elizabeth Hurley – would later assert in a sycophantic article published in the British press following Hugh's downfall with a prostitute. Borderline Second/First Class Oxford degree candidates are routinely given an oral examination – a *viva voce* – in front of a formal panel of senior Oxford dons as a last chance to make up crucial missing marks and Hugh's Finals papers, as far as can be determined, did not merit a *viva voce*.

Hugh's failure to secure a First was a keen disappointment to his tutors, however. New College had awarded him his scholarship on his likely potential to finish his three years on a note of scholastic triumph – which would bear fruit on the university's unofficial, if all-important, Norrington Table standing, the annual ratings of colleges based on their Final degree results. But Hugh's intellectual forte – according to tutorial partners – was bending his learning to provoke a quick giggle, or a flashily impressive shock, invariably siding with the least likeable characters in Shakespeare and making entirely inappropriate though very funny and quite cleverly argued claims for their chastity or wisdom, and insisting they'd been woefully misunderstood over the years.

Though Hugh's intelligence has never been remotely in doubt, and though he plodded through the revision for the summer exams, his approach to his studies, particularly with the distractions of *Privileged*, was never quite of the depth required to shine in the mind-numbing marathon of written papers that make up the Oxford English Language and Literature Finals. There was, perhaps, the tiniest crumb of comfort for the Second-Class-rated Hugh that the 1982 Oxford English Finals results threw up an odd anomaly.

In that year – according to a report in the *Guardian* newspaper published in November – only 31 Firsts were awarded in English, compared with the usual 40 or 41. Firsts in English were down by ten – or a whopping 25 per cent. Either 1982 was a singularly rotten year for outstanding English candidates (although Hugh's *Privileged* co-star Imogen Stubbs came flying through with one of the top Firsts in English at the university), or someone had moved the goalposts for marking the papers. The thoroughly Sherlock Holmesian case of the 'missing Firsts' created no end of fuss among both students and dons, and gave rise to a great deal of puzzled theorizing; but, as so often happens at Oxford, the anomaly was simply left to stand.

Meanwhile – as a direct result of the absurd hype surrounding *Privileged* – Hugh turned down a place at the Courtauld Institute in London to read for a Doctor of Philosophy degree in Art History after Oxford. The attentions of Hollywood had done their work. The groves of Academe had lost out to the distant lure of the Hollywood hills. But it was going to take him, after the initial early burst of interest from the London agents, far, far longer than he would have ever believed possible to make his mark.

TEN

'We all wondered, rather, what had become of him.'
*Old Etonian Gaveston friend of Hugh's
on the actor's post-Oxford obscurity*

Life immediately after Oxford did not present a chocolate box of promise for the 22-year-old Hugh. The crucial differences underpinning his own modest family background, and those of many of his genuinely privileged Gaveston friends – glossed over when they all made merry as students together – immediately began to tell in the harsher world beyond Oxford's ivied walls. The hard-up ex-student Hugh was in no position to indulge in any career-delaying globe-trotting after Oxford (one of his more colourful cohorts in the Gaveston crowd, one Paul Newman no less, splendidly took off touring a one-man puppet show round South America). Hugh had inherited his family's unyieldingly middle-class work ethic. He'd had his three years of undergraduate fun – now he had to get to grips with life.

Playing the perpetual student and living off his parents until he found his feet wasn't remotely an alternative – and would have found little favour with either of the senior Grants. Hugh had absolutely no desire to follow his brother Jamie into what he regarded with horror as the stuffy corporate world of J.P. Morgan. In this, Hugh was simply echoing Jamie, who often poked fun at himself for embarking on such a 'conventional' career path.

Although Hugh toyed with the idea of writing for a living, he had contributed only a few sparse theatre reviews to the student newspapers and magazines on which would-be journalists are traditionally expected to hone their skills at Oxford. Hugh departed Oxford conspicuously unburdened by the fat portfolio of earnest student articles demanded as a sign of genuine ambition by even the humblest provincial newspaper editors.

One by one Hugh saw his university mates gliding into their preordained, upper-middle-class futures. Daggenhurst was called to the Bar in 1983 – as was his elder brother Henry, a graduate of Oxford's Christ Church – and soon afterwards smoothly accelerated into a career in investment banking. Danny Daggenhurst later made a socially notable marriage to the only daughter of the Saudi Arabian arms-dealer, Adnan Khashoggi, Nabila. Nabila, wife of Daggenhurst (né Athon Karamanos), had famously once enjoyed the honour of having her father's yacht – the world's largest in private hands – named after her before an embarrassment of cash-flow problems forced Khashoggi to sell it on to Donald Trump, who promptly rechristened it the *Trump Princess*. Names are a notoriously slippery commodity among the jet set.

Other friends fell away into either élite newspaper or BBC training schemes, for which they'd quietly applied, long in advance of Finals. Meanwhile, the 'serious' actors from Oxford, the ones Hugh had both envied and privately despised for their commitment to the university's drama clubs, sailed serenely into RADA and other prestigious acting schools.

Hugh had only an embarrassingly thin sheaf of university acting credits, his oddball student movie role, a second-class degree – which effectively ruled out a higher academic career of any distinction – and, a disaster if you wanted to break into television or films, no Equity card.

For a young man who had launched himself into Oxford life with such splashy promise three years earlier, Hugh was looking awfully like someone who had managed to fritter away his opportunities. And, as an undergraduate who had learned to judge others superficially – the remorseless Gaveston creed – by how 'stylishly' they conducted themselves, the thin-skinned Hugh was uneasily aware of how richly any perceived failure of his own would, in turn, be enjoyed by some of his Oxford contemporaries.

He showed, too, a Peter Pan nostalgia for his Gaveston glory days, by eagerly showing up for the rather lame London reunions of the undergraduate society even as late as 1989 – a full seven years after his graduation. This was for a ball at London's Smithfield Market, titled 'Fowl, Flesh and Well-Hung Game', for which some guests, most unwisely as the warm May evening wore on, wore necklaces of dead game birds. Hugh – with Elizabeth Hurley instead of Mary Glanville on his arm – looked boyishly attractive as ever, stripped to the waist in skin-tight breeches.

Yet financially he couldn't even begin to compete socially with his wealthier Oxford friends. Hugh had learnt to exist with panache, and at modest expense, at Oxford. In London, living in his brother's Fulham flat, Hugh discovered that panache was a prohibitively expensive lifestyle. And the student film that had rekindled his acting ambitions, *Privileged*, released in June 1982 in the UK, and the following year in the USA, had also horribly backfired. While the film had brought him to the attention of the London agents, and sparked a flicker of interest from the prestigious talent-brokers of the William Morris Agency, it didn't win him a single follow-up break or solid job offer.

All the promise of *Privileged* itself had cruelly withered, too. As one of the actors in it sadly observed, 'In the end there was far too much advance hype. I think this caused some real resentment in the [acting] profession. There was really venomous criticism, which was extremely unfair because it *was* only a student film, but also understandable.'

In volumes of theatrical reminiscences – usually penned many years after the events experienced – actors' recollections of their apprentice years in British repertory theatre generally make it all sound perky, if occasionally beastly, fun: all that brave coping with cabbage smells in rented digs; the hilarious memories of boot-faced landladies parsimoniously counting out the breakfast cornflakes; and those marvellous, unforgettable moments when you can *feel* the magic being created on stage. But the reality of rep theatre is not only that it is hard, unglamorous work, it can also be a crushing disillusionment for young actors who have come either from a starry period of treading the boards at university or from the intense, often idealistic, rigours of drama school.

It is, perhaps, understandable that Hugh arrived at the Nottingham Playhouse, for his obligatory Equity-card-earning stint in repertory, in 1983, with singular ill grace. His hostility stemmed from the fact that he had, if only in his own mind, been within a whisker of being handed a one-way ticket to Hollywood. Unlike those of older actors who learn, from repeated cycles of rejection and success to build up protective scar tissue, Hugh's wounds felt painfully raw. He'd been made to feel so special – after all hadn't agents *personally* sought him out? Now he was back to being just another jobbing actor in a not especially glamorous – though respectable – provincial company. And he was genuinely nervous about his own green talents being rudely contrasted with other repertory actors who either had drama school experience, or had devoted their every spare minute at college to polishing their theatrical skills. The young Hugh fully expected to hate being at Nottingham. This proved a resoundingly self-fulfilling expectation.

At Nottingham Playhouse, Hugh very soon realized that his extraordinary looks – unlike at Oxford – certainly didn't gain him any preferential treatment. And although he has since created amusing thumbnail sketches of sheepishly finding himself playing 'third tree' or 'a shouting peasant' at Nottingham – and puts a comic spin on his mutual personality clashes with one of the theatre's directors, who – sources say – found Hugh 'arrogant' – the humiliation cut deep. Even at Latymer Upper, no one ever dared to cast Hugh Grant as 'a shouting peasant' – not since the lower fourth at any rate.

Arriving in the autumn of 1983 for the Playhouse's 20th-anniversary season, Hugh discovered himself on the lowest rung of the very world of self-conscious 'lovey-dom' he had so studiously avoided at Oxford. And he quickly learnt, too, that, short of a bomb falling on the rest of the cast (and preferably the director!), there was no chance of fast-talking his way into roles with any meat. He was doomed to crowd scenes and minimal speaking parts until he had thoroughly earned his spurs – attending *all* rehearsals for which he was called, like a jolly good trooper, and behaving with conscientious professionalism.

The same rule, of course, applied to every other junior member of the company. Ultimately, that was too much to ask of Hugh Grant. The effort was simply beyond him. Though he shared modest digs with other company actors, he seemed to prefer keeping himself to himself, ambling – often on his own – moodily round the picturesque streets of Nottingham, and clearly afflicted with a bad dose of professional pique.

The rewards of eventually being promoted to 'first tree', or even 'a peasant who one day gets to make a speech', were in the end just not worth the bother of taking seriously. Ironically, the one piece of acting Hugh Grant couldn't pull off at Nottingham was off stage. Though his wit and acute comic mimicry helped to make him popular with some fellow actors, his heartsick resentments over where he was, and what he was reduced to doing, were all too evident.

At the theatre, Hugh's roles included an uncredited walk-on in Oscar Wilde's *Lady Windermere's Fan*, and playing 'a waiter' in Thornton Wilder's *The Matchmaker*. In the company's production of *Hamlet* at least Hugh *did* get to announce the play's opening line – 'Who's there?' – as the officer Barnardo, but that part alone was not considered sufficiently taxing to spare the young actor from also doubling up as an anonymous 'Norwegian soldier'. Perhaps hardest of all to swallow – since he had, as a chit of a schoolboy, actually *co-starred* in Bertolt Brecht's *The Caucasian Chalk Circle* – were his bit parts in Brecht's *Mother Courage* as a 'soldier/boy clerk'.

These proved the last straw. Hugh's friend, the actor/co-writer Chris Laing, whom he met at the Nottingham company, has said that Hugh was booted out of his tiny *Mother Courage* roles, and was unceremoniously dressed down in front of the entire cast, for the crime of being late for an afternoon rehearsal.

Yet if Hugh was incapable of taking acting at Nottingham seriously, he was – in his own way – treating the business of acting itself seriously. Quietly and coolly he observed the behind-the-stage tensions – and petty malices – of a provincial theatre company in full swing and took note. He would later admit that this experience provided him with a rich mine of memories to draw upon for his merciless portrayal of a manipulative director in his 1995 film, *An Awfully Big Adventure*. His instinctive watchfulness, which Mary Glanville had remarked upon at Oxford, was still his most valuable asset in terms of feeding his slowly maturing acting skills.

Chris Laing has also teasingly described Hugh's constant companion at Nottingham as being the book *The Actor and his Body*, by Litz Pisk. A slim, precious volume written by an 'influential teacher of theatre movement' in the early 1970s, *The Actor and his Body* has not stood the test of time too well. Though it contains detailed practical advice on warm-up movements and relaxation exercises for actors, and is littered with uplifting chunks of poetry, it is impossible not to imagine Hugh doubled over with laughter over the book's more excitable passages about letting out one's breath to the sound of 'zzzzz', acquiring the trick of making one's eyes and tongue 'passive' and achieving the 'controlled, meaningful stillness of the bodily form'. If Hugh did take on board any of Ms Pisk's words of wisdom to young thespians, it seems likely that he – and Laing – also regarded the book as a delicious in-joke, all the better to relish because of its exquisitely pious approach to the mystical art of acting.

The meeting between Laing and Hugh at Nottingham was also highly propitious for them both. Together they discovered a shared and mutually competitive sense of humour – for surreally silly wordplay, puns and mimicry

– which they soon put to creative use for the benefit of the theatre company's entertainent. The sketch they presented, following the theatre's 20th-anniversary gala, and inspired by Nottingham's status as the supposed birthplace of Robin Hood, had a psychiatrist quizzing his patient:

'So when did you first realize you were "Merry"?'

'When I began going to "Merry" clubs and making friends with "Merry" men and using the "Merry" switchboard rather a lot.'

Thus the Jockeys of Norfolk – the satirical revue troupe formed by Laing and Hugh and later expanded, occasionally even including Hugh's post-Nottingham actress girlfriend, Beattie Edney – was born. But the serendipitous meeting with Laing – with whom he later shared a flat in London and formed a long and enduring partnership – was not enough to erase Hugh's bitter feelings about his brief foray into provincial rep. They never abated. It had proved one of the first occasions in his life that he hadn't been able, effortlessly, to dazzle his parents with his achievements, or bask in their quiet pride emanating steadily from beyond the footlights as he pulled off yet another star turn. And it rankled.

One Oxford contemporary recalls bumping into Hugh while he was at Nottingham and finding him in an unusually vulnerable state – 'extremely defensive, depressed and embarrassed, totally unlike the New College Hugh'. In any event, Hugh did not stay at Nottingham a moment longer than he could possibly bear it. After a brief fling, Hugh has claimed, with a theatre 'usherette' – whom he asserts he shared not only with another actor in the company, but with the young woman's regular boyfriend as well, which sounds like an exaggeration in search of an anecdote – and barely completing one season, Hugh fled back to London. His confidence had been badly shaken, yet – contrary to his later nonchalant claims that he 'drifted into films by fluke' – Hugh was distinctly more driven.

After a brief spell, according to friends, when he worked as a delivery boy for an upmarket London patisserie, there was a one-off modelling turn – strictly for the session fee – for a teen photo-strip publication, which was published in the 1984 *Secret Love Annual*. Here he posed as a sweet teenage romeo, named Brian, who rescues a girl from the clutches of her horrible beer-swilling boyfriend. All the photo-cartoon stories were about true-love confessions and dramas and took the highest moral ground.

To Hugh, this job was a huge joke, though the money – about £60 a day – was most welcome, as it was to the other 'models' who appeared in the same photo story, who included Hugh's mate and tennis partner from Latymer and University College, Oxford, Guy Bensley. (The issue was also greatly enjoyed by the unlikeliest readers of teen romances – Hugh's old university tutors, who were highly amused.)

Hugh turned his hand to no fewer than three other interim mini careers: quietly and rigorously attending film and television casting auditions, performing comedy and writing radio commercials. Some 'flukes', it would seem, require a little more spadework than others.

And, once again, Hugh would very soon find himself in the company of someone who urgently wanted to make him a star.

The Jockeys of Norfolk proved to be a very happy hiatus for Hugh, bringing him and his partners a measure of cultish acclaim on the comedy fringe circuit of London and – for the first time – allowing him to develop his own skills as a writer. The curious name is a playful borrowing of a piece of doggerel from *Richard III*. It is pinched from the warning given to Jack, nicknamed 'Jockey', the Duke of Norfolk, before battle. 'Jockey of Norfolk, be not so bold/For Dickon thy master is bought and sold' (V.iii, 304–5). There are no real jockeys of Norfolk, or indeed of any other county, in Shakespeare. But this is exactly the sort of daft wordplay Hugh loves.

The early-to-mid-Eighties was a jubilant and innovative period for stand-up and revue comedy in London. And both Oxford and Cambridge universities had, from the

Monty Python team through to new stars like Rowan Atkinson, Griff Rhys Jones and Stephen Fry, a first-class reputation for incubating successive generations of the best comic talents in Britain. With future television stars like Rik Mayall, Ben Elton and Andy De La Tour doing the club rounds of the more exalted venues, the Jockeys appeared on the more modest fringes, like the Canal Cafe Theatre and Islington's King's Head pub theatre.

Kit Hesketh-Harvey, a prodigiously talented revue comedian and screenwriter, became friendly with the Jockeys when he shared a dressing-room with them at the King's Head, which has the distinction of being the oldest pub theatre in Britain (Hesketh-Harvey would also later play a crucial behind-the-scenes role in restarting Hugh's film career). He vividly recalls the Jockeys' perhaps not entirely original signature sketch – a nativity scene done in the highly stylized manner of Britain's Ealing Studios films of the 1940s – with Hugh as the Archangel Gabriel stiffly announcing 'in terribly clipped English', 'Now look here, Joseph, I've got something terribly important to tell you. Your wife's going to have a baby.' To which an outraged Joseph replied, 'I say, how dare you! Are you tight?'

The skit, which included stereotypical cockney shepherds muttering about the weather, was performed at breakneck speed – and generally brought down the house. It perfectly played off Hugh's highly mannered, as yet unrelaxed, acting style.

The lads' most memorable sketch may, however, have been partly inspired by a lucky visit to one of the Edinburgh Festival's earlier comedy Fringe hits. In 1983, the spoof 'The Messiah' played at the Assembly Rooms. Just two actors – one the Royal Shakespeare Company's Jim Broadbent – in a very popular partnership named the National Theatre of Brent, retold the story of the nativity in a strikingly similar, absurdly accented manner. Comedy fans who caught both the National Theatre of Brent on tour and the Jockeys find it hard to rule out a purely coincidental link.

Hugh's then actress girlfriend Beattie Edney, who later

became a close chum of Elizabeth Hurley, occasionally joined the Jockeys on stage.

Another favourite Jockeys sketch enabled Hugh to flaunt his gift for wicked – sometimes cruel – observation of other people's physical foibles. Throwing himself into an impression of the popular British television naturalist David Attenborough, Hugh would roam the audience, pouncing on victims whom he would describe in terms of their animal characteristics. By employing a combination of meticulously rehearsed one-liners and genuine off-the-cuff sallies, Hugh turned this into a mini tour-de-force.

Hugh shared, by all accounts, a volatile relationship with the spirited and vivacious Beattie. There were 'lots of verbal kerfuffles', as one close friend says diplomatically – a recurring factor with all of his serious girlfriends. Yet Hugh appeared genuinely content with the Jockeys. He loved the intellectual challenge of discovering which comedy ideas worked on stage – and which flopped. And he was, for the first time since Oxford, once again enjoying the pleasant balm of fame. What's more, he adored the praise.

In the intimate arena of pub theatres, Hugh's beautifully chiselled, often androgynous, looks were not only immediately arresting but contrasted wonderfully with his facility for physical comedy – and hideous face-pulling. Gradually, throughout 1984–85, the troupe attracted a vociferous and loyal following of fans – including many old Oxford friends – and the flattering attentions of stage-door johnnies and joannas who delighted in sharing Hugh's self-deprecating, after-show banter.

'I thought I was deplorable in that sketch, didn't you?' he would ask, shamelessly trawling for inevitable compliments; and then, his eyes twinkling, 'You didn't think I was terrible? Oh, how lovely of you to say so!'

And, if employment on London's comedy circuits provided an uncertain living at the best of times, it could certainly be counted as 'stylish', always an uppermost consideration in Hugh's mind.

In vivid contrast with his Nottingham experience, Hugh

rediscovered an important truth with the Jockeys: that acting – if tickling pub audiences with a battery of silly accents and comic pratfalls could be called acting – could be *fun*. All they needed now was a lucky break, a boost to lift them out of the pub rounds and to enable them to give up their day jobs.

The Edinburgh Festival, held annually in August, and distinctly separated into two co-existing camps – the official august mainstream cultural programme of opera, ballet, theatre and music, and the Fringe, the joyous ragtag and bobtail of hundreds of student and professional plays and revues that spills throughout the great, grey, granite city – has proved a traditional showcase for major new comedy talent. Hugh was no stranger to Edinburgh. He had appeared in an Oxford student production of *Hamlet* on the fringe – performed, for reasons that vanished with the production, entirely in *Star Trek* costumes.

It was inevitable that the Jockeys would take their by now extremely well polished revue to the Edinburgh Fringe. In 1985 they coincided at the same venue – McNallys – also being used by Kit Hesketh-Harvey's *Kit and the Widow* revue. It was here that the Jockeys – but Hugh, above all – caught the influential eye of one of the foremost British TV chatshow hosts, who was featuring festival highlights on his programme, Russell Harty.

As Hesketh-Harvey cheerfully confirms, 'Russell Harty saw Hugh Grant – and there was a thunderclap!' The egregiously chummy Harty was – not unlike Mike Hoffman four years earlier – instantly and utterly entranced by Hugh's singular beauty, wondering why on earth this stunning boy wasn't already a star. Harty was adamant he would give Hugh and the Jockeys the public exposure he genuinely thought they deserved. The impulse was a generous one, if self-serving to the middle-aged Harty's tenderly rose-tinted – and distinctly unreciprocated – crush on Hugh.

'Harty thrust them hard into the limelight,' recalls Hesketh-Harvey. 'He put them on his show for a week during his coverage of Edinburgh, saying "here, everyone"

– meaning, of course, Hugh – "is a star!" ' Hugh's own take on the Jockeys' big television break is more mischievous. Though he was a model of winning and stuttery charm to the chat show host's face, he presents their meeting now as if he had been an ingenue encountering his first casting-couch come-on.

Hugh insists that Harty was considerably more camp behind the cameras than in front – threatening to spank the Jockeys 'very hard indeed' for having forgotten to provide a backing tape of the music they used. Sadly – for the late Russell Harty was known as a thoroughly decent television professional, who sought to keep his private life just that, and who would have taken great pleasure in seeing his personal Edinburgh discovery making it big – the nightly television exposure proved a death knell for the Jockeys of Norfolk. It was a stinging rebuff to Harty's – and his producers' – objective sense of judgement.

The sketches, which went down a storm to relaxed and indulgent fringe and pub-circuit audiences, came across on the small screen as puzzlingly limp, fey and embarrassingly undergraduate. The very presence of the cameras had knocked the lads off balance and, with it, their crucial comic timing.

Far from impressing comedy-bookers as tomorrow's television stars, the Jockeys resembled a bunch of self-impressed students hamming it up on home video, with Hugh's captivating features all but bleached out by immensely unflattering lighting. Harty very hastily drew a veil over his 'discovery' and extinguished the spotlight of publicity. The Jockeys had plummeted – in one roller-coaster week – from one of the hottest and most envied revues on the Edinburgh fringe to television's latest sacrificial lambs.

Yet it was a tougher, more pragmatic Hugh who rode out this new humiliation. The Jockeys had only been a part-time pursuit. Hugh had never been sure about the long-term future of the Jockeys and he had been supporting himself – as had his partners Chris Laing and Andy Taylor – writing and producing radio commercials for the

Cambridge-educated comedian, Griff Rhys Jones's London production company, TalkBack Productions.

The lads not only made a first-class team, bouncing jokes off each other, competing fiercely to cap one another's best lines – a comfortably familiar technique to Hugh from his early Latymer acting clubs – but created some award-winning campaigns for products like Brylcreem, Red Stripe Lager, the *Independent* newspaper and Mighty White sliced bread. In common with their best Jockeys' sketches, their most successful campaign ideas drew on the art of clever spoofing.

The Brylcreem hair products line still carried with it the unmistakable whiff of its 1950s heyday. Instead of denying this awkward aspect to selling the product in the 1980s, Hugh and his co-writers gleefully sent it all up, comically reinforcing the qualities of Brylcreem by using absurdly stilted BBC English-accented commentary: 'And here we are in the Mocha coffee bar in the heart of London's Soho district and a lot of young people are looking very smart. What keeps your hair looking so good?'

With Red Stripe lager, the team performed a similarly deft trick. They took the worked-to-death, and already widely spoofed, advertising gimmick of using 'trustworthy' Yorkshire accents to promote beer – and grafted it, with stylish inappropriateness, to the definitely non-Yorkshire product, Red Stripe lager.

The ads worked because they flattered the audience's intelligence. The underlying message was deceptively simple: hey, you're hip enough to get this joke – and that's why this product is for you.

The post-*Four Weddings* Hugh has also referred to this byway in his career as a genuinely satisfying period – and there is no reason not to believe him. He asserts, tongue firmly in cheek, that he felt like an adult for the first time in his life – with an office job and the 'manly' responsibility of turning up on time, and working late.

Yet, in recollections of his advertising stint, Hugh has also exercised his customary sly wit. 'I enjoyed the fact you could get all these top loveys for next to nothing. You could get Denholm Elliott for around seventy pounds an hour . . . "Sorry, Denholm, it's actually Mighty *White* Sliced Bread, not *Mighty* White . . ." Some actors hated us and couldn't believe it when they were introduced to producers who looked eighteen.'

A not so subtle reminder that hard times befall even veteran actors. This pose as a young Turk twitting the old guard is one to which Hugh would often return as he grew more famous, usually taking care to aim his barbs at actors who were – most conveniently – recently deceased. Denholm Elliott died at the age of 70 in October 1992, swarmed by personal demons, but having finally gained one Oscar nomination, for his role in the film for which Hugh was, coincidentally, gallingly rejected, *A Room with a View*, in 1985.

Following the Harty débâcle, Hugh became more determined to find legitimate acting work and doggedly did the rounds of the London TV auditions. Again and again, his porcelain pretty face and personal charisma made him the natural choice for casting agents. Yet, repeatedly, his lack of range and the curious fact that his charm did not seem to transmit well on camera blocked his progress with directors. Many times, friends say, he felt he had been more or less assured of a substantial part only to find this wasn't the case when final casting was announced. Hugh, however, was not quite ready to abandon his conviction that he needed only one lucky break.

His first made-for-TV movie came in 1985 with the ambitious USA/UK-financed Second World War tear-jerker *Jenny's War*, 'inspired by one of the most incredible true stories . . . of one woman's courageous quest for her only son behind enemy lines', according to the publicity material. Hugh received fourteenth billing in the four-hour drama behind TV movie stalwarts like Robert Hardy, Christopher Casenove, Elke Sommer and Dyan Cannon and won, not surprisingly, no notice at all from reviewers, who dismissed the well-intentioned production as coming 'straight from the bottom half of a 1940s Saturday matinée double bill'.

Hugh's earliest small-screen credentials also include a 1985 television play *Honour, Profit and Pleasure* – a celebration of the life of the composer Handel seen through the life of his friends. This credit, later dropped from his résumé, was for a slim role indeed. Simon Callow, of 1994's *Four Weddings* fame, had the lead as Handel. Hugh gets no official credit at all for what must have been a walk-on part.

The same year, however, saw the rather better received Central Television seven-part drama series, *The Last Place on Earth*, about the race to conquer the South Pole between the Norwegian Roald Amundsen and England's Robert Scott, and starring the leading British action adventure actor Martin Shaw. The lavish series was hugely hyped – as a kind of *Chariots of Fire* on ice – and it boosted the actor's status among his friends. (Hugh went on to play cricket for the dashingly named Captain Scott Invitation XI.) Hugh himself nurtured hopes that the production was 'starry' enough to win him a significant career break – though in the end his stiff-upper-lip role as Cherry Garrard flashed by without causing more than a ripple of interest in episode four.

So did, in October 1985, his appearance as the British diplomat and antiquary Sir William Hamilton in the Channel Four-sponsored TV drama *Lord Elgin and Some Stones of No Value*. This was a remarkably stolid piece of television, not merely dramatizing the controversial removal by Britain's Lord Elgin (played by Nigel Havers) of decorated sculptures from the ruined Parthenon at Athens in order to 'save' them for future generations, but unbearably inflicting upon the viewer a scene with Hugh and fellow actors, playing themselves *as* actors, solemnly debating the historical merits of both sides of the controversy. The part, though, appealed to the academic still lurking in Hugh, who cheerfully boasted that at least now he could 'spout Hellenism effectively'.

The following year he surfaced in the fifth episode – 'The Shadow' – of Thames Television's 1920s period drama series, *Ladies in Charge*, playing a minor character, billed tenth in a cast of ten, one Gerald Boughton-Greene. In June 1986 Hugh also popped up in one episode, titled 'The Demon Lover', of the long-running *Shades of Darkness* television series based on tales of the supernatural.

Somehow, television wasn't quite working for Hugh. No one gave him a shot at the juicier roles and he suspected he was in great danger of being forever cast in walk-on, upper-class-twit parts. Other actors, feeling themselves slipping into a rut, might have resorted to broadening their experience with stage work, and trusting that their brilliance might eventually come to the attention of television casting directors by this route. But Hugh had firmly rejected that option. He wasn't about to risk the humiliation of Nottingham all over again.

And, besides, there *was* an alternative.

ELEVEN

*'Just wait a few years, then you'll see who is going to
be the big star . . .'*

The director James Ivory on
Hugh Grant, 1987

Like every other fiercely ambitious young actor in Britain
in the mid-1980s, Hugh sensed that his strongest chance
of breaking through to Hollywood was by hooking up
with the Merchant–Ivory team. The illusion that Britain
had any sort of credible movie business at all in the final
quarter of the twentieth century was almost entirely
thanks to the unparalleled success of the Merchant–Ivory
film factory in selling deliciously romantic, intelligent
period images of the British back to an immensely tickled
Britain and to the rest of the world.

It is ironic, of course, that the team is regarded as a
British film industry success since the lion's share of
Merchant–Ivory's backing is almost always raised in America. The producer Ismail Merchant is Bombay-born, while
the director James Ivory hails from Berkeley, California,
and their literary collaborator, the brilliant novelist and
screenwriter Ruth Prawer Jhabvaler, is a woman of Polish
Jewish extraction, born in Germany, who fled to England as
a refugee, made her home in Delhi with her Indian architect
husband for 25 years and is now based in New York.

However, as a concept 'British cinema' can sometimes
be pretty flexible.

At least Merchant–Ivory actually *ran* a London office
and their extraordinarily fertile, 33-year-old creative partnership is now officially accepted as the most enduring in
the film industry, the *Guinness Book of World Records*
having given its crucial judgement on this matter.

By 1984–85, the Merchant–Ivory reputation for creating highbrow films (*Shakespeare Wallah*, *Heat and Dust*) on fairly lowly budgets and receiving warm critical attention was already secure. Also completed were their highly mannered period adaptations of Henry James's novels (*The Europeans*, *The Bostonians*). Now they were about to begin a series of adaptations of E.M. Forster's novels and – to the excitement of every agent in London – were scouting for British talent. Specifically British talent that would help sell Forster's visions of ravishing-looking, rule-bound, Edwardian Britain and Italy.

How, Hugh Grant must have wondered, could they *not* recruit Hugh Grant?

Like many other porcelain-skinned, drowsy-eyed lovelies who would repeatedly adorn the Merchant–Ivory period productions (Helena Bonham Carter, Rupert Graves and the future Oscar-winning Emma Thompson) Hugh, of course, already looked as if he'd been specially baked to perfection from a Merchant–Ivory recipe in a Merchant–Ivory Aga. Contrary to impressions, the Merchant–Ivory casting policy is not deliberately to give the same select coterie of attractive actors jobs for life by employing them over and again. Actors with whom they've previously worked are automatically welcomed back on set, no questions asked, for one reason only: to 'assist' behind the scenes – for nothing (save for the gourmet curries Ismail Merchant insists on serving to his casts and crew). And that remains one of the canniest examples imaginable of student drama production 'values' being transferred to the professional arena. Helena Bonham Carter, for example, frequently lent a hand on *Maurice* and got to know Hugh very well, even though she had no part in the movie.

The fact remains that Britain simply has a very small pool of A-list, or potential A-list, actors both experienced in movie work and available to work in the UK or in Europe – which is why the same lot seem to be apologetically tripping over each other in the loggia every time a new Merchant–Ivory comes out.

Hugh, however, to his great disappointment, failed to glitter sufficiently at the auditions for *A Room with a View*.

Though he'd lived his life in the shadow of E.M. Forster's London *pied-à-terre* and even spent his summer before Oxford pottering around the writer's beloved northern Italy, this gave him, cruelly, no special access to acting in films of the author's work. Not yet, anyway.

Later Hugh would jokingly claim that James Ivory's only reaction to his read-through for *A Room with a View* was a visible glazing about the eyes. Nevertheless, it was a worrying rejection, especially for the actor who was acutely conscious of exactly how well – or badly – his professional rivals were doing. Hugh saw, with a savage wrench, the serious-minded, public-school-educated James Wilby, with whom, of course, he had acted in *Privileged*, managing to secure his third walk-on movie role in *A Room with a View* (James Wilby had also appeared in *Dreamchild*). And the very hot Daniel Day-Lewis shook everyone – even the supposedly unshakeable James Ivory – by plumping for the part of Cecil Vyse, the unattractively supercilious fiancé of Lucy Honeychurch (Helena Bonham Carter).

After Day-Lewis's breakthrough London stage role – superbly taking over from Rupert Everett in *Another Country* – it was expected that he would prefer the far sexier role of the film's hero lover George Emerson. That went, in the end, to Julian Sands.

A Room with a View (1985) became an instant box-office and critical smash, bursting the confines of its 'art house' niche. Hugh was, understandably, intensely jealous. Its tone was exquisite. The hats looked marvellous. Helena became the new English rose, journalists and the public alike loved her link with true blue blood as the great-granddaughter of the Liberal peer Lord Asquith. Julian Sands was anointed as Britain's latest heart-throb, while Daniel Day-Lewis's early promise was spectacularly fulfilled and Maggie Smith revealed herself as a veteran at her peak. Italy shimmered perfectly. Merchant–Ivory had begun their E.M. Forster roll with a major hit and big blond Julian Sands was promptly pencilled in to play the lead in the next adaptation, *Maurice*.

This, too, wasn't a difficult period movie to get across to the rest of the world. Again it was about buttoned-up Edwardian Brits, this time about buttoned-up Edwardian British chaps loving each other too much at the posh British university of Cambridge. Granted that this is more or less what many Americans, and not a tiny number of European countries, seem to believe is the main purpose of Oxbridge education in Britain anyway, it wasn't a hard-sell concept.

Maurice is a fictionalized confessional of homosexual love with an awkward, wish-fulfillment, fantasy ending and was begun, in secret, by Forster in 1913 – a mere 34 years after homosexuality had been a crime punishable by death. He tinkered with the novel on and off for the rest of his life and was half right when he predicted there was no prospect of its being published 'until my death and England's'. The book finally appeared in 1971, the year after he died.

The novel tells the story of Maurice Hall and his struggle against his own homosexual nature in a society which was more than half a century away from legalizing sexual relations between adult men.

The heart-breakingly decent and ordinary Maurice is coaxed into discovering and identifying his homosexuality by his beautiful flirtatious aristocrat friend at Cambridge University, Clive Durham. In the end Clive persuades himself, at least, that he *isn't* homosexual, which leaves Maurice high and dry. Then Maurice meets Clive's lovely, working-class and uninhibitedly gay gamekeeper Alec, and the two live happily ever after.

Once again, Hugh was desperate for a role in the new Merchant–Ivory. Once again, he feared he hadn't made the grade – with principal casting all but complete, no word from James Ivory and filming about to begin in the summer of 1986.

Just eight days before *Maurice* went into production –

with location shooting at King's College and Trinity College, Cambridge, the stunningly well-preserved Linley Sambourne Victorian House in Kensington (also used for *A Room with a View*) and the gorgeously draped and many-chandeliered ground-floor dining-room of London's Café Royal all but confirmed – the unthinkable was suddenly announced: Julian Sands had withdrawn from the leading role. How he became unstuck from the production became the subject of much bitter debate, further muddied at the time by the painful break-up of the actor's marriage. There were dark mutterings about Hollywood offering Sands head-turning offers, in the wake of *A Room with a View*, and persuading him he'd simply become 'too big' for little British films.

Sands, who now lives in Los Angeles, coolly insists that, on the contrary, he had been more than willing to take on *Maurice*, but the film he'd been working on after *A Room with a View*, *Siesta*, had run badly over schedule. According to Sands, James Ivory had been apparently unwilling to rearrange the schedule for *Maurice* and no contracts had, in any case, been finalized.

In retrospect, Sands must have cursed the overblown, overrunning production of *Siesta*: this so-called 'experimental film', which also swallowed the talents of Jodie Foster, Ellen Barkin, Grace Jones, Isabella Rossellini and Alexei Sayle, was a resounding flop.

Now the Merchant–Ivory *Maurice* had to cast a new leading man in what seemed an impossibly short time. Thanks to taking the route Hugh had refused – performing in provincial theatre – the tall, blond and lovely James Wilby struck lucky. James Ivory had been deeply impressed with a performance Wilby gave on stage in Chichester. Yet, ironically, Ivory had reluctantly decided not to cast the impressive young actor in *Maurice* in a major supporting role in the film – probably as Clive Durham, the part Hugh ended up playing – because it was thought Wilby and the original star Sands looked too much like each other. With Sands out of the way, the problem vanished. James Wilby was told to forget about the tiny walk-on role he'd been given in the film: he was now the new Maurice.

It was a colossal responsibility for Wilby, who had just a little over a week to get to grips with the part. He very graciously later revealed to interviewers that, had James Ivory had more than a week to recast the role, he would almost certainly have chosen Daniel Day-Lewis instead.

And this time round, James Ivory hadn't glazed over during Hugh's casting interview, though he hadn't been a hundred per cent certain about the young actor, either. To Hugh's everlasting good fortune, *Maurice* was one of the Merchant–Ivory productions for which Ruth Prawer Jhabvaler was unavailable to write the screenplay adaptation. She was absorbed in writing her latest novel. Instead Ivory had gone to a very promising screenwriter who had a reputation for working fast and was also – a crucial consideration because of the film's collegiate setting – a Cambridge graduate. He was Hugh Grant's old comedy circuit dressing-room partner, Kit Hesketh-Harvey.

Hesketh-Harvey remembers that the director left the casting of Clive Durham almost to the last moment. 'At one point Jim [Ivory] canvassed me about who should play Clive. Hugh was high on the list and I did say, "Look, I've shared a dressing-room with this actor – he is wonderfully handsome, his accent is bang on, he's extremely bright and he'll make us all laugh."'

Hesketh-Harvey's generous endorsement was apparently taken on board, and Hugh – his dark good looks contrasting perfectly with Wilby's handsome fairness – was at last signed up as the stunning, though soggily self-deluding, Clive Durham.

Though Hugh later teased interviewers by describing Wilby as a fantastic kisser – 'the things he could do with his tongue!' – he has also claimed that making *Maurice* was an entirely terrifying experience. It wasn't his character's ambivalent homosexuality, though, that bothered the actor. Nor even that, away from the cameras, he had very little in common with the cautious and very thoughtful Wilby. What unnerved the young actor was James Ivory's belief that Hugh could bring to the surface the humour implicit (*extremely* implicit to be fair to Hugh) in the character of Clive Durham coupled with the director's notoriously laid-back directing style.

Hugh was, rightly, never able to convince himself that he was bringing the required dash of merriment to the part.

'Much of the terror of working with Jim is that he doesn't appear to direct closely at all,' confirms Hesketh-Harvey. 'He lets actors get on with it. Hugh wasn't told what to do at all. I hadn't realized he was quite so nervous but in fact I remember he didn't splash around between takes as a more experienced actor would have done.'

Hesketh-Harvey also recalls being struck by the two deeply contrasting sides to Hugh during filming: the exquisite-looking actor with the chilled-champagne voice who appeared entirely at ease in period costume and was impressively well informed about E.M. Forster, and the 'other' blokey Hugh, who talked football scores ad nauseam and once sent the make-up crew into a flap when he shuffled on to set one morning with a visibly swollen lip.

'It looks,' the screenwriter explains, 'like a continuity error in the film because you can see there's something wrong with Hugh's mouth *before* his character has a punch-up with [James Wilby's character]. But I gather he'd hurt himself playing football.'

Both Hugh and James Wilby campaigned vociferously, says Hesketh-Harvey, to be permitted to do their own riding scenes – to the total horror of the film's insurers. 'They were both raring to go. I would say that, as far as putting himself in physical danger is concerned, Hugh is absolutely fearless,' he says. However, the very proper concerns of the insurers prevailed – and in the end it is the (presumably more expendable) screenwriter Kit Hesketh-Harvey who can be seen as the galloping Clive Durham in the film's equestrian sequences.

The film was premièred at the 44th Venice Film Festival in 1987, where it picked up two awards: it was joint runner-up in the best film section and the award for best actor was shared by James Wilby and Hugh Grant.

In Britain, the film – released in November – earned Hugh prominent coverage in the gay press and brought him a sizeable gay following as well as a slew of good reviews. Many, though, carried a sting in the tail by contrasting how superb he was in the first half of the film as the undergraduate Clive with his unconvincing portrayal of Lord Durham as a settled country squire in the second half, which was generally agreed as belonging to the glued-on-moustache school of acting.

The reviewers were also unanimous in saying that the main weak point in the film was not the fault of the actors or the director. It was Forster who insisted that Maurice and his gamekeeper friend (played by the excellent Rupert Graves) should wind up discovering their perfect love for each other in a fairy-tale ending. 'A happy ending was imperative,' Forster wrote in a dignified note in 1960. 'I was determined that in fiction anyway two men should fall in love and remain in it for the ever and ever that fiction allows.'

In North America, where it had opened in September, *Maurice* promptly broke art-house box-office records and reinforced the 'Hugh Grant as Gay Icon' image. As Janet Maslin, of the *New York Times*, cooed, 'If audiences take away a sole representative image from *Maurice*, it might well be the sight of handsome, moody young Clive Durham ... resting his head voluptuously upon the knee of Maurice Hall's white flannel trousers.'

In Japan, *Maurice* touched some hitherto unsounded chord in the hearts of its schoolgirl population. Hugh Grant became to Japan's junior misses what Dolly Parton is to that island nation's more senior misters: an embodiment of occidental physical perfection. Hugh, of course, has long delighted in boasting about being Big In Japan and receiving sackfuls of origami dragons, pyjamas and barely comprehensible letters from devoted teenage girls. He has claimed he was even tempted to write some especially sensitive poetry and have it published in Japan with a romantic photo of himself, posing as Rupert Brooke, on the cover in order to make some cash out of his Eastern fame.

'Unfortunately, I don't want their love – I want their money,' he tells interviewers bluntly, defying them to disapprove; though Hugh was also later forced to apologize for any offence he may have caused after one too many comically accented imitations of 'dialogue' from the bad Japanese film scripts he'd been sent.

Why *Maurice* should have made Hugh so popular with girls is not difficult to fathom. The film offers a replay of *Romeo and Juliet* with gender instead of warring families as the big divide. Love that cannot be, because society won't allow it, is deeply appealing to post-pubescents, and in the UK as well as Japan the film attracted a significant amount of 'female repeater' trade – the inelegant term that refers to young women who will return half a dozen times or more to the same film.

Maurice, finally, brought Hugh his first real taste of fame, rather than the empty promises of agents or chat-show hosts. There were limousines and press conferences for the film's New York opening and Hugh enjoyed them all enormously. The actor – at last – found himself provoking gratifying squeals of recognition in London. These were significantly more frequent, friends recall, when Hugh would ever so casually stroll up and down outside cinemas where *Maurice* was actually showing! Far from never actively seeking fame, as he would later tell interviewers, Hugh absolutely relished it. For the first time, too, he was in demand for showbusiness interviews.

These, it has to be said, were not exactly triumphs of public relations. Hugh had not yet perfected a meet-the-press persona and he sent more than one journalist away gibbering with suppressed rage at his affected flippancy and tiresome sarcasm. Acting, he informed the distinguished film writer Minty Clinch, for an *Observer* magazine article, had been 'as easy as winking, it really has. I didn't even want to be an actor and I find it impossible to take it terribly seriously.' (Little mention of course, of the bitter early career disappointments, coaching by Schlesinger, the *Greystoke* fiasco or his recent accumulation of forgettable television roles.)

The spectacle of a new 'star' trying on a variety of personae for the benefit of the press – amusingly arrogant here, coquettish there, charmingly self-deprecating over here again ('Please tell me I wasn't absolutely the most awful thing you've seen in your life' was another line Hugh regularly used on journalists about *Maurice*) – is a very familiar one. And Hugh soon found it was going to take many years to get it right. Once again – after the initial fuss over the film's release had died down – Hugh realized that *Maurice* had not made him a star with the public overnight. Hollywood offers were conspicuous only by their absence. Rupert Graves and James Wilby grabbed the most column inches. To the world, Hugh Grant was still just another unknown with a lucky break behind him.

But, having sensed an original comic talent in Hugh, James Ivory for one was ready to sit back and watch patiently for it to flower. As Kit Hesketh-Harvey recalls, 'Beyond anyone else, [Merchant–Ivory] are real star-makers. When the film came out there was the most tremendous fuss being made of the other actors, which was quite right because they all did wonderfully and, to be truthful, the whole thing had been done in a screaming hurry.

'But Hugh got pushed to the background a bit. I said to Jim [Ivory], "Don't you think this is a bit odd?" and Jim just said, "Yes, but just wait a few years and *then* you'll see who is going to be the big star!"'

TWELVE

*'[He] is the archetypal hero ... except that he screws
a lot. He was fascinatingly ambiguous, pouring
his life into living and adopting Oscar Wilde's
maxim that the best way to end temptation is to
submit to it.'*

The director Gonzalo Suarez, to
Screen International, *1987, on the character
Hugh Grant portrays in* Rowing with the Wind

Hugh's romance with Elizabeth Hurley, the ingenue British actress he met the summer after *Maurice*, when filming *Rowing with the Wind*, came not a moment too soon for some of the actor's exasperated friends. Not that Hugh had affected any unusual airs as a result of the art-house success of his first Merchant–Ivory outing. Although Hugh was perfectly adept at acting the diva and mercilessly ribbing his friends about the colossal sums he was now earning – and they weren't – there was little question of any of his old Latymerian, or Jockeys, mates taking offence. They gleefully took to handing Hugh the entire restaurant bill at the end of West London evenings of shared curries and beers with the suggestion that he lighten the terrible burden of his own wallet.

However, in the months before taking up with Elizabeth, Hugh had begun tiresomely confiding his fondness for girlie magazines – the type located on the top shelves of newsagents' as opposed to the Soho hardcore variety. Wasn't it *frightful*, he moaned, that these vulgar pictures of females could arouse him? Did this mean that he was unable to form close relationships with real women? This is a question his confidants were, understandably, too nonplussed to answer sensibly.

Though the spectacle of young British males guiltily ogling magazines devoted to naked ladies is hardly an unusual one, Hugh's smutty-publication confessions were – it was felt – coming distinctly tardily. The actor was in his late twenties, not his late teens. Excuses of extreme youth, if any excuse was required to explain a sudden appetite for soft pornography, no longer really fitted. Hugh's was an admission that doubly discomfited his listeners. It seemed to confirm him more as oddly immature – his libido frozen in a Gaveston Society time warp in which the *show* of sexual naughtiness counted for everything – than as a man of exotically worldly tastes.

Yet Hugh also appeared to pose the question – isn't it just too *awful* of me to love this stuff so? – in a curiously sly manner, his blue eyes gleaming with interest as if waiting to pounce on an unguarded reaction of bourgeois shock . . . or disgust. What Hugh – in common with many highly self-absorbed and creative people – failed to consider was that his private urges and desires were not at all uncommon. Far from being aberrant or peculiar – as Hugh appeared to distinguish them – they were drearily run-of-the-mill. Perhaps, some friends decided more kindly, Hugh was simply overreacting to the 'gay icon' image *Maurice* had saddled him with and was somewhat clumsily reasserting his heterosexuality.

In any event, the actor's friends vastly preferred the familiar, acidly entertaining Hugh who described one very well-known actress with a lingering crush on him as possessing 'Brussels sprouts breath and badly shaved legs' to the Hugh who feebly complained that his dream girls were all splayed Playmates wearing suspenders and little else. In retrospect, of course, it is slightly alarming that Hugh began his relationship with Elizabeth apparently already troubled by his fixation for fantasy sex figures.

But, back in 1987, Hugh's friends breathed a sigh of relief when he returned from filming *Rowing with the Wind* with a new girl-friend, his ravishing 21-year-old co-star, Elizabeth Hurley.

For the next eight years – until the prostitute scandal of

1995 had Elizabeth tremblingly declaring that her own father wanted Hugh horsewhipped – the couple maintained a remarkable juggling act. Keeping two careers on the boil, maintaining apartments in London and Los Angeles and very publicly enjoying the material advantages their highly paid film work brought. To their closest friends, Hugh and Elizabeth seemed radiantly well-matched. And far from being patronized for being 'non-Oxbridge' by Hugh's university friends, the young actress inspired a very different reaction.

'She was so obviously incredibly street-smart,' says one. 'Very cool and observant. If there was any intimidating going on, it was coming from Elizabeth. She never came across as intellectual, but she was as sharp as a tack.'

Once again Hugh had a feisty, beautiful mate who could shield him from the unwanted advances of other women. Elizabeth not only sympathized with the stresses, the highs and lows of the acting profession, but hailed from a background that was, uncannily, a mirror image of his own.

The daughter of a (now) retired army major and a music teacher mother, Elizabeth was, like Hugh, a precocious and outgoing second child. She, too, knew the frustrations of living in a perpetual race to catch up with her much envied and copied elder sister Kate, just as Hugh had with Jamie. Elizabeth describes Kate, eighteen months her elder, who would go into another area of showbusiness as a screenwriters' agent, as inspiring her with intense feelings of jealousy during their teenage years by attracting boyfriends before she did. Yet the siblings grew close enough to share a flat once they'd left home, again like Jamie and Hugh.

In common with Hugh, Elizabeth enjoyed a sunny, stable childhood in an artistically inclined, conventional, middle-class family. At her home at Buckskin, near the London commuter suburb of Basingstoke, books were plentiful, meals were served on time and a good show of manners won firm nods of approval. Like Hugh, she had been ragged rotten at her local comprehensive for her plummy accent, which didn't fit in with those of many of her consonant-dropping schoolmates. Yet, despite the teasing, Elizabeth proudly stuck to the Received Pronunciation English she heard spoken by her parents.

Neither family was financially very comfortably off. Just as Hugh saw his own parents stretching their budget to guarantee him the best education they could afford, Elizabeth has recalled her mother, Angela, skimping on buying things for herself so she could purchase new tap-shoes for her daughter. Interestingly, both sets of parents seemed to feel it important that their children were aware that sacrifices were made on their behalf. There are, after all, methods of buying your child a pair of dance-shoes without signalling that you're going short yourself. And both Hugh and Elizabeth would share, as high-earning young adults, a naked delight in crowing about expensive purchases that suggests that these early lessons in money management misfired.

Hugh had his schoolteacher mentor, Colin Turner, to thank for his early acting ambitions. Elizabeth credits 'terrific' English and Drama teachers for pushing her in the direction of an acting and dancing career, as well as her parents for selflessly chauffeuring her to endless dance classes.

Where the pair radically differed, of course, was Elizabeth's rebel-by-numbers phase in her late teens. Around the time Hugh was absorbing the gloomy news that Hollywood was not, after all, panting for his presence and that his immediate future lay with Nottingham rep, the wilful Elizabeth was running wild. Almost overnight, it seemed, she transformed from a vivacious, bossy little girl who wept over *Watership Down*, adored pony stories and dutifully practised at the piano – to a fully fledged teen tearaway.

Punk was long dead to Londoners by the early eighties, but it still lingered stubbornly in provincial Basingstoke. Elizabeth, who was by her own admission seized by that most traditional of late adolescent enthusiasms – driving her parents up the wall – was an exuberant convert, bleaching her hair brassy white one moment, rinsing it blue the next, sporting a nose stud and sixteen rings in her ears and sashaying around town in leather mini-skirts and studded dog collars. As her parents held their breath and prayed – and her teachers foresaw a very sticky end to it all – Elizabeth threw herself into what passed for the 'punk club scene' in the seedier districts of nearby suburban Reading, while notching up the ultimate middle-class teenage thrills designed to *epater les bourgeois*, spending all night at Waterloo station after missing the last train home to Basingstoke, and shocking even 'punk' friends by her habit of neglecting to wear knickers.

The exhibitionist in her unleashed – and temporarily satisfied – Elizabeth then confounded the pessimistic expectations. She returned to the fold of school and family for her A levels in English, sociology and psychology, and later dropped in and out of drama school (sharing Hugh's scepticism over the benefits of being 'taught' acting) and ballet school before embarking on a professional career.

Fortunately, for the intensely ambitious Elizabeth, the rainbow-dyed hair could be – and was – grown out, the raccoon make-up scrubbed off and the earrings dumped in a drawer. The new London-based Elizabeth emerged from her punk chrysalis a bewitchingly lovely young woman with a long, lean, wide-shouldered dancer's body, a taste for the tiniest miniskirts and rather more experience of the vicissitudes of life than your average 20-year-old from Hampshire.

After working with a dance troupe, turning down a part as 'a Bond girl' – to her enduring regret, it clashed with other work – appearing briefly in a touring theatrical production of *The Man Most Likely To*, plus a smidgen of television experience in commercials and a lunchtime soap opera, Elizabeth finally met Hugh over dinner with the Spanish novelist-turned-director, Gonzalo Suarez.

In 1987 Suarez, by an odd coincidence, was then just one of three directors who were almost simultaneously struck with the idea of making a film about the English Romantic, Lord Byron. Very specifically, a film about the wild, if damp, summer Byron and his good friends the Shelleys (as in Mary, creator of *Frankenstein*, and Percy

Bysshe, radical atheist and genius) spent in Geneva in 1816 and their later life together in Italy.

Suarez's *Rowing with the Wind*, starring Hugh as Byron and Elizabeth as his mistress, a much smaller role, was released the same year – 1988 – as Ivan Passer's *Haunted Summer*. *Haunted Summer* starred Laura Dern and Eric Stolz, among others, and also recalled the wild, if damp, summer the Lord Byron (Philip Anglim) and his good friends the Shelleys – Mary and Percy Bysshe – spent in Geneva in 1816 and their later life together in Italy. Which, again, should not be muddled with Ken Russell's Euroflick *Gothic*, starring Julian Sands and Natasha Richardson, which took as its theme the wild, damp summer enjoyed by Lord Byron (this time Gabriel Byrne) and *his* good friends, Mary and Percy Shelley, in Geneva in 1816 . . .

The trio of Byronic film-makers must have been practically tripping over each other on the shores of Lake Geneva!

Gonzalo Suarez was defensive on the subject of Hugh's Byron being compared with anyone else's, telling *Screen International* in 1987 (with a view to putting a million miles between his film and Ken Russell's psychedelic romp in particular): 'My film does *not* deal with drugs or diabolisms or deliriums. It is about people who have the guts to live outside the conventions of their time and the courage to cope with the consequences.'

Rowing with the Wind, however, Elizabeth's first film, did have the unique distinction of igniting the most glamorous showbusiness relationship of the 1990s. Making the song, 'Something Stupid (Like I Love You)' by Frank and Nancy Sinatra – which was playing in the cafés of Spain while they filmed – into their 'own' song, Elizabeth and Hugh tumbled headlong into an intense friendship, and then romance. Elizabeth played, with ease, the exquisite Claire Claremont, Mary Shelley's then seventeen-year-old stepsister who became Byron's mistress.

Hugh has gallantly confirmed that his initial reservations at accepting the role of Byron in a 'Europudding' movie (it was shot in Spain, Norway, Switzerland and Italy) were greatly alleviated by his first sight of the long-haired, sexily short-skirted Elizabeth as his screen love-interest at that introductory dinner with the director. Elizabeth has always maintained she fell for Hugh's sharp sense of humour – and his romantic white breeches – an interesting comment in the light of the couple's later fondness for private fancy dress. Defending his role in *Rowing with the Wind*, Hugh seldom fails to add the charming *faux-naïf* explanation: 'If people say come to Spain and we'll pay you, you know, *hundreds* of thousands of dollars, and there's lots of pretty girls and even if you know the film's not going to be terribly good or properly released . . . it's *very* difficult to say no.'

Nevertheless Hugh was made to suffer for his salary. The part required the actor to spend many queasy hours bobbing in a small open boat in order for the perfectionist Suarez to capture exactly the right Turneresque blood-coloured sunset; by the time the shot was in the can, Hugh was a deep Turneresque green. He is not someone who has ever boasted about his great sea legs.

The film was awarded second prize, 'the Silver Shell', at the 1988 San Sebastian Film Festival – one of the second-tier European film festivals held in the tiny Basque seaport – and won polite reviews but, reportedly, no major inter-national distribution deal except in Hugh Grant-loving Japan (a disappointment to the director, who had cast Hugh partly because *Maurice* was expected to make him the next big hot British property).

One festival reviewer earnestly congratulated Gonzalo Suarez for having had the moral fibre to 'eschew the scenes of orgy and concentrate alternately on the wry comments and *bons mots* of Byron' – not exactly a recommendation to have them stampeding to the cinemas!

Nor did *Rowing with the Wind* establish Hugh and Elizabeth as a promising screen couple. No directors came running to sign them up together. Yet the film was an important watershed for Hugh, not only because it brought him a new girlfriend. It seemed to sharpen his often saving sense of self-ridicule. The only spin he *could* put on stomping around Spain in a fetching wig while pretending to be a long-dead poet was a ruefully comic one. He seemed to stop modelling himself in terms of his screen roles – the mannered hooray of *Privileged*, the smarmy aristocrat of *Maurice* – or clinging to the belief that Hollywood was just one lucky break away.

To friends he began to refine a new David Nivenish persona, by simultaneously apologizing for doing such a 'ridiculous job' as acting while hinting, in a deafening fashion, that it was all a tremendously high-earning lark. At times Hugh even sounded as if he was reworking some of Niven's better one liners. His charming 'hundreds of thousands of dollars and lots of pretty girls' line seems to echo closely Niven's cunningly pitched comment about the absurdities of his profession: 'Can you imagine,' the inimitable light-comedy king used to enquire mischievously 'being *wonderfully* overpaid for dressing up and playing games?'

As Hugh embarked on what was to be, for the next six years, a strictly B-movie career, it seemed at first that Elizabeth was set to be the more successful of the two. The year after she met Hugh and barely twelve months since launching herself as an actress, Elizabeth appeared to have landed *her* first crucial career break with the lead in Dennis Potter's acclaimed television adaptation of the wartime drama *Christabel*. The series, about an Englishwoman married to an anti-Hitler German lawyer and their life in Nazi Germany, won some excellent reviews and whipped up a storm of publicity of the 'unknown English beauty scoops a starring role' variety – though the actress seemed an oddly youthful choice to play a tweedy, heroic, married mother-of-two. Its promise, however, was illusory.

None of the scripts that came her way in the wake of the series came near – in Elizabeth's opinion – to matching the quality of *Christabel*. And it was after doing publicity for the BBC series in America, after it had been bought for US television, that she plumped for staying on in Los Angeles – breezily declaring that she would give Tinseltown her best shot 'until my thirtieth birthday', which doubtless seemed a lifetime away.

In reality, Elizabeth ping-ponged between Europe and Los Angeles, ever willing to pose for magazine fashion layouts to remind British directors that she was still available for prominent roles yet adding very little quality work to her own résumé. Like Hugh, Elizabeth likes to draw a comic veil over her more forgettable films, like *The Skipper* ('they thought it was a masterpiece, but it was nonsense'), in which she co-starred with another publicity-adoring actress, Patsy Kensit. Yet, unlike Hugh, Elizabeth had yet to perfect the publicly mortified pose, 'and, of course, I was *terrible* in it too', preferring to lay the blame on the film's makers instead.

By all acounts, making *The Skipper* was hell in every way for everyone concerned. The thriller, in which Elizabeth played a psychopathic hairdresser from Leeds, a role that might have alerted her earlier to the film's poor promise, took months to shoot, mainly in Malta, in a 110-degree heat with everyone's nerves frazzled by the physical discomfort of shooting on board a yacht, Elizabeth falling out, reportedly, with her German co-star Jurgen Prochnow, Patsy Kensit openly rowing with the director and both actresses complaining that they weren't being 'sufficiently appreciated' on set. The shaken director, Peter Keglevic, was quoted in one magazine as saying, 'Something so strange happened. I don't understand young women any more. Crudely put, today's men must be more and more afraid that today's young women will kick them where it hurts . . .'

At least, however, Elizabeth did not have to suffer the double indignity of seeing her new actor boyfriend's career eclipsing her own. None of Hugh's films released in 1988 appeared to present any special threat, though the plot of one of them might in later years have given her pause for thought. Hugh had been cast as a lonely white man on the loose in a strange country – who is lured into scandal by having sex with a dark-skinned beauty.

CHAPTER

THIRTEEN

*'Beneath the translucent material, her brown breasts
seemed slightly paler, a shade of damask, and I was
overwhelmed, terrifyingly, by that sight. I knew she
had put on that obscene and delicious costume for
my benefit.'*

from Bengal Nights *(1933) by Mircea Eliade*

'Hugh Grant is bland.'

from a review of the film Bengali Night *(1988),
based on the 1933 novel*

With *Bengali Night* (*La Nuit Bengali*) Hugh became, if
not a film star, at least an international globe-trotter.
Filming on location in India was required for this saga of
forbidden love, a kind of *Bridges of Madison County* set
in and around Calcutta, which appealed strongly to
Hugh's love of at least being *seen*, by his mates, to pursue
a suitably glamorous life.

Hugh also tends to prepare for film roles by reading
around them, and the project genuinely pricked his intellectual curiosity. Based on a steamily erotic, semi-
autobiographical, confessional novel written, surprisingly,
by a renowned Romanian divinity scholar, Mircea Eliade,
Bengal Nights was about the stigmatizing consequences of
a sexual relationship – at the tail end of British Raj India
– between a white Western male and a precociously
sensuous young Bengali Hindu girl.

In the film, Hugh plays Alain, an ex-patriot French
engineer invited into the home of his chummy Bengali
employer to convalesce after a bout of malaria. Vulnerable, lonely, yet already ardently attracted to the mysteries
of Hinduism, Alain becomes sexually obsessed with his

employer's voluptuous dark-skinned daughter (played by Supriya Pathak). A torrid affair begins, conducted in desperate secrecy, but Alain's belief that he might, eventually, be accepted as a suitable son-in-law by his employer (Soumitra Chatterji) is shown to be wildly optimistic.

When their affair is betrayed, in spite of some sympathy from the girl's mother (the Indian screen star Shabana Azmi), the lovers are brutally parted for ever. He is cast out of his enraged employer's home, while the girl is utterly disgraced, and both are doomed to live the rest of their lives in regret.

The uninhibitedly passionate avant-garde novel on which the film was based was published in Romania in 1933, but became a huge best-seller only when translated into French in 1950, just five years in advance of the benchmark publication of Hugh's all-time favourite novel, *Lolita*, which deals, of course, with a strikingly similar theme about the dark lusting of an older man for a much younger, coquettish woman. Yet the impossibly romantic real-life denouement to Eliade's 'novel' would have been ruled far too contrived for fiction. Over 40 years after their love affair, the once gorgeous Bengali girl who inspired Eliade's book happened to read it and subsequently, though keeping her identity a secret, wrote her own 'fictionalized' account of their relationship and its aftermath, very touchingly entitled, *It Does Not Die*. Eliade himself died in 1986 at the ripe, if regretful, age of 81.

Although, as usual, Hugh fussed about 'finding' his character, particularly as he was in the hands of an untested first-time director, his role as Alain didn't appear to be too much of a stretch from previous parts. Once again, as in *Maurice*, the film was period, this time the 1930s, with his character required to look anguished in fetchingly distressed linen and the plot revolving around a love that unyielding society will not permit. Hugh looked young – perhaps too young – and beautiful as the naive cultural outsider.

But the actor didn't entertain any hopes about the film significantly boosting his career. Its budget was modest (22 million francs) and it was a 'mongrel' production, a French-British-Indian collaboration that would not have been widely seen outside European art houses. In truth, it is not a Hugh Grant film that would have been widely seen *inside* European art houses either. Not because it was a terrible film, or a trashy one – its heart was in the right place, even if its plotting and continuity weren't. The overwhelming drawback of *Bengali Night* is that it doesn't actually make sense.

After the affair is exposed, Alain winds up, a shattered man, back in the miserable Calcutta boarding-house whence he had come. Yet what he was doing there in the first place and how he came to be suddenly employed by Chatterji's character remain one of a number of puzzling little mysteries left dangling in the film (although dealt with explicitly in the original novel).

'Ambitious but muddled,' said the reviewers of *Bengali Night*, although it was felt that blame, if any, should be laid at the inexperienced feet of its director, Nicolas Klotz. Hugh was thought to be 'bland' as Alain, though tolerable in the love scenes with the enchanting Supriya Pathak. However, it was also wondered by reviewers what precisely the fine English actor John Hurt was doing in the film. That is, the puzzle was not what John Hurt was doing *in* the film, but what John Hurt was *doing* in the film. Owing to holes in the plot – perhaps we should call it *Abridgements of Calcutta's Madison County*! – cinemagoers were left confused by the *point* of him.

Hurt plays Lucien, a sour-faced wandering international photojournalist who appears to be an old acquaintance of Hugh's character. His function, apart from hating India, seems unclear. Hurt's character hates India so much that he leaves the country soon after he arrives. And that's the rather abrupt end of John Hurt's role in *Bengali Night*. Hugh later explained that he had approached John Hurt while filming, for any useful tips he might have on acting technique.

He recalled: '[John] said he didn't have any technique at all. He said, "I don't know what the fuck I'm doing." '

Hugh took this to be a spirited statement about the essentially irreducible nature of the craft of acting: given his uncertain role in the movie, John Hurt was probably talking much more specifically.

Bengali Night finally did mark Hugh's career taking off – but sideways. He wasn't a star, he still suffered rejections at auditions – for Steven Spielberg's 1988 movie *Empire of the Sun*, for example – but he was certainly employable and living a life that was often removed from his London friends (when he was away on location) and suited him very well. Hugh loved to return from location, like a hunter from safari, to hole up with Notting Hill friends brimming with fresh anecdotes about tyrannical directors, rotten scripts, being 'forced to get into bed with pretty girls for a living' and larding his stories with whoppingly indiscreet asides about actresses.

With his wicked eye for observation, particularly for physical peculiarities, Hugh reduced friends to helpless laughter with imitations of his female co-stars and ribald gossip. And film work, as he never failed to remind his friends, was – no matter how terrible the results – terribly well-paid! When Oxford friends teased him about the smallness of his parts in the movies that did achieve general release, like *White Mischief*, Hugh would promptly agree he'd been *appalled* at his treatment on the cutting-room floor because he had, in point of fact, been assured he had won the lead role. Fact, of course, was never so entertaining as pure fiction. Dogged by the abject fear of ridicule that affects many actors, Hugh always sought to out-ridicule himself first.

FOURTEEN

'Kiss Me, Hughie!'
Greta Scacchi to Hugh Grant
in White Mischief, *1987*

White Mischief (1987), directed by Michael Radford, is based on the true story of upper-class Brits indulging in all sorts of sexual shenanigans in 1940s Kenya, when they should, of course, have been back home in the UK volunteering to melt down the family silver for the War Effort.

Hugely enjoyable, if rather long, the film stars Greta Scacchi and Charles Dance as doomed lovers in a cleverly embroidered version of a real scandal that rocked decadent, morphine-taking white Kenyan 'Happy Valley' society. This was reinvestigated for an elegant *Sunday Times* article by the celebrated critic Cyril Connolly in 1969, then turned into a book after Connolly's death by his co-author, an Eton-educated American journalist (not the actor), James Fox.

Dance played Josslyn Hay, Earl of Erroll – the murder victim – Scacchi his mistress, Diana, who was also the young wife of three months of Sir Henry 'Jock' Delves Broughton. Jock Broughton was tried and acquitted of the murder, but found 'guilty' by the *Sunday Times* investigation and the compelling book afterwards.

It is not, however, a movie that displays the full range of Hugh's talents. This is largely because a good fifty per cent of his role is over and done with before the opening credits are shown. Blink immediately *after* the opening credits and the rest of Hugh's contribution is over too.

Although any actor would be proud to have *White Mischief* on his professional résumé – it looks good and strongly suggests that you were rewarded handsomely to swan round Africa in fabulous taupe-linen jodhpurs for several months – there is actually a tiny part of the movie that is not set in Kenya at all, but in England, and that's where Hugh enters, and very speedily exits. In compensation for *not* wafting around Kenya, at least Hugh gets to roll around with an ethereally beautiful Greta Scacchi, who desperately begs him on screen, 'Kiss me, Hughie!'

The actress has not got his real name and his *White Mischief* name mixed up, Hugh is called Hughie in the film because he is playing Hugh Dickinson, a Harrow-educated Royal Army Signals character. Though his part in *White Mischief* is undeniably small (he gets billed near the bottom of the supporting actors) Hugh, to his credit, gives it everything he's got.

We first meet him galloping, very competently indeed, alongside Scacchi on a gloriously sunny 1940s day across the magnificent English country estate of the Scacchi character's much older, doddery, aristocratic husband-to-be (Joss Ackland in towering form). From the way Hugh says, 'Good morning, sir; very sorry about your lawn' (the one he and his stallion have evidently just *totally* ploughed up) to Joss Ackland's character, it is breathtakingly obvious that he's also been enjoying ploughing the man's fiancée. Which is quite a lot to pack into a line about a lawn.

Scacchi as Diana says something about the gardener fixing it and then the opening credits roll. When they're done, we are in a softly lit London boudoir with Scacchi and Hugh, presumably post-coitally, though both are clothed, drinking champagne. Hugh has his collar open and his tie undone.

'Well, here's to love,' he says, in a tone that effectively combines wistfulness and reproach. 'Very funny,' shoots back Scacchi. 'You don't think he's rather old?' asks Hugh, referring to Joss Ackland's character. 'I like older men,' she replies wantonly, adding after a pause, 'They have more money.' Then Diana lolls back on the bed, revealing that she is wearing an even ruder version of the halter-top dress Marilyn Monroe famously wore in *The*

Seven Year Itch, and says 'Oh no' as the air-raid sirens begin.

Cut to air-raid shelter with Hugh and Greta playing Lord and Lady Muck (she has added a big white mink stole to her outfit) down among the *hoi polloi*. Hugh is still trying to put her off the idea of marrying the doddery old aristo just for money, but without sounding too pompous or moral about it.

'My mother married for a title and look what happened to her,' he says. This is not a bad line, except that it immediately has the effect of making you incurably curious about his character's mother. We simply aren't given a clue. Scacchi's next line is 'I'm *not* your mother, thank God.' Then Scacchi does her 'Kiss me, Hughie!' bit.

Hugh enthusiastically obliges and the actress rakes her scarlet nails through his beautifully floppy hair. 'Now, tell me that you love me,' she teases, to which Hugh responds – in precisely the buttoned-up, stuttery, embarrassed fashion that would make the world fall in love with him six years later in *Four Weddings* – 'I – I love you. You know I do.' *We* know he does, too.

Hughie then pours more champagne (they remembered to take the bottle with them from the boudoir to the air-raid shelter) and displays some lovely comic inflections when he tells Diana she won't find any tigers when she goes out to Africa – only 'ostriches, baboons, hyenas . . .' He mouths 'baboons' particularly enchantingly. (The point is that when she gets to Kenya she does indeed find herself among ostriches, baboons and hyenas – of the upper-class, white-trash, human variety.)

And that is the extent of Hugh Grant's *White Mischief* role. A total of eight lines in a one-hour-and-fifty-minute movie. From the next scene onward, the action is in Kenya and never leaves. It is wonderfully kinky – sort of *The Piers Gaveston Society Goes On Safari* – with superb supporting performances from John Hurt (Hugh's co-star in a film the following year *Bengali Night*) and Trevor Howard, looking more robust here than in the film *he* made the following year with Hugh, *The Dawning*.

Although we are not told what title was owned by the unknown husband of the mother of Hugh's character in *White Mischief*, this part qualifies for fourth place on Hugh's gradually lengthening big-screen list of beautiful, charming, classically repressed, upper-class English types, his Lord Adrian (in *Privileged*) being first and his Lord Durham (in *Maurice*) second with Lord Byron (*Rowing with the Wind*) third. By the end of the following year, Hugh would have added two more hereditary barons and an upper-class twit to his repertoire. Dramatically speaking, Hugh Grant was not, at this stage in his career, quite ready to spread his wings.

FIFTEEN

'Of course he couldn't remember his lines. They had to have them all on idiot boards.'

Hugh Grant on acting with
Trevor Howard in 1988

'Trevor Howard was not well. But it was extraordinary. The moment he appeared in front of the camera, all the energy leapt into him.'

Joss Ackland on acting with
Trevor Howard in 1988

Another one of Hugh's flotilla of 1988 films is *The Dawning*, one of those curiously stillborn British efforts that promise, in theory, to be chillingly brilliant and mop up at the awards ceremonies, and then fail conspicuously to do anything of the sort. (This one picked up just half of one small prize.)

At first glance the cast appear straight out of the top drawer, two starry veterans (Jean Simmons and Trevor Howard), plus one international superstar in the making (Anthony Hopkins, with whom Hugh would be acting, with far more congenial results, five years on, in *The Remains of the Day*), combining with the fresh young talent of Rebecca Pidgeon and Hugh.

This period piece about the Irish Troubles and based on a Jennifer Johnston novel has Pidgeon making her screen debut as a romantic, apparently orphaned eighteen-year-old naif, Nancy, who lives with her aunt (Jean Simmons) and grandfather (Trevor Howard) in a splendid Georgian seaside house in 1920s Southern Ireland. She fancies herself in love with Hugh's character, a handsome ex-soldier turned stockbroker of, unfortunately, near certifiable witlessness. Hugh's main contribution to the film is proving that even his sublime looks can lose out to an abundantly Brylcreemed hairstyle.

Then Nancy discovers an armed stranger on the run (Anthony Hopkins) hiding in her beach hut. Persuading herself that he might be her missing-presumed-dead father, she rashly agrees to run secret messages to Dublin for him – only to witness an appalling escalation in the 'troubles' with the massacre of a dozen British soldiers.

Sadly, this attempt to locate the political turmoil of the period in the sexual and intellectual awakening of an eighteen-year-old middle-class Irish girl failed to captivate. The reviewers noted the film's apparently impeccable credentials, gave Hopkins a pat on the back, and then swiftly sent it packing.

The odds were always stacked against this being the film that would establish Hugh. *The Dawning* marked the farewell screen appearance of the widely loved and ad- mired Trevor Howard. The sight of Howard, fragile and faltering in a wheelchair – which had as much to do with his obviously waning health as with the plot – and barely capable of displaying even intermittent flashes of his talent was painful to behold. In his almost immediate previous film *White Mischief*, in which Hugh had a tiny part, Howard had managed to convey some spryness.

Yet Hugh had little tolerance for Trevor Howard's frailties, describing to interviewers – *after* Howard's death in 1988, of course – how the actor was still liberally knocking back the whisky, 'despite the fact he had vir- tually no internal organs because they'd all dissolved in alcohol', and was entirely reliant on 'idiot boards' for his lines and even then failing to get them right. Hugh also claimed, perversely, that he thought the sentimental indul- gence shown to the elderly, dying actor was 'patronizing', and mimicked the more purple pronouncements of other members of the cast about Howard: 'They kept saying, "Oh, the old bugger, he's still got it. He's mahvellous – so funny in the rushes!" ' Hugh's caustic wit is least attractive when it is aimed at a vulnerable target and targets seldom come more vulnerable than a one-time screen idol summoning his strength, rightly or wrongly, to give one final performance for the road.

Hugh, in a supporting role, was outclassed – and few young actors wouldn't be – by Anthony Hopkins in a starring one. Hopkins had already begun his own mid-career blossoming (with the hit stage play *Pravda* in 1985) and was starting to reach the exhilarating form that would carry him through to the 1992 Oscars. In *The Dawning* Hopkins 'subtly demolishes the rest of the cast', as one reviewer not so subtly points out. In any case, the movie was a discovery vehicle for Rebecca Pidgeon, not Hugh Grant, and Hugh's character was a distinctly unappetizing one in the first place.

As if all that wasn't enough, Robert Knights's panicky and lumbering direction had the effect of a runaway tank: everything got flattened in the way. Hugh has said, insightfully, of his performance in *The Dawning* as 'a sort of Anglo-Irish foolish young man', that it was one of the occasions 'where I thought I was being unnaturally good and turned out to be unnaturally bad . . . I don't know, I made too many faces . . .'

The experience, though, was not entirely without its compensations for Hugh – among them, the privilege of acting with the virtuoso Hopkins, if not the whisky-slugging Howard, and allowing him to alight briefly from the Euro co-production gravy train. And it did, at least, manage to sidle off with a half-claim on the jury prize at the twelfth Montreal World Film Festival in August 1988 – sharing it with the more watchable Indian offering *Salaam Bombay!*

SIXTEEN

*'I think we have another reptile loose on the
premises.'*

Hugh Grant in
The Lair of the White Worm

1988 was also the year of Hugh Grant in *The Lair of the
White Worm,* in which the worm received a longer credit
than Hugh Grant. It is a movie that does not (and critics
tend to be united on this) belong in the absolute first rank
of Ken Russell's many notable oeuvres. In fairness, the film
– a kind of Very Rocky Wriggly Horror Picture Show – in
which Hugh is beginning to show twinkles of promise, is
far from being among the worst few miles of celluloid that
Russell has produced to date either. It compares remarkably well with his 1977 *Valentino,* for example. (Though
most directors' films do, in fact, compare well with Russell's 1977 *Valentino.*)

There is reason to argue on Russell's behalf however
that *The Lair of the White Worm* proves the veteran
enfant terrible film maker to be, yet again, a little too
avant garde for his own good. The movie was an adaptation of the hitherto little-known last novel written by
Bram (author of *Dracula*) Stoker and anticipates, by a
good five years, the popular cinematic fangfest of the
nineties, which saw in toothy succession Gary Oldman as
Bram Stoker's Dracula, Jack Nicholson in *Wolf,* Tom
Cruise in *Interview with the Vampire,* and Mel Brooks's
Dracula: Dead and Loving It.

Yet fangs were not yet the fashion in 1988 and *The Lair
of the White Worm* did not inspire an immediate host of
imitators.

Russell adapted Stoker's 1911 novel himself and produced as well as directed the film (his sixteenth). It betrays, not surprisingly, Ken Russell's fingerprints on every frame. The phallic symbolism is laid on with a shovel and you are meant to notice, in spades, exactly who is wielding it. (Hugh would have to wait almost six years, until John Duigan's *Sirens*, to co-star with so many penis substitutes again.)

An aptly named Scottish archaeologist Angus Flint (Peter Capaldi), whose Scottishness is visually underlined by his habit of playing the bagpipes when he isn't visually underlining his profession by staring at the ground and saying, 'Aha! Very interesting!', unleashes the usual terrible chain of events after digging up a huge, worryingly worm-shaped, ancient reptile's skull somewhere in the Lake District. Ken Russell fell helplessly in love with the Lake District in 1967 when he was scouting for locations for his film *Rossetti*, and judged that Cumbria would pass very nicely for Iceland. He has since made his home there and frequently libels the place on film.

Mr Flint soon learns that the area is riddled with worm mythology and sets about discovering all he can about local lore with an uncomplicated country lass Mary Trent (Sammi Davis) and her rather more sophisticated sister Eve (the name is not accidental) played by the beautiful and genuinely blue-blooded actress Catherine Oxenberg.

Enter Hugh in a variety of super brocade waistcoats as Lord James D'Ampton, a lovely local toff with a family connection to a legend about a knight who slayed a local wicked giant serpent. Once a year there's a ye olde worme party at D'Ampton's place to commemorate the vampishly vermicular days of yore. Stratford Johns (once a British household name as the big copper with the beetling eyebrows in the *Z Cars* TV series) is reduced here to playing – wickedly well – Hugh's manservant, Peters.

There is also an actor called Paul Brooke who plays PC (as in Police Constable) Erny, and who one US critic very sweetly refers to as Mr P. C. Erny. Enter, too, Amanda Donohoe (in one of her last film roles before swapping

London for Los Angeles and signing up for the US TV series *LA Law*) as Lady Sylvia Marsh, the other local toff, a 'sort of worm-related priestess' according to one slightly uncertain review, with a kiss curl in the middle of her forehead and, occasionally, walrus-length plastic fangs. The normally uninhibited Donohoe has said of her role in *The Lair of the White Worm* that it caused her to seriously question her future as an actress. 'I was standing there in full blue body make-up and nothing else, and suddenly I thought, "Will I get away with this? Will I ever work again?" '

Of course she did – and Hugh now says this remains one of his favourite films, before *Four Weddings*, and insists it is also one most likely to be appreciated by those of his fans serving substantial prison sentences for serious crimes. As he told one US journalist: 'There are a few maniac kind of waiters or something who say "Hey, *The Lair of the White Worm*, great movie, man," and then you know that they're about to go off to McDonald's and machine-gun a hundred people.' Like a legion of actors and actresses before him, Hugh rapidly learnt that Russell's attitude to acting approximated less to the mysterious art described by the gentle Ms Pisk in *The Actor and his Body* than, arguably, any other director in the world. Hugh told interviewers: 'It would be impossible to say that he's every actor's dream. Instead of saying, as directors generally do, "Darling, it's fabulous. But – you might try this?", he'll say, "Well, fuck what it feels like to you, just do what I do. Here – watch me!" That tends to be how he directs. Especially in the afternoon, after lunch.'

Though it didn't mark a watershed for Hugh, *The Lair of the White Worm* saw the more perceptive critics beginning to acknowledge Hugh's forte. His slyly comic skills were noted. The *New York Times* especially enjoyed the way he said the line: 'I think we have another reptile loose on the premises.' The British reviewers admired the sangfroid he brought to the role. But Ken Russell was no more interested in creating a film as a showpiece for Hugh's comic talents than Polanski would be, with *Bitter Moon*, four years later. (In the British director's autobiography which covers this period, poor Hugh doesn't rate a single footnote mention, while Donohoe is lavishly praised – with Russell highly optimistic about her natural star qualities and his film as the appropriate vehicle for displaying them.) It is also probably closer to the truth to describe both Donohoe's and Hugh's performances as ironic, rather than comic. This is often what happens to actors who agree to be in a Russell film; it is a way of signalling to the audience, 'Of course I know this *looks* perfectly ridiculous, but it just might turn out to be a classic.' To his friends, Hugh declared he had low hopes that this latest work might be rated as high art. Considering that *The Lair of the White Worm*'s credited cast list included six maids/nuns, seven soldiers/witchdoctors, Jesus Christ and the worm itself – the audience was informed that it came in three different sizes – Hugh couldn't really say anything else.

SEVENTEEN

'It was the nadir of my career.'
Hugh Grant *on*
The Lady and the Highwayman

In the last of his 1988 movies, first broadcast on PBS television in the USA in January 1989, Hugh played a character whose identity had to remain a secret behind a mask for almost the entire length of the action. This requirement was not the setback it might seem for the young actor's emerging profile, however. The film was *The Lady and the Highwayman*. If Hugh mentions it at all in his interviews, it is with the comically defensive disclaimer that it represented 'the nadir' of his career, although he will simultaneously point out that the part made him bags of cash.

The explanation for all this mumbling about nadirs and cash is evident from the first frame of *The Lady and the Highwayman*. The film is exquisite rubbish. It was big-budget – by British film standards – costing four million pounds. That is £300,000 more than *Four Weddings* would cost over five years later. Though prettily filmed, expertly directed, well-produced and devouring the talents of a glamorous if not quite A-list cast, it was – fatally – erected upon the collapsing pink blancmange of a romance by the excessively prolific doyenne of the genre, Dame Barbara Cartland.

Yet it cannot be dismissed out of hand. *The Lady and the Highwayman* was one of four British-made Barbara Cartland adaptations that looked, briefly, to puff a life-saving breath into the UK film industry at a time when – overlooking Merchant–Ivory – an obituary was once again being prepared for the business. All four were produced by the flamboyant British entertainments mogul and unashamed Cartland fan, Lord Grade.

The film also united Hugh with another, rare, Oxford University-educated actor who had struck Hollywood gold himself also playing a repressed Englishman who collides with a feisty, outspoken American woman, two decades before Hugh did precisely the same in *Four Weddings*. He was Michael York, who co-starred in the 1972 cult and Oscar-winning classic *Cabaret* opposite Liza Minnelli who played unbuttoned Sally Bowles. Perhaps there *is* only one breakthrough Hollywood role for English actors. Here York, who, like Hugh, got a second-class Oxford degree in English, is reduced to playing one of Britain's best-known dirty-old-man kings, Charles II, in what publicists rather helplessly call a 'Restoration romp'.

Hugh is his right-hand swordsman, Lord Lucius Vyne, a.k.a. the Silver Blade. The original publicity notes for the film – which also starred Lysette Anthony (a goodie), Emma Samms (a baddie), Oliver Reed (a *bad* baddie), Gordon Jackson, John Mills and Christopher Casenove – trumpeted:

> Set in the turbulent 17th Century of Charles II. THE LADY AND THE HIGHWAYMAN features all the cut and thrust of Roundheads and Cavaliers. On the very day Lady Panthea is forced to marry the lecherous Christian Drysdale, she is dramatically freed forever from his brutal clutches by a mysterious masked rider – the Silver Blade.
>
> Introduced to the court ... her youthful good looks soon draw the attention of the King himself. The King's mistress Lady Barbara Castlemaine flies into a jealous rage and with the aid of the devious and sinister Sir Philip Cage succeeds in implicating her in the death of her own husband [the one Hugh's character had kebabed]. Innocent of the charge, Panthea is arrested and put on trial. Conducting her own defence she refuses to save herself by revealing

the identity of the Silver Blade and is wrongfully sentenced to death . . .

Thanks to a plot twist and the terrific timing of the Silver You-Know-Who, there is a happy ending.

Each of the Cartland films (Hugh was only in this one) was speedily put together, with six weeks of location shooting and wrapping in ten weeks. Each was directed by the highly experienced and personable John Hough, a director who cut his teeth on the original TV *Avengers* series, which may explain why Hugh, as the horribly bewigged Silver Blade, so strongly resembles Diana Rigg. Hugh was, according to Hough, a very handy rider and was cast 'because everyone was starting to say that he was the next big British star. It made perfect sense. We'd all seen him in *Maurice* and he was starting to do more television.' Perhaps.

The most irksome aspect to the Cartland films is that viewers are being asked to watch a cast of fairly well-known thespians either not bothering to hide the fact they don't regard these roles as the make or break of their careers – or possibly simply fighting a losing battle against terrible dialogue. For example: 'Then die! You and your little puling greenstick maid!' And – as Hugh loved to crow – all were getting paid handsomely for the privilege.

One can only believe Hugh implicitly when he insists this really was a film he did purely out of naked greed. The good news is that, after the four Cartland novels were filmed in the 1980s, there were no plans to make any more. The worrying news is that there are another 600 Dame Barbara Cartland romances awaiting option.

As the late eighties folded into the nineties, Hugh was no nearer achieving the Holy Grail of movie stardom but he was working steadily and, unlike the pickier Elizabeth in her flat above Sunset Strip across the Atlantic, accepting more roles than he turned down. He loved returning from filming, flush with cash, to cut a dash taxi-riding between London nightclubs – one of his close mates was later the flamboyant Piers Adam, the owner of the SW1 London Club – dancing, flirting, and picking up the tab for girls' drinks.

Hugh had been banned from driving in 1986 after being convicted on a second offence of drink driving, the first having been only the previous year. For actors, though, a driving ban is actually far less onerous than it can be for other folk, since chauffeured transport is routinely laid on by film and television companies. Living in one of London's most taxi-dominated areas, Hugh was hardly inconvenienced at all. His main complaint to old friends – which he made with a regularity that slightly belied the archly comic spin he put on his words – was that he didn't get recognized *nearly* enough.

'I was,' said one old Oxford friend, 'forever running into Hugh in clubs. He'd be fussing over his hair in the loos and moaning that nobody had asked him whether he was Hugh Grant! He said it was extraordinary how much film and television work you could do and still not be recognized.'

Another film industry colleague of Hugh's says, 'Of course I knew who Hugh was around this time but I'd never really chatted to him much until we met at some flash London party. I was just trying to be nice and said, 'Are you resting between films at the moment?' He blew up – though in a typically over-the-top comic way, shouting, 'That's a *dreadful* thing to say to an actor; what an *appalling* question to ask an actor! How could you!' I spent the rest of the party trailing after him apologizing profusely. It turned out he'd already done five films that year, but no one knew a thing about them.'

At another memorable London party – held in a converted church with freely flowing Absolut Vodka slammers in place of communion wine – Hugh turned up, again fresh from shooting, in the almost ludicrously baggy shorts that were becoming his sartorial trademark. Hugh had been all charm – and sly boasts about the money he was earning – when an impromptu and somewhat tipsy game of football-cum-indoor tag began among a number of male guests, including some old Latymer and Oxford mates.

The simple aim of the game was to tackle whoever had possession of the ball. Watching the game from the safety of a balcony above the dance area, observers noticed a fascinating and far-from-innocent pattern emerging. Hugh was being passed the ball ten times more frequently than anyone else, which meant he was tackled ten times as often. For all his friends' phlegmatic boasts that Hugh was just another Latymerian who happened to be in films, here was suddenly a rare opportunity to rough up the best-looking actor in London in the name of fun. Hugh was repeatedly slammed into from all sides and the game stopped barely short of all-out assault, leaving him red-faced, winded and bruised. His behaviour, guests noted, was considerably lower-key after the rough-housing and there was less talk about his income.

Meanwhile Hugh continued to rack up the parts, with *Impromptu* in 1989, which he has described as the worst wig film of his career. He told the UK's film magazine *Premiere*, 'I never came to terms with my wig. Something had gone horribly wrong in the fitting in Paris and they'd made it big enough for two Hugh Grants to wear at the same time. It was all right from the front but from the side it was like wearing Dougal on your head.'

Impromptu is a biography-with-liberties-taken about nineteenth-century composers and artists, done in an over-blown, feverishly bosomy, sub-Ken Russell style, with scenes of horses ridden by drunken poets defecating on literary manuscripts in ladies' boudoirs. *Impromptu* was almost strangled at birth with a highly limited general release in both the UK and the USA, before meekly accepting premature video retirement. Yet the film does represent a crucial shift of key in Hugh's career.

Hugh had indicated to friends that he'd become suffi-ciently unsure about his film work at this point that he was even toying with the idea of trying for a London stage play. *Impromptu*, however, looked more promising. This movie at least gave him second billing to the brilliant Australian actress Judy Davis, and the chance to flex his comedy skills under the eye of an award-winning Broadway director, the long-time Stephen Sondheim collaborator, James Lapine.

By no means a masterpiece, *Impromptu* was certainly not an entirely bad film either. It is a movie that Hugh has officially declared himself being 'fond of', which translates more specifically as 'I'm really quite proud of this one in a funny sort of way.' In other words, should Hugh ever happen to solicit an interviewer's personal opinion of *Impromptu*, it would be most unwise to slap him on the back, roar with laughter, and say, 'Never mind, perhaps the money made it all worthwhile.'

Impromptu is a 'period romp', a kind of *Carry On Up the Keyboard*, about the weedy Frederic Chopin (Hugh, hampered by a *mittel*-European accent) being hotly pursued by the cross-dressing, female French novelist George Sand (Judy Davis) in 1836.

Not all the dialogue is dreadful. At one point the lovesick George Sand hurls herself before Hugh's Chopin, begging the composer to permit her to pour out her feelings for him. 'I only need a minute of your time, then I'll go,' she promises. 'Very well, I'll give you exactly one minute,' he replies crisply, and promptly launches into his 'Minute Waltz'.

But some dialogue *is* dreadful, as when Sand, bursting into a room, says to Chopin, 'I am your slave and you have summoned me with your music.'

Chopin to Sand: 'Madame Sand, I must ask you to leave my private quarters.' One can very nearly hear Barbara Windsor and the late Sid James making the same exchange, only making it a lot funnier.

The part required Hugh to learn to mimic competent piano skills. Julian Sands, the missing actor from *Maurice*, who turns up here as a well-built Liszt, explains that they were taught to play their pieces just as if they were learning dance steps: 'One finger here, then move it here, and here, now faster', and so forth. While Emma

Thompson, as a rich and silly patroness of the arts, proves – as ever – that her talents will melt even the most curmudgeonly reviewers' hearts. Her small role won plaudits everywhere.

Nevertheless, the reviews were very mixed. One, in the usually even-handed American journal, *The National Review*, was entirely withering, referring not only to Hugh's Chopin as 'wimpy and twitty', 'babyish' and 'nerdy' and Sands's Liszt as 'listless', but beginning, '*Impromptu* must be the most pretentious, silliest, and inadvertently funniest film in years.'

Hugh's role in *Impromptu* also reveals how he is beginning a definite, if subtle, shift into the territory that would eventually make him a star: his Chopin is at first dismayed and repelled by George Sand's forthright sexuality. The woman is a foreigner after all (French to Chopin's Polishness). He is the passive male, the object of ardour, the pursued not the active partner. Then he figures she may not be such a bad thing after all. Cue fireworks. This is very much the stuff of which a *Four Weddings* heart-throb would be made.

Hugh was also proud enough of *Impromptu* to spend one London party, shortly after the film was released, posing almost permanently beside a piano – being played by another Oxford graduate, a composer – and requesting Chopin, 'because, you see, I've just played him in a film'. It made a delightful scene – until the irate people living next door to the party stormed round to demand that the 'horrible racket' be turned down because they couldn't sleep!

In the spring of 1989, American television viewers were offered three hours and 20 minutes of almost undiluted Hugh Grant in what one reviewer described as not so much a biographical mini-series as an extraordinarily lengthy 'champagne commercial'. This was the French-Canadian production of *Champagne Charlie*, with Hugh in the starring role as Charles Heidsieck, the founder of the Piper Heidsieck champagne label and the entrepreneur responsible for bringing the fizz to America under Abraham Lincoln. Why a highly romanticized account of a wine salesman's life should have been judged worthy of 200 minutes of prime-time television is never satisfactorily answered. Films with champagne in the title are notable, without exception, for failing to live up to their sparkle.

Some attempt to give the movie historical depth was attempted by shoehorning in the tensions of Civil War America, and Hugh's character was shown to be torn between his wife at home in France and whooping it up as the toast of Manhattan with a stereotypical southern belle mistress. Hugh also had star billing but, then again, there wasn't one other name that was instantly familiar – or even vaguely familiar after a great deal of thought – among the rest of the 37 credited cast members.

Professionally, this was not a part to highlight on his résumé. It simply didn't indicate anything about Hugh's ability or screen charisma that hadn't already been proven in other roles. It was another production that Hugh added to his 'I did it for the filthy lucre' list, later sending himself up as appearing in *Champagne Charlie* as a 'fat sweaty drunk' on account of the champagne freely available on set.

Privately, Hugh and Elizabeth, back from LA on one of her frequent visits, held a small party to show the *Champagne Charlie* video to friends in his Earls Court flat. Hugh provided liberal amounts of Piper Heidsieck – a gift from its grateful manufacturers – while keeping up an extravagantly ironic commentary about the awfulness of his acting.

To his credit, Hugh later promoted the product hailed in the mini-series, if not the mini-series itself, like an old pro. He agreed to be seen lunching alongside such assorted 'celebrities' as the showhost Nicholas Parsons and, rather more impressively, the character actor Herbert Lom for the official London launch of yet another vintage-year Heidsieck, even declaring loyally, and totally untruthfully, 'Delicious stuff – I never drink anything else!' for the benefit of the press.

The same year, 1989, saw Hugh making and appearing in his last purely financially motivated made-for-television movie, an adaptation of a Judith Krantz three-handker-chief period blockbusting novel, *Till We Meet Again*. This was filmed over the summer on a variety of hospitable, picture-perfect locations, including a vineyard near Santa Barbara, California, rural Sussex and the dales and moors of Yorkshire. Hugh had fifth billing in a credited cast of eight, which starred his old *Lady and the Highwayman* cohort, Michael York, and it was shown on British television shortly after Christmas that year, to no very startling effect on his career.

By October, Hugh was on set again, miscast perhaps, but in a film that was, at least, intended as serious art.

Though David Leland's 1990 film *The Big Man* (released as *Crossing the Line* in the USA in 1991) was not ideally poised to bring Hugh's talent for light comedy to the attention of Hollywood, it did aspire to a certain high-mindedness that had been lacking from previous Hugh Grant films.

First and foremost, however, the feature was intended as a star-making vehicle for the Irish actor Liam Neeson. At the end of the 1980s, with his Oscar-nominated best-actor performance in *Schindler's List* four years away, Neeson, then living in LA, was being touted as just a step away from the romantic lead roles dominated by the Hollywood 'fab five' of Tom Cruise, Mel Gibson, Harrison Ford, Dennis Quaid and Kevin Costner. *The Big Man* was supposed to fix this oversight for Neeson.

Based on a William McIlvanney novel, the movie was sold to America as a *Rocky*esque fable about a Scottish miner, Danny (Neeson), who is desperate to find a means to support his family after becoming a casualty of the British Coal Strike. Anxious to regain his status in the eyes of his middle-class wife Beth, played by Joanne Whalley-Kilmer, Danny is in a vulnerable state when approached by a mysterious Mr Fixit from Glasgow's dodgy under-ground circles called Matt Mason.

Hugh was not quite ready for such a stretch of character. The mysterious Mr Fixit was played by Ian Bannen, who persuades Danny to enter an illegal bare-knuckle fight. But Danny isn't too sure about this and agonizes with his cheerfully sleazy friend, Frankie. Cheerful sleaze wasn't yet Hugh's metier either.

America's favourite Scotsman, the comedian and actor Billy Connolly, played Frankie. And, when Danny does decide to fight, his wife ups and leaves him for her sexy Scottish lover Gordon, finally Hugh's part. Though he did manage a convincing Scottish burr, Hugh held little hope of being singled out as an actor to watch.

Fortunately, if only because it is often intensely irritating for actors to have small and easily overlooked parts in wildly successful movies, the film did not establish Neeson as the Ballymena Stallone. Commentators on both sides of the Atlantic described all the performances as solid and convincing but the film as 'less dramatic than anaesthetizing'. One reviewer, clearly torn between loathing the movie and appreciating that the actors did what they could, was even reduced to the old formula beloved by English masters reviewing disastrous school productions: 'Every member of the cast is as good as the circumstances allow.'

The movie, which is probably of interest only to those who fancy a nostalgic rant about the state of Britain and the coal industry under Prime Minister Thatcher, went to video and promptly dropped out of sight.

One credit that has quietly dropped off Hugh's standard post-*Four Weddings* and post-scandal film résumés is his role as the gay American son of a wealthy middle-class widow played by Julie Andrews in the made-for-television movie *Our Sons*. Broadcast in the USA May 1991, it was – incredibly – only the second major American network movie to deal with AIDS and gay men, rather than AIDS and haemophiliacs or AIDS and viewer-friendly children, in the six years since the benchmark drama made by the same director, *A Touch of Frost*.

From the perspective of 1995, with a comparatively healthy plethora of hugely popular and highly intelligent gay-themed plays on both sides of the Atlantic (*Love! Valour! Compassion!* in New York, *My Night with Reg* in London) and some fifteen lesbian and gay characters regularly appearing on primetime US TV shows, the media comment stirred up by *Our Sons* seems archaic. Repellent, even.

Yet the unusually frank tone of the drama – for its time – and its airing just two years after advertising worth a reported $1 million was, shamefully, yanked from a 1989 episode of *thirtysomething* that featured two male lovers merely *talking* in bed, won Hugh more than his usual share of attention for *Our Sons*. Though Hugh maintains that he loathes playing Americans because they seem to 'squash' his personality, he pulls off a credible performance as a young man revealing to his mother that his companion of three years is dying from AIDS complications.

James (Hugh) begs his mother Audrey (Andrews) to try to reconcile his lover with *his* estranged mother Luanne (played by the former sexpot actress Ann-Margaret in camply slumming form and in an even worse wig than Hugh has often worn). The trashy mobile-home-residing Luanne has rejected her son for eleven years because of his homosexuality – a 'perversion' she considers the devil's own gum-rottin' candy, while the sophisticated Audrey believes she has rather graciously come to terms with her own boy's sexual orientation.

The twist to the drama is that, provoked by Luanne's powerful, if bigoted, honesty, Audrey and James are forced to accept they are not nearly so beautifully adjusted as they believe. Mutual hostility has been quietly humming all along beneath the liberal façade of their relationship.

The unusual presence of the regal screen star Andrews, in her first made-for-TV movie, helped to whip up a flurry of articles about homosexuality and AIDS as suitable subjects for mainstream small-screen fare. (Coincidentally, 1991 also saw the USA's first lesbian primetime kiss, if one that pandered to male fantasy, courtesy of Amanda Donohoe, Hugh's old *The Lair of the White Worm* vamping partner, in *LA Law*.)

Suddenly, the mere fact that *Our Sons* had been made and screened at all became more important than the muttered objections from some critics about the gloss of the whole package – the Americanized British grande dame Julie Andrews, slick soap-style camera work and the subterfuge of dealing with AIDS primarily as it affects two mothers from different social classes rather than the men themselves. (One critic even complained, bizarrely, that Hugh and his co-star Zeljko Ivanek were *too* moving in their scenes together – though none were 'intimate' – and drew attention away from the female characters.)

For Hugh's irreverent schoolfriends, however, the main gossip point of his latest casting was not Hugh's sensitive acting. It was that he'd finally got to act with Walton-on-Thames's original singing-nun-on-the-run from *The Sound of Music*, Julie Andrews, some fifteen years after playing a von Trapp daughter in his own school's production.

But, back in Britain, it wasn't Hugh who was grabbing headlines at all. It was his girlfriend, the beautiful, willowy, five-foot-eight Elizabeth Hurley. In contrast to Hugh's hardly pragmatic approach to his craft – if the money's decent, take the cheque and trash the role in interviews if it doesn't work out later – Elizabeth had been more circumspect. Surfacing briefly in series like *The Chronicles of the Young Indiana Jones* and other decorative but relatively low-key parts, Elizabeth had become better known for complaining, in captions for luscious British magazine fashion layouts, about the humiliations of auditioning for roles that weren't *terribly* good in Los Angeles, being rejected by the ageing Warren Beatty for 'looking too young' for another part and for personally rejecting 'quite offensive roles' by the score.

Suddenly, in 1991, Elizabeth seemed to have landed her second breakthrough role, after Christabel, as Ken Russell's hand-picked Lady Chatterley in the much-hyped forthcoming BBC adaptation of *Lady Chatterley's Lover*.

Though the soft porn actress Sylvia Kristel had starred in an X-rated film version of the novel in 1981 (opposite Nicholas Clay as the gamekeeper Mellors), and there had even been a not-so-sleep-inducing Radio Four *Book at Bedtime* adaptation in 1987, which prompted a noisy campaign of complaint spearheaded by Mary Whitehouse, no explicit television version had ever been contemplated.

It was to be a world first. And Elizabeth, after a promising response to her audition, was understandably ecstatic. It was a sexy, classy, reputation-making role. She'd loved the book at school. As, of course, had Hugh.

Lady Chatterley's Lover was to be for Elizabeth what *Greystoke, Lord of the Apes*, had been for her boyfriend nine years earlier. A mere chimera. And a bitter professional disappointment. Though the actress was given to understand the part was all but hers, casting had not been contractually confirmed, nor was the four-million-pound funding for the production secure.

Unlike Hugh, who had at least been able to keep the Tarzan misunderstanding a secret among friends – until he was ready to turn it into a polished anecdote after he shot to fame – Elizabeth went public with her *Lady Chatterley* news. Posing for newspaper fashion layouts and confiding that Hugh liked nothing better than for her to dress up in tiny, tight hotpants and knee-length white boots – which would be mistaken for a hooker outfit in Los Angeles, she quipped suggestively – Elizabeth played up her coquettish side for all she was worth.

She would be embarking on this sensationally steamy role with her eyes 'well and truly open', she teased. She confessed to ripping up pages of her teenage diaries because of their 'embarrassing' contents and 'breaking my arm' falling off a table dancing at the Wag Club in London. She and Hugh had once been threatened at gunpoint while on holiday on the Caribbean island of St Lucia by an irate local who refused to take no for an answer when he offered to be their guide. Hugh had once lost a one-thousand-pound Cartier watch she had given him as a gift. Her idols, she claimed, included Rupert

Campbell-Black, the dashing upper-class rotter hero of Jilly Cooper's novel *Riders* – 'I fancy him like mad!' – and the books by her bedside included Dostoevsky's *The Brothers Karamazov*, Nancy Mitford's biography of Louis XIV, *Le Roi Soleil*, and, in apparently delightful eclectic contrast, *Rosettes for Jill*, 'an old pony book I used to read when I was fourteen'.

Like Hugh, Elizabeth loved to give the impression that her life was every bit as frolicsome as the books she adored. 'I'm always in the middle of some drama or other,' she told one interviewer lightly.

Her passion for Nancy Mitford is especially revealing. Mitford's genius was, of course, for simultaneously satirizing and glamorizing the antics of upper-class hedonists intent on 'amusing' themselves at any price. Elizabeth assured one interviewer that she was sure Nancy Mitford would have been 'just as entertaining [as her novels] in real life'. Elizabeth seemed determined to believe that Mitford's writings – some of the finest satirical comedy of this century – were, in fact, news bulletins from a fabulous social Front.

Isolated in Los Angeles and surrounding herself with English friends like the journalist William Cash, an Evelyn Waugh acolyte himself who also struck a pose of languid amusement and patrician disgust at the vulgarity of Hollywood, Elizabeth badly needed the *Chatterley* job back in England. It was not to be. The whole production was put on ice for a year, mainly because of funding problems, according to BBC sources. Ken Russell's television version, aired in the summer of 1993, had a more experienced actress, Joely Richardson, as Lady C, Sean Bean as Mellors and Hugh's old *Privileged* and *Maurice* rival James Wilby in brilliant form as the cuckolded cripple, Clifford Chatterley.

It was a wrenching time for the young actress, though Hugh, say friends, was a model of support and genuine kindness. He had been through exactly similar cycles of wild hope and crushing despair himself and he knew it was every actor's nightmare to declare publicly that a sought-after role had been landed, only to see it all turn to ashes.

Hugh's career, in contrast to Elizabeth's, was gradually turning itself around. And, unlike the Los Angeles-based Elizabeth, Hugh did not endure the same isolated lifestyle. Though filming kept him away from England for long weeks at a time, he could slot right back into his London peer group through his beloved football.

CHAPTER

EIGHTEEN

'For when the One Great Scorer comes
To write against your name,
He marks – not that you won or lost –
But how you played the game.'
                    Grantland Rice (1880–1954)

All Hollywood movie stars, especially when they are
brand-new movie stars, talk very animatedly about the
subject of 'keeping my feet on the ground'. Sometimes
stars cite one parent in particular who assists in this
peculiar rite, as in 'my mum makes certain I keep my feet
on the ground, bless her', rather as if the woman were
employed to crawl around on her knees ready to pounce
if daylight should suddenly pour beneath the soles of both
the movie star's boots simultaneously. It was football,
ironically, that used to keep Hugh Grant's feet on the
ground.

Hugh's beloved football has been a constant in his life
from childhood. In his senior Latymer days he'd listened
raptly to the former soccer star Stan Bowles, a regular at
the bar of a pub near the school, the Ravenscourt Arms,
as the ex-international held court with his opinions on the
latest transfers and results. During and after Oxford,
Hugh vociferously supported the bottom-of-the-third-divi-
sion-bumping Fulham (and claimed to enjoy roaring, on
the terraces, 'We are Fulham, we are *Fulham*' to the
strains of Rod Stewart's 'We are Sailing'). He was, friends
recall, as tediously intimate with the minutiae of football
statistics as he was, far less tediously, with the ruder parts
of D.H. Lawrence.

Throughout the late 1980s Hugh played energetically
for a number of Sunday-league London teams, including
the acting and media-dominated Marney Team (named for

the road lived in by the team's founding member Tim Whitby, Hugh's old steadfast New College pal). He also played for the grandiloquently titled Victoria and Albert Museum team, whose members included staff from the London Museum. During this time he played against teams from the VAT offices, the Natural History Museum and the Notting Hill All Saints' Restaurant side, run by the restaurant's owner, a loyal and close mate of Hugh's, Rupert Smith.

Hugh even managed to be the centre of attention in football. Many players remember one game between the excellent side Hugh played for when he had time between acting jobs, the Clapham Rovers, and a noticeably more streetwise and nakedly aggressive team from south of the river. The two met for the usual South London Sunday League weekend fixture.

The ball bounced off-side at one point and Hugh, suddenly, grabbed it and stood defiantly clutching it even though the referee hadn't made a decision on who had touched the ball last. It was Hugh's air of premature ownership that inspired a rival player with the brilliant idea of trying to grab it back.

'Hugh absolutely refused to give up the ball, no matter how hard the other guy tried to get it away from him. It was very funny to watch,' says one player. 'At this stage he should have just handed it over – otherwise, frankly, you're going to get into a fight. But Hugh wouldn't give in; he just stood there holding on for grim life but refusing to get belligerent about it.'

When the referee ruled in favour of the other team, Hugh slowly jogged on to the pitch, threw down the ball, turned to the mountainous rival who'd been trying to get it from him, puckered up, and said, loudly, 'Oh, go on then, big bottom!'

His rival, say team-mates, was dumbfounded.

'He was speechless. He hadn't the slightest idea how to react, and Hugh knew it,' says another friend. 'That's Hugh's idea of fun. You've basically got these fairly macho guys who get seriously freaked out by this strange, camp personality that Hugh puts on. I mean the language is all pretty ripe – you fucking cunt, you wanker. But Hugh always played it his own way.'

Says another old university friend, 'The guys we play against aren't thugs. Of course not. Let's just say referees got occasionally beaten up in the car park. Yet after the game, Hughie would be the total lovey in the changing-rooms. It would be 'lend us your shampoo, darling', 'mind the soap, now'. None of the other sides would go *near* him in the showers. To be honest, you have to be very, very sure of yourself to get away with that sort of kidding. No one else dared to go anything like as far.'

Hugh's decency as a player – on and off the field – is also well known. 'He is a useful, good-hearted player and that is saying a lot when you see what happens to some middle-class types on the football field. You see some unbelievable egos coming out,' says an old friend.

Another remembers how, when he broke his ankle during a game, Hugh was the only team member to ring him up afterwards to ask, genuinely concerned, how he was. 'He's brave too. I've seen him elbowed in the face when it was bloody hard to say if it was accidental and keep going. He doesn't even try to keep away from the rough stuff. We've all seen him with blood pouring down the side of his face.'

Though Hugh's later notoriety would curtail returning to these friendly London matches, he also kept himself fit playing tennis – returning often to the old courts of his youth at Ravenscourt Park, 'very competitive with a great serve', according to a film-business friend, Paul Raphael.

The year 1991 was also when Hugh met the director Mike Newell for the first time. Hugh loved the leisure time that highly-paid film and television work brought him while he was 'resting' between jobs, and teased friends mercilessly about envying him for being free of responsibilities while they were burdened with 'squalling brats'. Nevertheless, he kept a very beady eye on his own bank account.

Hugh later mocked other actors for hiring themselves

out at an hourly rate for voiceovers, but he did exactly the same. Newell met Hugh while taking the French actress Juliette Binoche through a camera test. The director needed an actor to read Binoche's cues to her – and Hugh was available for the job, as Newell later explained:

'Every actor has ups and downs in his life and I think that was probably one of Hugh's downs.'

However Hugh was also starting to complete better-quality work. In the BBC's drama *The Trials of Oz*, he played the hippy magazine editor Richard Neville. Neville was, famously, the real-life Australian editor of the psychedelic anti-establishment magazine, *Oz*, published from 1967 to 1971 in London – before it was extinguished in a blaze of publicity with the successful prosecution of its 'Schoolkids' issue for obscenity. Neville got a fifteen-month sentence, though it was reduced on appeal to four months, in Wormwood Scrubs after one of the most entertaining trials since that concerning *Lady Chatterley's Lover*.

One of the arguments during the trial was over the magazine's graphic illustrations of Rupert Bear's penis. Hugh turned in a good performance – in a shoulder-length hippy wig – as the childishly sex-infatuated and self-obsessed Neville. And the film that would change his life was just around the corner. Not *Four Weddings*. But Roman Polanski's *Bitter Moon*.

NINETEEN

Number of times Roman Polanski mentions Hugh Grant when promoting his film, Bitter Moon, *in interviews in 1992: zero*

Although neither director nor co-star could have possibly predicted it, Roman Polanski's mordantly witty slice of erotica, *Bitter Moon*, was the movie that would, at long last, ignite Hugh Grant's career.

Not that it would happen overnight. The fuse the film lit was a lengthy one. *Bitter Moon* was released in the UK and Europe in the early autumn of 1992, after a cool rather than frenzied reception at its Edinburgh Film Festival première that year. But the American public had to wait another eighteen months, until March 1994, before they were permitted to see it.

Nor was it because Polanski appeared to have any special intuition about Hugh's potential as a world-class heart-throb. The catchline on the original advertising posters for the film was the rather limp 'some lovers never know when to stop', instead of 'Hugh Grant – the untold S & M story!'

It is significant that, when interviewed at great length in Paris in September 1992 by the British feature-writer Zoë Heller for the *Independent* newspaper, Polanski had plenty to say about his latest movie, about its themes concerning the fleeting nature of sexual passion and its uneasy relationship with love. He even had a fair amount to say about Zoë Heller's attitudes towards sexual passion. But, Heller now recalls, she didn't once mention Hugh Grant in her interview because Polanski didn't once mention Hugh Grant either.

The movie was, in fact, nakedly intended as a star vehicle for Polanski's beautiful and intentionally nakedly displayed wife, Emmanuelle Seigner, whom Hugh's character – a stuffy Eurobond trader on a cruise ship – madly fancies.

The hauntingly beautiful and graceful Emmanuelle is 33 years the film-maker's junior; a fact that, if mentioned, usually prompts from Polanski a very robust 'so fucking vot?' But *Bitter Moon*'s unique value to Hugh lay in giving him the chance to show off, once again, his maturing gift for comedy – just at a time when a quietly fashionable British director called Mike Newell happened to be beginning *his* search for a star to carry off a low-budget project, a little thing provisionally called *Four Weddings and a Funeral* . . .

Working with Roman Polanski is seldom dull. Exasperating, exhilarating, alarming and exhausting, perhaps, but rarely a bore. *Bitter Moon*, shot in and around Polanski's home-in-exile, Paris, was no exception to the general rule. Hugh soon learnt that the locker-room legends about Roman Polanski were, in the main, absolutely accurate. The ever bookish Hugh had even taken the trouble, typically, to read Polanski's autobiography – which goes into detail about his training at the Lodz film school, as well as the hideous murder of his wife Sharon Tate by the Charles Manson gang in 1969 and his theories on film – to prepare for working with him.

Hugh was especially entranced by the way the tiny (five-foot-five) Polish-born, French-naturalized Polanski took control of everything on the set – even down to the humble task of rigging microphones. He had, said Hugh, no compunction at all about elbowing electricians out of the way to fix a wire, or showing the camera crews their job, with a cry of 'No, fuck off, guys, I'll do it, gimme the stuff!'

Bitter Moon, which explores Polanski's pet preoccupation with the eroticism of erotica observed, was also a noticeably Gallic-flavoured production. There was wine with meals on set, something totally unthinkable in Hollywood, and totally unaffordable in Britain.

And no one in the cast or crew could ignore the

spontaneous shouting matches between Polanski and the effervescently Parisian Seigner, nor the frequent protestations from her that she was fed up with film acting anyway. A former model and now the mother of Polanski's child, Seigner has since rather disarmingly explained that she never harboured a truly passionate desire to be an actress anyway. That was Polanski's dream for her. Which is possibly why the earlier 'star vehicle' her besotted husband directed her in, *Frantic* – with Harrison Ford as co-star looking permanently on the verge of a genuine nervous breakdown – also failed to set the world on fire.

Nevertheless, Hugh, like many far more senior Hollywood actors before him, soon fell victim to the notorious Polanski habit of giving his actors line-readings. This is when the director will painstakingly act out a part himself, in front of the actor paid to do it. He will even demonstrate the intonation he wishes given to a line of dialogue, right down to the stress on a particular syllable.

Polanski will then expect the actor to parrot him flawlessly when the camera rolls. It is an approach that is not always soothing to an actor's ego. The latter may have flattered himself, not unreasonably, with the assumption that he was hired for the film because he had the necessary instincts and skills to breathe life into a certain character, not because he had an uncanny ability for mimicking Roman Polanski, minus the heavy Polish accent.

(When *Chinatown* was filmed, the crew was secretly terrified that its star Jack Nicholson was one day going to revolt against this highly controlled approach to directing – and actually repeat on camera a line precisely as Polanski had uttered it, Eastern European inflexions and all. That day never quite came.)

Though Hugh did not particularly care for being given syllable-by-syllable line-coaching – 'not the ideal way to direct' – he has said very firmly that he genuinely relished the experience of being guided by a copper-bottomed, old-fashioned, foot-stomping artistic European director. Hugh also claims he was too terrified to ask Polanski just how funny *Bitter Moon* was meant to be, in case he discovered it wasn't intended to be funny at all.

Once a school mimic, always a school mimic, Hugh made 'doing Polanski' one of his best comic turns at film festivals. To the delight of journalists, he would snap into a superb, rapid-fire impression of the director in maestro mode, liberating a temperamental torrent of f-words, concluding – back in character as Hugh Grant – with the observation, uttered in a puzzled British tone, that, 'It wasn't like working on a Merchant–Ivory film, y'know.'

Hugh has joked, too, that when he once asked the director, very timidly, for a clue to his character's motivation during a key scene, Roman threw up his hands in exasperation shouting, 'Oh God, I don't know! I have no idea! You sort out the motivation and show it to me!' This sounds much too good to be untrue. It is part of the Polanski lore that he has a film fixed in its entirety in his imagination before he shoots a single frame, and that he is concerned only with getting that version translated as accurately as possible into film, and not with a character's interior motivation. Hugh also says that if a drunk scene was required, Polanski would simply bark 'for fuck's sake, have a drink!'

On set Hugh established an enduring, platonic friendship with the exquisite English actress, who plays his wife, Kristin Scott Thomas. They would, of course, act together again in *Four Weddings and a Funeral*, when her off-set remark, 'Oh [the part of Charles] it's just like him. *That's* Hugh!', would be widely quoted as an endorsement that the film's Hugh and the screen Hugh were one and the same, despite the actor's denials.

Shortly after completing *Bitter Moon* the actress told me, during an interview in London, that she found Hugh Grant entirely captivating in his ultra-Englishness – adding perceptively that he was brilliantly funny in the role. Scott Thomas, who is married with children, also said, equally perceptively, and with more than a hint of unease, that she wasn't entirely sure how the film would be received by the critics. Indeed, like Hugh too, Scott Thomas implied that

Polanski had been less than forthcoming about exactly how *he* saw the film.

When it came to publicizing the film, Hugh delighted in telling journalists slightly improper tales-out-of-school about Seigner. 'She's one of my favourite people – but she's wicked. There's a scene where I had to kiss her in front of Roman, and as soon as we broke away, she'd say, "Oh, Oog, how could you do zat! You put your tongue in my mouth. Zat's dis*gust*ing!" And I hadn't. I mean, I just hadn't! Not with Roman standing behind me. So it was tough.'

To journalists, Hugh also playfully twitted Seigner for her lack of inhibition, claiming that her bare breasts became an over-familiar sight – hardly surprising in view of the sexually explicit part she was playing, but a great line for reminding fans how very daring Hugh Grant's career had become.

In *Bitter Moon* Hugh and Kristin play a strait-laced English couple, Nigel and Fiona, who are trying to fan the embers of their rapidly cooling marriage with a luxury cruise. On board they meet a creepily disgusting American failed writer, the wheelchair-bound Oscar (played by the 52-year-old American actor Peter Coyote, who seems to have made a career of these unattractive types), and his sex-bomb wife Mimi (Emmanuelle Seigner).

Oscar tells the story of his and Mimi's relationship to Nigel, via a series of sexy flashbacks, whose response indicates that inside every buttoned-up Englishman is a goggling voyeur panting to be unleashed or, possibly, tied up.

Critical reactions to the film were most peculiar. In Britain, it provoked the usual slew of sniffy articles along the lines of 'dirty old Roman does it again' – as if Hugh's character represented Polanski's outrageously condescending judgement of British sexuality, an unwanted sermon on the national mount as it were. The British, of course, loathe it when the French come over all superior about sex, as if they invented it. Bringing up Agincourt sometimes helps.

Yet some of the more serious English film critics pronounced *Bitter Moon* the best work of Polanski's career since *Knife in the Water*, the Oscar-nominated film that bounced him into the international arena over 30 years earlier. On the European mainland they didn't, on the whole, quite appear to get *Bitter Moon* either. The mainstream reviews were either hesitantly hostile or sycophantic.

Polanski later complained to the very worthy US cinema magazine, *Film Comment*, in 1994, when the film was released in America, 'You know, I already forgot about this movie. Now when you ask me about it, I realize it's really nasty and funny at the same time! That was always our intention. Unfortunately, some people, like the critics here in Europe, don't dare to laugh at a Polanski film. But the public does laugh. When I saw it in a cinema I was really thrilled, because every bit we intended to be funny came out the way we wanted. But it's a very nasty humour.'

One can't help noticing, however, that in the Zoë Heller feature interview the one word Polanski doesn't apply to the film is 'funny'. It appears to be a purely retrospective judgement.

Yet in America – where the film had gathered dust for over eighteen months because no one quite knew how to market it or how to explain its highly unusual satirical-cum-sexually-sensational 'tone' – the critics seemed to have no trouble at all understanding what Polanski said he was up to all along. The US film trade paper *Variety* was unusual in its scathing 'Polanski approaches rock bottom' opinion.

When it was finally released in March 1994, to coincide entirely opportunistically with *Four Weddings*, it was being described as the 'long-awaited' Polanski film as if it had been somehow lost in the post.

Review after review applauded Hugh's priceless comic skills. 'Polish that Best Supporting Actor Oscar,' one lengthy review cosily urged Hugh. '*Bitter Moon* is *Love Boat* meets *Last Tango in Paris*, a feverishly goofy psychodrama,' crowed New York's *Newsday*. Hugh had provided a 'faultless pastiche of an emotionally consti- pated Sloane'. He was, according to *Time* magazine, 'an archetypically repressed British husband', which doesn't say a lot for the international image of British husbands. The USA may have forced Polanski to jump bail and flee to Europe after he admitted sex with a thirteen-year-old girl in 1977, but it remained generously appreciative of his skills as a director.

Having made the film, however, and seen it released in Europe with no substantial impact on his career, Hugh simply had no inkling that it was about to turn round his life. He gamely got on with his next 'Europudding' movie, *Night Train to Venice*.

In 1993 Hugh popped up in two films playing a journalist. This was not the stretch it might initially appear. Neither of the roles required him to act remotely like a sleazy sex-scandal stringer for the Sunday tabloids. Both of his 1993 journalists talk in clipped, upper-class British man- ner and the second happened to be a newshound who was also the godson of an English lord.

The first film was *Night Train to Venice*, a Euro-muddle of a production that should never have left the platform.

Night Train to Venice is one of those thoroughly annoy- ing efforts that look as if they were passed by a committee clutching a checklist of crucial Euro considerations. Not so much *Jeux Sans Frontières* as *Cinéma Sans Frontières* at its worst. It is very nearly cinema *sans* any sort of point at all. It is remotely possible that Hugh thought this movie might one day gain cult status.

The most important consideration of a Euro-film is always, firstly, will it feature scenery from all over Europe, thus qualifying for pan-European investment? As the title suggests, the film ends in Venice but begins in England and travels – *all the way across Europe on the Orient Express!* (*Huit points.*)

Secondly, is there any chance of Eastern European involvement? Indeed there was. The movie's excitable score was recorded in Cracow – though this, according to the producer in one magazine article, involved the film-makers in a nasty brush with the Polish mafia. (*Neuf points*.)

Thirdly, does it feature actors with that elusive but all-important 'cross-frontier appeal'? Absolutely. Hugh Grant had already starred as a Pole (Chopin) opposite a Frenchwoman (George Sand) and a Hungarian (Franz Liszt) in the Anglo-American film *Impromptu*, as well as an Englishman (Lord Byron) on holiday in Switzerland and Italy in the Norwegian-Spanish film *Rowing with the Wind*.

In addition, the film had the fine character actor Malcolm McDowell, who some fans, quite mistakenly, assumed perished after making *A Clockwork Orange* – perhaps because of all the violence it featured. In fact McDowell has been very successfully Off-Off-Broadway-ing and Euro-filming ever since and, thanks to *A Clockwork Orange* playing constantly in one cinema in Paris, remains a major cult icon in Europe. This makes his casting in *Night Train to Venice* all the more Euro-appropriate since the part he plays is not a million miles removed from the nasty knife-wielding Alex of Kubrick's 1971 nastypiece. (*Dix points* on both counts.)

Film buffs will also remember that McDowell shot to fame in the hip 1969 anti-public school film *If . . .* – in the last scene of which our anti-hero was seen jubilantly machine-gunning down his public-school fellow pupils on Speech Day. It is quite appropriate that McDowell should turn up on *Night Train to Venice* as a character intent on torturing the star of 1982's homage to Oxford, *Privileged*.

The plot of the film, which was promoted as a 'new-age' thriller, is extremely thin. Hugh is an investigative journal-ist who has written a blockbusting exposé of the neo-Nazi movement in modern Europe. Entrusting the care of the manuscript to nobody but himself (not even to a fax machine, the fool!), he decides to escort the papers per-sonally from England by train to his anxious Venetian publishers.

The Orient Express being what it tends to be in the movies, the journey is not without incident. Passengers pivotal to the plot – including an actress (played by the actress Tahnee Welch, daughter of Raquel), an ageing ballerina and a camp entertainer – get on and off the train.

There is a mysterious stranger on board, known only as 'the Stranger' (McDowell). It is generally a pretentious sign when film characters are simply identified as 'the Stranger'. 'The Stranger' is in control of gangs of violent skinhead thugs stowed away on board. As if this wasn't well nigh intolerable, the story keeps flashing back to the angst-ridden memories of the main characters. Hugh later told *Vogue* magazine that the single most embarrassing memory of all his Euro-pudding movies was 'being chased down the Orient Express train by twelve Dobermann dogs, a transvestite and Raquel Welch's daughter without her clothes on, while I screamed. I was in my underpants as well, I recall.'

All in all, *Night Train to Venice* – which was premièred at the 46th Cannes Festival in May 1993 and which, budgeted at $5.8 million, cost almost $800,000 more to make than *Four Weddings* – appears to be something of a genre-bender, one part thriller to one part psycho-drama to one part political comment. (*Trois points.*)

The Remains of the Day did not have a spectacular effect on Hugh's career, but it helped to halt his tentatively crablike progress in the very early 1990s. This was also his first big-screen movie, after *Maurice*, about which Hugh didn't either need or want to be comically defensive. Hugh's friends were long inured to hearing the carefully polished put-downs that greeted any enquiry about his work – 'a *devil* of a load of nonsense in which I am *frighteningly* bad and for which I received the most *enormous* amount of money . . .'

For one thing, it wouldn't have worked on *The Remains of the Day*. ('Well it's an adaptation of an *appalling* Booker Prize-winning novel by Kazuo Ishiguro and nobody had the *foggiest* idea what they were supposed to be doing and I don't think the director, James Ivory or something, had even *read* the book, and I'm in this *awful* bit opposite some strange Welsh person called Anthony Hopkins – he's just been made a knight, could that be right? – and the whole thing was simply too *gruesome* for words . . .'). For another thing, it simply wasn't necessary.

With two Oscar-winning stars, Hopkins and Emma Thompson (for her 1992 role in *Howards End*), and helmed by the same *Howards End* Merchant–Ivory team back to full strength with the brilliant Ruth Prawer Jhabvala adapting the novel for the screen, *The Remains of the Day* was gold-plated. To his great credit, Hugh – in a small supporting role – shimmered with charm and talent as the journalist godson of James Fox's morally misguided Lord Darlington. The movie of Ishiguro's superb novel, about the behind-the-scenes appeasement of closet Hitlerites in 1930s upper-class Britain, was unerringly faithful to the text.

Hugh's best scene comes when Darlington has inexcusably instructed his butler Stevens (Hopkins) to furnish his godson with a rough idea of the facts of life on the eve of the boy's marriage.

'There's no need to make a song and dance of it. Just convey the basic facts and be done with it,' barks Darlington to Stevens. Stevens approaches his master's godson in the gardens and attempts a little speech about the 'birds and the fishes'. With a gleaming side-parting and expression of indulgent mischief and affectionate exasperation chasing across his features like sunlight glancing through a rainstorm, the on-screen Hugh responds to the butler's dignified stumblings: 'I am more of a fish man myself. I know more about fish. Freshwater and salt.' Later, though, Hugh would gently twit Anthony Hopkins by insisting, disingenuously, that the senior actor displayed 'such a lot of *technique*' in their scenes together.

By the time he'd finished shooting *The Remains of the Day*, Hugh had already signed up for John Duigan's *Sirens*, to be shot in Australia, the film for which the production of *Four Weddings* was slightly delayed. Mike

Newell had caught Hugh in *Bitter Moon* and was prepared to consider him for *Four Weddings*. After auditioning him, Mike Newell was ready to wait for him to return from Australia. This was his man.

TWENTY

*'Whatever people's aspirations to higher feelings, it
still comes down to pure lust.'*

Hugh Grant, 1993

Hugh's long, hard apprenticeship in films and television
paid off spectacularly in 1993. In many respects his career
more closely resembles those of the old Hollywood stars
under the long-disbanded studio system than a modern
actor. Both Cary Grant and David Niven – with whom
Hugh is most often compared – had spent years quietly
learning their craft, virtually unnoticed, in studio assembly-line movies before their star appeal was coaxed forth
in their early thirties.

Hugh's Euro films and art-house work, unseen by mainstream audiences, had also sheltered him behind a similar
shield of anonymity while he was developing his skills.
Initially Cary Grant was just another handsome English
actor whose sense of humour was too subtle to be picked
up by the camera – until he was cast as a ghostly prankster
in *Topper* (1937) and landed his breakthrough role in *The
Awful Truth* the same year. This was the benchmark
Depression romantic comedy that presented the world
with the bemused, richly comic Cary Grant persona that
made him an idol.

The conservative – and uncertain – Cary Grant had even
attempted to buy himself out of his role in *The Awful
Truth* – for $5,000 – in a fit of sheer panic over the
brilliant Leo McCarey's deliberately offhanded approach
to directing. Though Hugh didn't try to buy his way out
of *Four Weddings*, he, too, had a movie like *Topper* that
hinted strongly at his true potential, *Bitter Moon*, and
found himself, as a result, in the hands of a director he

found every bit as unnerving as Cary Grant's Leo McCarey – Mike Newell. Yet before the two could team up in the late summer of 1993, Hugh had two other projects to complete. *The Changeling* for the BBC and John Duigan's fantastical *Sirens*.

In *The Changeling*, a bloodsoaked Jacobean melodrama which Hugh filmed at the BBC's Wood Lane Television Centre – just down the road from Latymer's playing-fields – he was cast as the infatuated yet highly principled Alsemero, with Bob Hoskins and Elizabeth McGovern co-starring. When Hugh came to publicize the drama, shown in the UK in December 1993 and the USA in April 1994, he was his characteristic larky self, telling interviewers, 'I do a lot of shouting, which is very unlike me. I even manage to squeeze out a tear. I was so proud of it that I wanted to keep it in a glass.'

However, in an internal interview he gave to the BBC's in-house drama publicity department, Hugh reveals himself rather differently, admitting that he not merely reread the original play by Middleton and Rowley, first acted in 1622, but had fastidiously studied the obscure penny-dreadful hack-work upon which the play was based: John Reynold's 1621 publication *God's Revenge Against Murther*. Hugh had swotted up the role with his usual attentive diligence.

He also throws some revealing light on his interpretation of his character, who falls in love with a woman caught up in a murderous love triangle. Alsemero has devoted himself to chastity and to the revenge of his father's death:

'In the late twentieth century, it is very difficult for people to get hold of the idea of somebody dedicating himself to vengeance and to good works. But when [my character] sees Beatrice-Joanna he falls head over heels in love – that is why it hits him so hard when he discovers her infidelity. He has allowed himself and his beliefs to be betrayed and all his pent-up neuroses about women suddenly erupt. The play is very much a bitterly cynical portrayal of love. Whatever people's aspirations to higher feelings, it still comes down to pure lust.' For Hugh, the play was not so much a tragedy as 'a very, very black comedy'.

If the 90-minute Jacobean drama, shown on BBC2, could hardly compete with Elizabeth's 1993 Hollywood success as a kick-boxing air stewardess in Wesley Snipes's action adventure *Passenger 57*, Hugh wasn't too worried. Even as he flew to New South Wales, Australia, to film *Sirens* in the late spring, Hugh heard he'd got the lead role in the Mike Newell film that almost every young actor in England was chasing, *Four Weddings and a Funeral*. It was a perilously close call. Newell was very seriously considering other actors. But a delay in getting the finance together for the film worked in Hugh's favour. There would just be time – with a little extra delay for Hugh to honour his commitment to *Sirens* and get back to England for filming. It had been Hugh's *Bitter Moon* performance on top of a scintillating audition that had finally made up Newell's mind.

TWENTY-ONE

*'If every relationship was utterly open and people
felt under an obligation to reveal every aspect of
their mental life then no relationship could really
survive.'*

The director John Duigan on
Hugh Grant's empathy with his
repressed character in Sirens, 1994

As usual, Hugh prepared meticulously for *Sirens*, which
was loosely based on the life of a notoriously Bohemian
Australian artist, Norman Lindsay, who died in 1969 at
the age of 90 and had been a lifelong obsession of the
Australian director, John Duigan. Hugh spent time observing Anglican ministers in Chichester to prepare for his part
as a buttoned-up Oxford-educated clergyman, Anthony
Campion, travelling to his new Australian parish in the
1930s, with his wife Estella (Tara Fitzgerald).

Before settling in, they pay a visit to the controversial
erotic artist Norman Lindsay (Sam Neill) at his lushly
Garden-of-Edenish estate in the aptly named Blue Moun-
tains, with the aim of persuading him to withdraw a painting
of a crucified Venus from a major art exhibition. The couple
become gently unhinged – at first outraged, then seduced – by
Lindsay's philosophies and his trio of naked live-in models,
including Sheela, played by the luscious Australian super-
model Elle 'The Body' Macpherson in her big-screen debut.

Filmed around the remote goldmining town of Sofala,
five hours west of Sydney, and also at the gorgeously
rambling house that had originally belonged to Lindsay
(now run by the Australian National Trust, where the
artist's statues, half man, half woman or beast, are still
studded around the grounds), *Sirens* was an ideal erotic
comedy vehicle for Hugh.

He was relaxed enough on set to improvise. For instance, one unscripted moment that remains in the film came when a fly landed on his toast at the end of a breakfast scene and Hugh launched into a little Winnie-the-Pooh-ish line, 'It came in on my honey, into my tummy, made me feel funny', which an enchanted Duigan thought so perfectly in character, he insisted it stay in.

Elle Macpherson also revealed that Hugh kept the cast and crew amused devising silly word-games on set. One was called 'Sheep, sheep, come home'. Hugh particularly relished, too, one of the film's in-jokes: Duigan had the hotel featured in the movie named the Sir Charles Dilke Hotel, after the famous Victorian English radical politician, who looked to be Gladstone's successor until a sex scandal, in which Dilke became involved with a married woman who was not his wife and was smeared in a subsequent divorce case, led to his defeat at election in 1886.

Already a firm admirer of Duigan before *Sirens*, Hugh – ever the cineaste – had been particularly struck by the director's coming-of-age films *Flirting* (1983) and *The Year My Voice Broke* (1987), describing the poster for *Flirting*, three girls doing up their suspenders, as 'unforgettable'. Hugh also claims that his own Oxford background gave him a vital key to playing the role of a vicar who 'discovers he's not as groovy as he thinks he is', because of memories of dons who were 'quite ready to quote the more steamy passages from Joyce, and indeed of Lawrence, and they could talk about orgasms and penises but you couldn't imagine them actually having sex at all', as he told one magazine with his usual droll humour.

Duigan also had the highest respect for his new star, telling one newspaper, 'Hugh empathises with the character and takes the audience on quite a surprising arc. Initially he's rather ridiculous, but later on is revealed as a vulnerable man who's deeply in love with his wife and anxious to understand the changes going on in her. At one point he says to her, "It's good to have some secrets" – and I think that's a persuasive argument. If every relationship was utterly open and people felt under an obligation to reveal every aspect of their mental life then no relationship could really survive.'

Yet Hugh had no time to rest after the shoot wrapped, or to hang around with 44-year-old Duigan, who had become his newest 'best friend' (they shared a distinctly lavatorial sense of schoolboy humour). The cast and crew of *Four Weddings* were impatiently expecting him back in England with production starting on 31 May 1993. For the first time in his career, Hugh Grant had an entire film riding on his presence alone. It was, he said later, one of the most thrilling moments of his life.

From the moment that *Four Weddings* passed into cinema history as the most successful British film of all time, it was easy to forget the struggle of its birth. After completing his script, the Oxford-educated, sublimely gifted comedy writer Richard Curtis (who scripted the *Blackadder* television series and the 1989 Jeff Goldblum/Emma Thompson movie *The Tall Guy*, and is one of the main writing talents behind the British Comic Relief famine aid) spent an entire year with the producer Duncan Kenworthy and director Mike Newell polishing the screenplay and struggling for funding.

To bring the movie in on its astonishingly slim initial budget of £3.75 million (investors included PolyGram, Channel 4 and Working Title productions), the film's makers deferred chunks of their salaries and devised a shooting schedule which – famously – required almost no overnight hotel stays for the actors, with Essex (close to London) standing in for Wales (too far away) and the Scottish lake location shots obtained by a cameraman on his holidays. (The Scottish wedding was shot at the Alton Hotel in Birmingham.)

The leading role seemed tailor-made for Hugh, exactly the image-solidifying comic part he needed to capture the public imagination. But the actor felt ill for much of the breakneck-paced shooting, from a mixture of nervousness, exhaustion and hay fever. He felt, too, under intense pressure from his exacting Cambridge-educated director, Mike Newell, not to coast through the role of the bachelor Charles, but to play the truth of his character.

Nor was Newell a 'personality' director, like Roman Polanski or Ken Russell, who would absorb the blame if the whole venture flopped. He had an excellent, diligently earned, professional reputation, directing the brilliant BBC movie about an annoying film extra, *Ready When You Are, Mr McGill*, *Dance with a Stranger*, *The Good Mother* – starring Diane Keaton and Liam Neeson – and the 1993 Golden Globe-winning *Enchanted April*.

Hugh was also well aware of the quality of the script and admired Richard Curtis tremendously.

'It was,' according to another actor who tested for Hugh's part, 'the best and tightest script anybody had seen around in ages. It had "hit" written all over it. Everyone knew, if they got it right, that it was going to be the next Great British Thing.'

Even the luxury of being able to return home to his Earls Court flat at the end of the day's shooting, instead of to a foreign hotel room, was offset by the cruelly early starts required by the location shooting at stately homes – the Capability-Brown-landscaped Luton Hoo in Bedfordshire and the Georgian manor house Goldingtons in Sarratt, Hertfordshire.

Though Hugh believed heart and soul in the movie, and wished desperately for its success after a career studded with so many disappointments and broken promises, he hated the madcap pace of its making and was both relieved and drooping with fatigue when *Four Weddings* wrapped in mid-July after a 36-day shoot.

With a gap before his next film commitments Hugh holidayed with Elizabeth, played tennis with old Latymer and new film friends, including John Duigan, and heard, to his growing delight, the increasingly encouraging bulletins about the post-production *Four Weddings* and *Sirens*. Hugh was also quietly buffing the public-speaking skills that would stand him in such marvellous stead when it came to the 1995 Golden Globes Awards.

Film festivals and awards ceremonies now number in their hundreds around the world, with only the top thirty or so – from the Oscars down – being covered in the mainstream press, and only the starriest of all on television. In November 1993, Hugh was in a new role as one of the guest presenters at the Felix European Film Awards in Berlin (Felix is the name of one of the characters in the comedy, *The Odd Couple*; Oscar is the other).

One of the film critics present recalls, 'Hugh was co-presenting the award for best actress with Alan Rickman. There was the usual roll-call of parts up for the award, and after each one, Hugh joked, "We *both* were desperate for that one, weren't we?" or "That's another girl I would *completely* have done; I really fancied playing her!" It had clearly all been rehearsed between the two of them and it was far and away the funniest speech of the event.'

Hugh was also relaxing in high style in the lull before what he'd been warned was certain to be a marathon publicity tour for *Four Weddings* in America in the new year. No party, be it book-publishing, magazine, London club, or geared to films, seemed complete without Hugh, variously in his outrageously baggy shorts or black tie, with or without Elizabeth, drinking champagne, and felling girls like ninepins with his wit and charm, though, as usual, ever ready to offer a devastatingly unkind summation of a girl's looks or voice in asides to friends.

'My view of Hugh,' says one loyal old Oxford mate, also in films, 'is that he blows too hot or cold. If he withdraws his charm, which he does like he's knocked a switch, you feel yourself in a very cool place indeed ... His social antennae are too finely tuned for his own good. The lingua franca of the film world is almost entirely flattering – "Oh Hugh, you were marvellous; that was wonderful" – and Hugh seems insatiable for it in other parts of his life, too. At the same time, Hugh is appallingly rude about people, even old friends, who he'll dismiss for looking "seedy" or "blousy". But when the sun peeps out again in Hugh, it shines on everyone!'

* * *

Hugh – without Elizabeth – was a guest during the same pre-Christmas party season, at an elegantly lavish London bash hosted by one of Britain's top glossy magazines. Afterwards some of the revellers, including Hugh and a male friend from Oxford, who appeared to be distinctly tired and emotional, went on for supper at a restaurant in the Old Brompton Road. After unsuccessfully trying to order oysters, and settling agreeably for asparagus and 'heaps of champagne' instead, Hugh and his friend were joined at their table by some of the society lovelies who had also been at the party. Halfway through the meal one of the women turned to her side plate – only to find it occupied not by thinly sliced brown buttered bread but the limply displayed penis of Hugh's companion.

Sensing a joke but not finding it hugely amusing, she caught Hugh's attention and – motioning in the direction of the problem – murmured that she didn't believe the contents of the plate were quite what she had ordered.

'No,' said Hugh, 'I don't think so for one moment either.' And, without missing a beat, he whisked his friend and the problem away from the table and out of the restaurant door, returned to pay everyone's supper bill – a not inconsiderable amount – soothed the ruffled feathers of management and went off to see his friend safely home in a taxi. David Niven, it was agreed by those remaining, could not have performed any more graciously himself.

Four Weddings premièred in the USA as the curtain-raiser to the Sundance Film Festival at Utah in January 1994, and promptly put an end to what was starting to be whispered as 'the Sundance curse' – the theory that any film opening this festival, established by Robert Redford in 1983, would be carrion at the box office. While Mike Newell's dreamy Celtic boy-and-a-horse adventure *Into the West* (1993) was the most recent of a small number of films to kick off the festival and then fail to light up the world's cinemas, the distributors' main frustration was that there hadn't been a smash from Sundance since 1989's *sex, lies and videotape*, which also starred Andie MacDowell.

Co-starring with Andie MacDowell in *Four Weddings and a Funeral* – the film that was to transform Hugh into an international heart-throb, 1994

Above With Georgina Cates in *An Awfully Big Adventure*, 1995

Below A painful experience with Julianne Moore in *Nine Months*, 1995

Hugh's leading ladies in *Sense and Sensibility*, 1996: Emily Francoise (*above*) and Emma Thompson (*below*)

Above Hugh with Liz Hurley before his fall from grace, 1992

Below The perfect couple at the première of *Four Weddings and a Funeral*, 1994

Left Tuesday 27 June: Hugh is arrested by Hollywood vice officers

BK4454813 06-27-95
LOS ANGELES POLICE: HWD

Below Friday 30 June: Hugh tries to explain himself to Liz Hurley

Left Divine Brown, prostitute

Below Divine Brown, celebrity

Right Disgraced: Hugh with a sullen-looking Liz at the première of *Nine Months* in 1995

BK4454822 06-27-95

LOS ANGELES POLICE: HWD

One man and his dog, July 1995

In 1994 Mike Newell pushed all thoughts of *Into the West* into the far distance. He was back in the tiny un-chic mountain ski-resort town of Park City, undaunted, with the highest hopes for his new film and his star, with PolyGram willing to flex its mighty marketing muscle behind the distribution if the première results were good.

The Sundance Festival, which is now almost rated as the American Cannes, acts as a showcase for many conspicuously 'arty', 'political' or independently made films in search of distribution deals. Andie MacDowell dutifully put in an appearance at the start of the festival, but disappeared early. Unlike Hugh, she is married with children. This left Hugh, who had come straight from New York and Los Angeles, suffering from flu and having received, with Elizabeth, a token shaking in bed during the January earthquake, forced to make himself available for a numbing number of interviews to promote both *Four Weddings* and *Sirens*, which was also premièred at Sundance.

Ironically, it was a bit of an uphill struggle where *Sirens* was concerned because at the festival the 'buzz' about the film – that is, the mixture of publicists' hyperbole and genuine gossip – was not about Hugh at all, but all about the lusciously displayed curves of the model Elle Macpherson, who plays the siren model Sheela, and who was also at the festival. This would all change dramatically by the time *Sirens* was on general release.

Despite Hugh's claims that he hated doing the flesh-peddling rounds of meetings at the festival, he did a remarkable job disguising the fact, joking merrily that the free plastic alarm clocks handed out to journalists – a nod at his film character's constant lateness – cost more than he'd been paid to star.

One leading Australian film and TV journalist, Jenny Cooney, who managed to secure a one-on-one interview with Hugh in Utah, says, 'He pushed himself harder than anyone else. He came very near to fainting halfway through it. Everything was going fine, when he suddenly turned deathly white and said, "I'm sorry, but I seem to be about to faint." Then he took a deep breath and made a joke about wearing the wrong type of shoes, recovered and carried on. To be honest I wanted to take him home with me on the spot and give him some soup.'

Even Robert Redford – who was officially said to be so wrapped up in the post-production of the latest film he had directed (*Quiz Show*, about the scandals that rocked the big-prizemoney TV shows of the 1950s) that he could appear at only one Sundance press conference – made time to meet Hugh behind the scenes.

Hugh, typically, has now turned their meeting into a joke that, at first glance, appears to be against himself: claiming that Redford virtually ignored him in favour of chatting to Elizabeth Hurley after the three had lunched together. It is not, of course, harmful for one's image to reveal that your girlfriend's charms are evident to the guy who got to share Demi Moore with Woody Harrelson in *Indecent Proposal* and Katherine Ross with Paul Newman in *Butch Cassidy and the Sundance Kid*.

The notices from Sundance were fabulous. For the makers of *Four Weddings*, the final benchmark test was: would the film – which opens with its memorable string of f-words – play well in that bastion of conservatism, Salt Lake City itself? It played sensationally in Salt Lake City. Then came dazzling test-screening results from both coasts (screenings were held in the upmarket New Jersey suburbs and in Santa Monica, California), which pointed to Hugh's heart-melting public-school looks and persona as the movie's main selling point. These persuaded the film's USA distributors to release it over a month earlier than planned, at the start of March – a dead period for new releases – rather than towards the end of April.

Hugh promptly agreed to the suggestions of executives from Gramercy Pictures – PolyGram's independent distribution company – to embark on a saturation self-marketing blitz across America. New stars on the rise invariably make heady copy and Hugh, bearing the gift of his pawky charm aloft, marketed himself with aplomb. He agreed to meet journalists for coffee, breakfast, lunch, in his hotel suite, in the bar – name the restaurant – or after dinner. He met them, wearing a party hat and munching popcorn on late-night talk shows and slurping cappuccino on the early-morning television shows.

He discussed his sinus problems and Andie Mac-Dowell's dribbling during the *Four Weddings* tea-drinking scene with equal ease. He rode horses for fashion layouts, posed handsomely in handsome suits beside bicycles à la Oxford University days, poked fun at almost every earlier role he had ever played ('Gosh, I was *appalling* in that!') and even permitted journalists glimpses of his pyjamas – sometimes patterned, sometimes pink – sweetly laid out in his hotel bedroom.

Hugh was a breath of spring to an America jaded by a cruel East Coast winter and a January West Coast earthquake.

As *Four Weddings* quivered on the brink of commercial release, almost every major newspaper and magazine had its Hugh Grant piece ready to go ('I feel absolutely ba-nah-nahs,' says Hugh Grant pulling out a tissue and dabbing his red nose.) By this point, not even a New York press-screening of *Four Weddings* that coincided with one of the worst snowstorms of the winter could stand in its way. Only 14 out of the 65 VIP press invited made it to the cinema. One of them was the veteran syndicated columnist Liz Smith. It's a winner – and Hugh Grant looks ready for US stardom, she pronounced serenely.

Weddings Fever had begun.

TWENTY-TWO

*'Charles (Hugh Grant), the thoroughly English best
man, delivers a funny pre-toast speech that
principally concerns himself – his favorite topic, one
suspects – rather than the happy couple. As the
festivities wind down, he encounters Carrie (Andie
MacDowell), the attractive American guest with
whom he fell in love at first sight earlier in the day.
"Great speech," she offers, indicating self-
involvement is no flaw in her book.'*

Waspish review of Four Weddings,
Terry Kelleher, New York,
Newsday, 9 March 1994

Richard Nixon, asked how history would remember him,
is said to have replied that it all rather depended on who
was writing it. In retrospect, the former American President might have added that it all rather depended on
which movie opened opposite his funeral.

In the event, Nixon's damp spring burial cortège in
Yorba Linda, California, was no match for the column-
inches devoted across America to the simultaneous unveiling of *Four Weddings and A* (altogether another) *Funeral.*
Within little over a month of its American release, the film
was number one at the box office, loved – almost unani-
mously – by critics across both seaboards, and attracting
bigger audiences, in terms of week-on-week increases,
than either of its rivals, the AIDS and Auschwitz mega-
movies, *Philadelphia* and *Schindler's List.*

The 'official' accounting became a running story in itself
– a film made for under three million pounds finally
garnering over $260 million worldwide (the modest pro-
duction budget does not, of course, take into account the
marketing costs, said to be 'many times' the initial figure).

Sirens, released in the USA just after *Four Weddings*, underwent a panicked promotional remake (just as *Nine Months* would do the following year in the wake of the prostitute scandal). The hot selling point of *Sirens* had always been the naked Elle Macpherson. As the prematurely released *Four Weddings* pulled in the queues, Miramax realized in horror that it wasn't the heavily hyped nude Macpherson with her carefully prepared catchline of 'I've put on twenty pounds for this role' that it needed to push, but the fully clothed actor playing the prattish cleric – Hugh Grant.

A rash of scarlet, measly, last-minute stickers alerted the American public that *that* Hugh Grant in *Four Weddings* was the same as *this* Hugh Grant in *Sirens*. They appeared across the Australian film's posters. This sticker-plaudit approach – which smacked of amateurish piggy-back marketing – was rapidly scrubbed: in favour of a whole new billboard campaign for *Sirens*, showing Hugh running his fingers through his dishevelled, distinctly *Four Weddings* hairstyle, alongside a sexily smiling, bare-shouldered Elle Macpherson, with whom he has no significant direct relationship in the film. (This was, absurdly, stiffly described as 'a coincidence' by Miramax spokespeople, despite the fact that in *Sirens*, Hugh's hair is, for the most part, damply pomaded to his skull and has little resemblance to his *Four Weddings* style.)

Four Weddings made Hugh an international star. There were double-page advertisement spreads in *Variety* and *Screen International* as the film passed the $100 million mark and gloating British press articles saying that the US had 'fallen' for a Brit movie along the lines of David versus Goliath. *Chariots of Fire* (1981), a previous benchmark British success, had taken 'only' a comparatively puny $60 million; *The Crying Game* (1992), $62 million; *Much Ado About Nothing*, the highest-grossing British-made film of 1993, $22 million; and *The Remains of the Day*, also 1993, just under $22 million. *A Fish Called Wanda* had never made the number-one US slot.

Even as Hugh filmed Mike Newell's *Four Weddings*

follow-up, *An Awfully Big Adventure*, budgeted at £2.4 million, in April 1994, playing a twisted, gay provincial theatre director in post-war Liverpool, the congratulatory faxes were winging their way to his London agent.

Four Weddings simply hopped from hype to hype. The film – released in some 40 countries – topped the box office in places as diverse as Japan, the Lebanon, Brazil, Iceland and Germany. In Paris, it drew even larger attendances than *Jurassic Park*. With the exception of the same Spielberg behemoth, it became the second-highest attended movie ever in Britain. Elizabeth's stunning appearance in the borrowed £2,540 Versace dress, stapled together with 24 safety-pins, at the film's May London première at the Odeon, Leicester Square – with Hugh pictured peering grinningly down in gallant delight at her slim yet buxom cleavaged form – made magazines round the world. The London première had, of course, been planned as a major event with the Odeon decorated like a church – complete with full-throated choir – the crowd of around 3,000 outside given confetti to throw and a party at the Naval and Military Club in Piccadilly afterwards.

But in Britain *that* frock – which both Hugh and Elizabeth insisted had been a last-minute choice – and that alone pushed the premature death of the Labour leader John Smith off the front pages.

Elizabeth, who had no part in the film, had made herself part of its mythology. The couple romped onwards and upwards. American newspapers began to carry free advertisements for the hotels featured in the film, urging readers to book themselves in for a *Four Weddings* experience of 'inglenook fireplaces, oak-beamed ceilings ... and 16th century paintings'. More interviews appeared with Hugh confessing, disarmingly, how miserable he'd been during filming and how he'd been sure he'd have to emigrate to Peru because he looked so bad in the rushes. The more he talked down his own part, the more he was hailed as Britain's suave antidote to the pumped-up all-action icons of Stallone, Willis and Schwarzenegger.

The more sincerely Hugh insisted that he really wasn't

as lovely as his screen character, and pointed to his *An Awfully Big Adventure* part as showing his 'bitter and nasty' side, the more his remarks were interpreted along the lines of David Niven's cheery disclaimer that he discovered a mean streak in himself after one or two too many gins – so had stopped drinking gins!

Four Weddings continued to cast a Midas glow all around. The estate of another Hugh – the poet Wystan Hugh Auden – enjoyed a sudden bonanza as anthologies of his selected works, including the poem read so movingly at the funeral scene by John Hannah, were rushed into best-selling reprint as a film tie-in entitled *Tell Me the Truth About Love*. In the UK the book made the best-sellers lists for over 30 weeks – right through to 1995. The *Sun* headline? 'Dead poet is groovy due to hit movie.'

The American edition, unlike the British, didn't feature Hugh on the cover, but contented itself with a purplish peel-off sticker proudly announcing, 'Includes the poem featured in *Four Weddings* . . .', which could be removed by punters perhaps unwilling to admit they'd been moved to buy poetry as a result of a comedy film.

Hugh, a lover of Auden from university days, was quietly proud of the literate tone of the movie. By a coincidence, of which he was well aware, *Four Weddings* – produced, directed, written by and starring Oxbridge alumni – saluted earlier Oxbridge stars. Years earlier the great Chaucerian scholar and Oxford don Nevill Coghill had claimed he had taught only two men of genius: one was Richard Burton, the other W.H. Auden.

By the end of summer 1994, *Four Weddings* had become a 350,000-video-cassette rental blockbuster in the USA; in November the cassette became available in Britain, and again broke sales and rental records. The White House, reportedly, tracked down the *Four Weddings* London florist noted in the film's credits, and booked him to organize a glittering Washington event – by transatlantic fax.

Seven years after James Ivory had made his prediction about Hugh, it had all come true. This time it was his co-stars – Andie MacDowell, Kristin Scott Thomas, Simon Callow, James Fleet, Charlotte Coleman, John Hannah, David Bower and Rowan Atkinson in cameo – who got slightly pushed to one side in the trample to anoint Hugh. Small wonder that he occasionally got his quotes mixed up! It is difficult to judge now whether it was on the set of *Four Weddings* that a make-up lady mortified the actor by asking him, when he had to take off his shirt for a scene, 'Do you want definition painted in?' – or whether it was on the set of *The Changeling* or *Bitter Moon*, as Hugh has it in various interviews.

At the Cannes Film Festival in May, Hugh and Elizabeth luxuriated, courtesy of PolyGram, at the magnificent Hotel du Cap – infamous for accepting only cash payment to settle bills – and relished their insulation from the *hoi polloi* of the main festival 40 km away. They were finally living as bona fide stars, in a £750-a-night suite, with scripts delivered by courier, bundles of press clippings arriving to be giggled over daily, seats at the festival's opening movie, *The Hudsucker Proxy*, and more interviews – for Hugh – with the *New York Times* and top British magazines.

In June Hugh received star billing in a London charity football match, 'The Other World Cup', over every other television celebrity team-mate where he signed autographs, posed for Polaroid snaps with fans and declared that he 'loved every minute of the attention'.

The following month Hugh and Elizabeth were both back in France, at the Ritz Hotel in Paris – Hugh's favourite bed-and-breakfast – as VIP guests of Gianni Versace for the designer's latest collection and in the gratifyingly starry company of Prince, Sylvester Stallone and Bryan Ferry.

The perks of Hugh's fame were, of course, double-edged for Elizabeth, who had to endure the spotlight of publicity on her boyfriend lighting up the murkier corners of her own past.

Tabloid 'revelations' focused hard on Elizabeth's wild teenage past with the *Sun* running the headline, 'She wore no knickers and dated a punk called Septic'; and the *Daily Star* imploring its readers, 'Did you go wild with wayward Liz?' The titbits about Elizabeth – her membership of the Reading punk scene, or what passed for one, and the publication of some rather nasty Lolita-ish photographs the actress had willingly posed for but which surfaced against her will in the British magazine *Loaded* – infuriated her. Nevertheless, she also conceded that they helped her image.

Britain has always seemed to need at least one beautiful rebel actress daughter of an army officer running amok in the shires, and Elizabeth filled the position left vacant by Charlotte Rampling, herself an officer's offspring. In the 1960s it had been Ms Rampling's unconventional and distinctly swinging domestic arrangements with two chaps at the same time that had the nation convulsed over its morning tabloids. In the 1990s, Elizabeth was an ideal replacement.

Like Hugh, she sought to control publicity by courting it on her own terms. When the *Modern Review* attempted to republish the pubic-hair-revealing shots of her that had bobbed up in *Loaded*, the actress successfully threatened to sue the magazine, fell out spectacularly – not surprisingly – with its then editor Toby Young, a former friend, and complained about his 'outrageous' behaviour to the *Sunday Times* magazine.

To publicize the *Sunday Times* interview, Elizabeth posed for the magazine's front cover in a skimpy lilac shift being blown by a wind machine, to reveal a smooth flash of bare buttock, while teetering in a Daliesque pair of black leather boots with foot-long nail-spike heels protruding. Inside the magazine, Elizabeth appeared naked except for a strategically placed feather boa.

She also 'permitted' her close friend, Henry Dent-Brocklehurst, a one-time miserably public-school-educated (Stowe instead of Eton, as he'd have preferred) heroin addict who had cleaned up his act, to offer comments on her real personality to the *Sunday Times*. The young, unmarried aristocrat, whose family owns a 1,000-year-old

Cotswold castle, explained he met Elizabeth through friends when he was in Los Angeles setting up a video production company and recovering from the heartbreak of a failed relationship. Elizabeth put him up in her Sunset flat for two months and her 'kindness', said Henry Brocklehurst – as he is known informally – sealed their friendship.

He was part of the actress's coterie of English friends: Julian Sands, the ex-Bond Timothy Dalton, William Cash and the designer Elizabeth Emanuel. 'Elizabeth [Hurley] doesn't like people who are serious,' Dent-Brocklehurst told the *Sunday Times*. 'She can't stand people who are pompous or pretentious . . . she likes to surround herself with boys and girls whom she can mother.'

After Saturday cricket parties in Los Angeles, Elizabeth would serve traditional roasts and Yorkshire puddings, making 'an extra effort to make sure that the puddings were ready, that the custard was just the right temperature.'

Though Elizabeth's patchy acting credits had been widely noted in the press, she had at least been fleetingly back on the British small screen in the spring of 1994 in the popular period film series *Sharpe*, set in Napoleonic France. With Elizabeth's prodigious talents for self-promotion, could, Britain wondered, the pop-up Elizabeth Hurley period calendar cookbook be very far away?

TWENTY-THREE

'Is this really *the next James Bond?'*
Daily Mail, *12 May 1994*

Hugh, too, had his unflattering share of press attention.
The headline in the *Daily Mail* on 12 May 1994 could
hardly have been less respectful. 'Is this *really* the next
James Bond?' it asked, with a gurgle of disbelief. The
picture alongside was a close-up head-and-shoulders portrait of Hugh rather peevishly plucking at the furry collar
of his leather jacket, his hair visibly and fussily gelled –
possibly a publicity still from the 1985 South Pole adventure series, *The Last Place on Earth*.

Could it be true, queried the accompanying article, that
an actor whose girlfriend claims she sews name-tags in his
clothes is about to become James Bond No 005 after Sean
Connery, Roger Moore, George Lazenby and Timothy
Dalton? The question was not meant to be rhetorical.

The stories that Hugh was under consideration as the
next Bond were, on the whole, an unwanted embarrassment which ran and ran – on both sides of the Atlantic –
for a clutch of very specific reasons.

First, in the UK it gave the freshest possible boost to the
'overnight sensation of *Four Weddings and a Funeral*'
juggernaut just at a time when it was running dangerously
short of fuel – and with the opening of *Sirens* at the end
of July a little too far off to help.

The idea of Hugh in the part was both astonishing and
implausible but not downright insane. For the first time,
too, the public hadn't already been saturated with acres of
PR flummery about the new Bond. The identity of the fifth
British superagent was not due to be revealed until later in

the summer, but the star of the TV thriller *Remington Steele*, Pierce Brosnan, was widely and correctly assumed to be the mystery man. Brosnan turned down the role when offered it eight years ago, after Roger Moore retired, because of other contractual obligations and no one was seriously considering a left-field candidate.

And because Brosnan had indeed already been signed for the role, the gossip about Hugh, and indeed a whole raft of other names suddenly said to be under consideration, was regarded as both free advertising and a rather enjoyable aquarium of red herrings by the Bond publicists. The Hugh Grant angle lit up the world just like the good old days of *Diamonds are Forever*, when the publicity wrote itself.

In America the five-times-a-week *Entertainment Tonight* show even ran a telephone poll shortly after the first Hugh-as-Bond rumours had surfaced to see who was the most popular choice.

Brosnan came first but the American public endorsed the rumours: Hugh got a healthy vote along with Mel Gibson, Liam Neeson and Ralph Fiennes. A few people responding to this poll, who were assumed not to have quite grasped the question, voted for Emma Thompson.

As so often happens when a rumour catches the imagination of both journalists and the public, stories start to cross-pollinate. So a story in the UK press which confirms that Hollywood rumours do exist about Hugh as Bond is taken by the US press as proof that these rumours ought to be taken seriously. It is quite a sport to crouch in the middle and watch the whole process. By the time Brosnan's address on Bond Street was confirmed, one very influential US magazine, privy, apparently, to the inner workings of Hugh's mind, said he'd passed on the role because he wasn't allowed to make Bond as droll as he liked ('in words David Cassidy never used, I think I'll kill you . . .').

Secondly, it provided an ideal opportunity in the UK for a small Hugh Grant backlash; the chance to signal that while America may have 'discovered' a new British star, that didn't mean Britain had to genuflect every time his name was mentioned.

In addition, while casting the new Bond is no longer an Event, ever since a *Daily Express* readers' poll advised the producers Cubby Broccoli and Harry Saltzman that a certain Sean Connery, then the star of Walt Disney's popular *Darby O'Gill and the Little People*, would be the ideal Fleming hero back in 1960, the British press still takes an unusually proprietorial interest in the matter.

Finally, denials from actors that they are considering or have been offered a certain part are notoriously untrustworthy. Actors always pretend they aren't remotely interested in roles until they are signed because, understandably, they have no wish to become labelled henceforth as Mr so-and-so, 'the James Bond reject'. You only have to look back to August 1993 to find Bond number four, Timothy Dalton, cheerfully promising that his next Bond movie – the one Brosnan has now made – would be 'the best ever'. At the time, no doubt, he did intend to make it.

In private, Hugh was insisting to friends that this one really was untrue. The part had never been offered to him. The possibility of the part hadn't even been discussed. Yes, a remake of *The Saint* had been mooted but the Bond stories were a total fabrication. Even Hugh, who had weathered the exhaustion caused by his heroic international plugging of *Four Weddings* and *Sirens*, and who had loved the attention being an accredited movie star initially brought him, felt fed up. The press, it seemed, could make up and print anything it liked as long as it had the words 'Hugh Grant' in it.

And in spite of the private denials and the ones wearily repeated to the media, that he hadn't the faintest idea about the origin of the Bond rumours, the story wouldn't die.

His suitability or unsuitability for the role was chewed over on TV, radio and in the papers and, when Brosnan *was* confirmed in the role, it was loftily said that Hugh had either been pipped at the post or been offered the part and turned it down. Just like, in fact, the actor to whom he was being closely compared, Cary Grant. Incredibly, before he took the advice of *Daily Express* readers, Cubby Broccoli's first choice for *Dr No* in 1962 had been the then 58-year-old Cary Grant.

The likeliest source of the story is a misunderstanding between one of Britain's major bookmakers, William Hill, and the leading and very highly regarded serious international movie-business publication, *Screen International*.

Its editor-in-chief, Oscar Moore, says, 'We were being asked by William Hill for a list of actors most likely to be considered for the role and we gave them the usual names – Pierce Brosnan as the most likely by far, Jason Connery, the ones everyone in the business was talking about and the ones we knew had been considered at some time or other.

'Then someone wrote on a bit of paper "Hugh Grant" and this was duly communicated to the bookmakers. In fact his name had been written down as a joke – simply because everyone was talking about him. No one had any idea it would be passed on seriously. No one had any idea it would be taken seriously if it did get passed on.

'The next minute the papers were full of Grant-as-Bond stories.'

The magazine even subsequently, and entirely honourably, contacted Hugh's agent at ICM to explain how it may have inadvertently started the publicity blaze.

'But I don't think his agent understood,' says Moore. 'In fact he insisted that Hugh was already reading the scripts! By this time I think he was getting mixed up with *The Saint*, for which Hugh was being considered. It must have been the craziest time.'

Friends say that the early summer was one of the toughest periods for Hugh. The euphoria produced by the rapturous reviews of the film had long evaporated. He was already infected with the standard new-star paranoia – that people didn't love *him*, the real Hugh, but only the fictional screen persona. He hadn't yet learnt not to care what was written about him.

Not caring what is written about you is not a cynical or lofty attitude for a movie star. It is essential. It is also hard. Even a close-lipped veteran like Paul Newman made the mistake, about a decade ago, of responding personally to what he considered an excessively stupid piece of gossip repeated in a well-known American tabloid. His complaint became public and the two have been slugging it out ever since. It is not a winning sight.

In a noticeably thin-skinned – even naive – moment, Hugh complained to his old Oxford friend and former Piers Gaveston Society chum, the *Sunday Times* writer Geordie Greig, 'These people shoving scripts at me don't care about me or my world one bit. All they care about is that someone else perceives me as hot.'

Which is about as neat a definition as there is, and from the horse's mouth too, of what the phrase 'movie star' actually means.

By his own admission, Hugh had been forced to beg Mike Newell for the part of Meredith Potter in *An Awfully Big Adventure*, which was filmed in Dublin rather than Liverpool, where it is set in 1947. Not because it was another starring role, for the story is principally about the dark coming-of-age of a stage-struck girl, played by the newcomer Georgina Cates. But because Newell wasn't immediately convinced that Hugh was right for the part.

Hugh's determination to be seen playing, as he described the role, 'a predatory and egotistical monster who has used and discarded a string of vulnerable young men and women' won over the director. Newell later joked that he'd used 'the acerbic, chilly, whiplash side of Hugh that I had to keep suppressing in *Four Weddings*.'

The shoot, though, was not without its tensions, as Hugh found himself unusually intolerant of the standard tedium of film-making. It was hardly surprising. Hollywood was hammering on his door with offers that outstripped the entire budget of the film. Journalists visiting the set found the actor moodily identifying with the part – 'Potter is a nasty piece of work, and that's what I'm becoming' – and preferring to shut himself in his trailer making long mobile-phone calls to Elizabeth, rather than lark about with the crew between takes.

Hugh's next project – also agreed before *Four Weddings* – was *Restoration*, which began filming at the end of May in North Wales, Shepperton Studios and the West Country. The film, a farcical Restoration comedy which reunited Hugh with his *Privileged* director and scriptwriter Mike Hoffman and Rupert Walters and starred Robert Downey Jr, provided only a cameo for Hugh, as a seedily amoral painter at the court of Charles II. True to his promise to himself to take on as many varied parts as possible after playing so many repressed Englishman roles, Hugh camped it up before reporters visiting one of the locations – the Somerset mansion Brimpton D'Evercy – in full make-up, high heels and ruffles baring his newly yellow 'rotting' teeth and insisting a cosmetic cold sore he'd especially liked had been wiped clean on the instructions of the producers because 'we don't think Hugh Grant should have a cold sore.'

However, none of the cast could entirely overlook the tabloid investigation into Elizabeth's past then going full swing. One of Hugh's co-stars on *Restoration*, David Thewlis, told an American magazine on set, 'Each time you open the papers, it's like the *Daily Hurley*.'

The final film commitment left to honour was *The Englishman Who Went Up a Hill but Came Down a Mountain*, shot in North Wales in the late summer and early autumn of 1994 and reintroducing Hugh to his *Sirens* wife, Tara Fitzgerald (who remained unshakeably loyal to her co-star even after the prostitute scandal – sending him a private message of supportive love). If Hugh's caustic remarks about the staff at the hotel where he stayed – and a hotel to which he admitted he *insisted* he be moved – later left an unpleasant taste in the mouth, there was no doubt that the actor seemed on buoyant form on location, giving out autographs by the ream, posing good humouredly for snaps with extras and enduring ribs from the crew about the weekly American polls that were naming him 'sexiest man alive'.

Hugh's presence in the film, which had a budget of just £2.8 million and was almost entirely American-financed, guaranteed the movie's success. By the end of 1994 – with his development deal with Castle Rock made public and simply adding to his lustre – there was scarcely a film or entertainments publication on either side of the Atlantic that had neglected to feature Hugh in its annual 'halls of fame'.

The actor who had begun the year in bed feeling the tremors of the Los Angeles earthquake rode it out on a tidal wave of public adulation and approval. And there were still the industry awards for *Four Weddings* to come.

TWENTY-FOUR

'It's tragic how much I'm enjoying getting this ...'
Hugh Grant, 21 January 1995

At the 52nd annual Golden Globes Awards held on Saturday, 21 January, at the Beverly Hilton in Los Angeles, Hugh Grant sent up Hollywood so stylishly that Hollywood couldn't help but love him back all over again. The Golden Globes have traditionally become, as the actor Michael York once neatly put it, 'the interim handicappers' odds for the upcoming Oscar sweepstakes.' They are awarded by the eclectic bunch of the Hollywood Foreign Press Association, an odd, mainly freelance, assortment of correspondents whose credentials have frequently been questioned over the years, yet who have come to be trusted – more or less – in accurately predicting the most likely winners on Oscar night.

Unfortunately, for Hugh, the Oscars don't include a category for best actor in a comedy. Fortunately, The Golden Globes do.

'It's tragic how much I'm enjoying getting this,' he began as he accepted the award for his 'champagne bubble' *Four Weddings* role. 'It's heaven. Right up my alley. I can't *tell* the Foreign Press Association how much I admire them. It's with *tremendous* ill grace that I grudgingly acknowledge the contribution of a few other people.' (A sound-barrier-breaking wave of laughter as the audience realizes that this is not merely going to be one joke followed by the usual 'No, but seriously, folks, I really do feel honoured', but was to be a comic tour de force.)

'I *suppose* Richard Curtis wrote quite a funny script. I

suppose Mike Newell directed it quite well under difficult circumstances. Though with tremendous bad temper, I might add.'

By the time Hugh thanked his agent Michael Foster at ICM (from which he was soon to depart) for having won him the part 'by sheer dint of being extremely small and extremely vicious', and mentioned 'my girlfriend Elizabeth Hurley, who put up with easily the nastiest, most ill-tempered, prima-donna-ish actor in English cinema for six weeks and then came back to *me*, which was really nice,' he was the hit of the evening.

The veteran, syndicated American showbusiness columnist Liz Smith in an irony-free post-Globes round-up called 'Golden moments, golden thoughts', declared, 'Best on-stage: Hugh Grant, who solidified his stardom with the night's wittiest, most irreverent speech. If Hollywood was charmed by him before, now he is worshipped . . .' The *Daily Telegraph* opined that Hugh was 'the sort of Englishman whom it has become fashionable in certain circles to knock as being out-dated, even irrelevant or embarrassing.'

With a Golden Globe in hand, and the presentation in December of the 54th Golden Apple Award for male discovery of the year from the Hollywood Woman's Press Club, Hugh – with Elizabeth glimmering at his side – appeared invincible. Hugh won huge laughs appearing on British television for the 1995 Comic Relief appeal in March to snog with the ample British comedienne Dawn French in a comic copy of Elizabeth's Versace dress.

But both Hugh and Elizabeth genuinely loathed one bout of publicity that was genuinely out of their hands. The actress had to run the gauntlet of dozens of press photographers after arriving from New York for an appearance at Southwark Crown Court on 22 March to give evidence against a gang of young women who had mugged her for ten pounds at knifepoint in Kensington the previous November. A passing van-driver who had helped pursue the muggers was hailed as the UK's most envied 'white knight'.

The trial, which made the front page of *The Times* and resulted in convictions, seemed perilously near to publicity overkill. The trial, as *The Times* reported, was 'brought forward to ensure that Miss Hurley could be with Mr Grant in Hollywood for the Oscar ceremony next Monday [March 29]' – a rare footnote to robbery cases heard before at Southwark Crown Court.

The 67th Academy Awards, or Oscars, ceremony failed to add further crowns to Hugh Grant or *Four Weddings* and his moment in the spotlight, as co-presenter with Andie MacDowell, during which he playfully elbowed his graceful co-star aside in an attempt to replay his Golden Globes triumph of wit, misfired gauchely. Yet the couple now belonged to the premier Hollywood ranks, joining – fashionably late – the post-Oscars *Vanity Fair* party at Mortons with Elizabeth in plunging beaded white, shoulder to shoulder with a guest list that ran from Anthony Hopkins, Jon Bon Jovi and Tony Curtis to anyone famous at the XYZ end of the alphabet.

In April, in London, at the British Academy of Film and Television Arts awards evening, *Four Weddings* won five of its eleven Bafta nominations, with Hugh picking up the Peter Sellers Award for Comedy. He joked of Elizabeth's borrowed John Galliano pink flamenco-style frock – which she wore braless – 'She has been very *supportive* and stood *firmly* by my side even when her dress split on the night of the première and we had to bung in a few pins.' While the compère, Billy Connolly, commented – of Elizabeth's appearance – 'That was very pleasant, I must say. Jiggling should be an Olympic event.'

TWENTY-FIVE

'*All at once I saw her bare arm. The colour of the skin struck me – it was a shade I had never seen before: matt brown . . . the strange quality of that sombre brown [flesh] . . . it was the flesh of a goddess or a painted image . . . I had the vague feeling that the memory of [the girl] was already connected in some way to my most fugitive thoughts and desires . . . The idea both amused and disturbed me . . .*'

Guilty – and prophetic – thoughts from the
character played by Hugh in his 1988 film,
Bengali Night *(quotation from the
fact-based novel on which the film is based,*
Bengal Nights, *by Mercea Eliade)*

By early June 1995, there were precious few young actors who wouldn't have bargained with the devil to be Hugh Grant. In March his girlfriend Elizabeth accumulated yet another glamorous layer to her image as the new face of the cosmetics giant, Estée Lauder, replacing the super-model Paulina Porizkova. At the London launch, Hugh dutifully appeared at her side, looking shambolically chic in an open-necked shirt and a mustard-yellow faux old-fashioned tweed suit complete with knitted waistcoat – as if fresh off the family grouse moors.

At the press conference held at the Manhattan's Royalton Hotel to announce the 'news', the atmosphere was tinged with genuine excitement. To America, which had not been fed a year's worth of tabloid tattle about the actress's wild teenage past, raunchy photos and less than brilliant screen career, Elizabeth was a fresh discovery: a gorgeous, poised, radiantly beaming young woman bearing the romantic endorsement of that impossibly sexy Brit, Hugh Grant. The event reached the traffic-snarling, crowd-pulling, flashbulb-popping level perhaps only Elizabeth Taylor and Richard Burton used to be able to command when they hit town. Estée Lauder publicists, cannily, refused to confirm in advance whether Hugh would attend Elizabeth's ceremonial elevation to supermodel status. Hugh duly turned up, of course, but kept his appearance tantalizingly brief, in deference to Elizabeth's moment in the spotlight.

On both sides of the Atlantic Hugh was popping up as a celebrity charity poster boy. In March, his face and name launched the Macmillan Cancer Appeal's Great Tie and Scarf Auction which announced, 'A fabulous collection of ties and scarves, many with signed messages from famous personalities including Hugh Grant, John Major, the Prince of Wales, Joan Collins . . .' Even the heir to the throne had to queue behind Hugh's name. In May, Hugh smiled sensitively from billboards all over New York as the Herb Ritts poster boy for an AIDS benefit.

The same month Elizabeth was placed fourth in *People Weekly* magazine's annual round-up of the 50 Most Beautiful People In The World, after Halle Berry, the *ER* star George Clooney and Demi Moore. Hugh had made the same list the year before. '[Hugh and I] stand in front of the mirror deciding, if we have a baby whose features it should have,' Elizabeth teasingly told the magazine. 'Her beauty is horribly marred by her ears,' Hugh chipped in waggishly. 'She looks like the F.A. Cup.' The magazine obligingly translated the quip for its US readers, explaining that this cup was a 'soccer trophy'.

Hugh's own career was in orbit – and in the experienced hands of some of the most influential executives and directors in Hollywood. He even had his own development deal with Castle Rock – the cash-rich Hollywood mini-studio run by the movie director Rob Reiner (*When Harry Met Sally*) and financed by the American media mogul Ted Turner. So anxious was Hollywood to get into 'the Hugh Grant business' that Castle Rock was prepared to pay for Hugh to commission his own star-vehicle scripts as long as the studio got first refusal on making the film.

Hugh set up his own film production company, based across the street from the Natural History Museum in smart South Kensington, for this flattering purpose, naming it Simian Films. Hugh told interviewers on television in America and in British magazines that the unusual name – meaning ape-like – had been inspired by Elizabeth's observations that he resembled a monkey and specifically denied that it was a gleeful just-look-at-me-now nod to the Tarzan casting fiasco he experienced in 1982. But knowing Hugh's passion for Nabokov's *Lolita* anti-hero Humbert Humbert and the actor's fondness for literary allusion, it is tantalizingly possible that the following self-parodying line from the novel may have assisted Hugh's choice: Humbert is addressing the reader directly: 'I do not know if . . . I have sufficiently stressed the peculiar "sending" effect that the writer's good looks – pseudo-Celtic, attractively simian, boyishly manly – had on women of every age and environment. Of course such announcements made in the first person may sound ridiculous. But every once in a while I have to remind the reader of my appearance . . .' (Chapter 24).

It would be only too typical of Hugh to lay a false trail about something so trivial as the derivation of his film company's name while privately relishing with Elizabeth a literary in-joke, which makes exactly the *opposite* point about his looks.

By June 1995 Hugh had made the all-important status transfer from his old agency, International Creative Management, to the starrier, more powerful arms of the Creative Artists Agency, which represents the biggest Hollywood names like Spielberg and Hoffman – and delighted at seeing his defection to A-list management being solemnly reported in the trade press as an 'inevitable move' for someone of his potential box-office clout.

When, in the spring of 1995, the Hollywood paper *Variety* released its annual worldwide box-office sales for the hottest stars of 1994, Hugh came in twelfth, behind, hardly surprisingly Tom Hanks, Arnold Schwarzenegger and Jim Carrey, but *above* long-established Hollywood royalty like Harrison Ford, Julia Roberts, Sharon Stone, Sylvester Stallone, Bruce Willis and even Mel Gibson.

No one was remotely predicting *Four Weddings*-sized success for Hugh's new film, *The Englishman Who Went Up a Hill but Came Down a Mountain*. Nevertheless it became the USA's top-grossing independent film the first weekend it opened in mid-May.

Elizabeth and Hugh sparkled at the première and Hugh, champagne glass in hand, and his merchant banker brother Jamie posed happily for gossip-column photographers at the post-première party.

It opened in the UK in August in fifth place – beaten only by the juggernaut summer movies *Casper*, *Batman Forever*, *Judge Dredd* and *Free Willy 2*. The post-scandal Hugh, by then, was in no position to attend the London première for fear of attracting the wrong kind of publicity. In America, however, *The Englishman Who . . .* was still in the top five fattest independent earners by mid-June, having pulled in a respectable $9 million.

The reviewers, on the whole, politely – rather than ecstatically – welcomed the director Christopher Monger's 'whimsically comic tale' of how, in 1917, an entire Welsh village bands together to get a local hill reclassified as a mountain – thereby literally putting the village on the map – by piling fifteen feet of earth on top. Hugh's approach to US publicity for the film, in which he played an uptight British mapmaker, had been genuinely relaxed and, wisely, scaled down to the modest size of the movie. 'Small budget, tweed jacket . . . can do this standing on my head,' he joked about his part, while laughing to US television news reporters that he had discovered he could speak Welsh while on location – but only when 'completely drunk'. If this film didn't add much muscle to the 'Hugh Grant business', neither did it dim his appeal to established fans. Nor did its comparatively limited success damage his industry standing. Hugh had, after all, agreed to the role *before* the release of *Four Weddings*, and the film was not therefore judged as *the* crucial 'follow-up' project.

One studio executive commented, 'If Grant weren't such a big name [*The Englishman Who . . .*] would be considered an art-house hit. But people are expecting a huge hit film because he's so big these days.' That much-needed 'huge hit', was, it appeared, just around the corner.

By late spring 1995, the advance hype on Hugh's all-important summer big-budget movie, *Nine Months*, was sufficiently dazzling for the film industry's trade paper, the *Hollywood Reporter*, to note – with standard overstatement – that Hugh's 'asking price has soared. He is now in the $6 to $7 million area – right up there with Brad Pitt . . . His new asking price will place him in the company of not only *Interview with the Vampire* star Brad Pitt but Richard Gere and John Travolta . . .'

Madame Tussaud's was also busy preparing to put Hugh in the waxwork company of Madonna, John Major, Luciano Pavarotti et al. Hugh joked in advance about his unveiling at the museum in late August: 'They either do it without your cooperation, in which case the waxwork is very poor, or you go in and every line in your scrotum is measured. And that's what I did.'

Even the bombing of Elizabeth's latest films, *Beyond Bedlam* and *Mad Dogs and Englishmen*, could not dent the couple's glamour, just as the repeated duds turned out by Burton and Taylor had not had any detrimental impact on their status. *Beyond Bedlam* won some notoriety for failing to get a certificate rating for its video release from the British film censors, though its plot alone – as summarized here for the catalogues of the British Film Institute – should have warned the actress that the film was likely to go the same ignominious, critically drubbed way as *The Skipper*: 'During the treatment of a revolutionary new drug, a serial killer finds himself able to telepathically transmit his evil beyond his prison cell.'

Hugh, wittily indiscreet as ever, told one American magazine that *Beyond Bedlam* was 'unspeakable. It was a chancre, I think we can safely say that.' (A chancre is an ulcer in venereal disease.)

Mad Dogs, with Elizabeth as an upper-class heroin

addict, was also put to sleep by lethal invective: 'hysterically overwritten nonsense'; '[Elizabeth's] performance generates the kind of excitement you get watching paint dry.'

Though Elizabeth was stung by the barbs, she was protected by friends like William Cash and Henry Dent-Brocklehurst, who were quick to reassure her that *of course* the nasty media were going to be out gunning for her because of her success as a model. In his collection of essays on Hollywood, Cash even goes so far as to refer flatteringly to Elizabeth's one big-budget film, *Passenger 57*, as 'her most recent big budget movie' as if he were overwhelmed for choice.

Meanwhile the now hugely expensive Hugh was obediently playing the star interview game, delighting the *Nine Months* publicists by grabbing the July cover of *Premiere* magazine, one of America's most popular and least vapidly gushing movie publications, as well as appearing half naked by a pool in a photo layout by one of his favourite photographers, Herb Ritts, for *Vogue* – again, in July.

To both magazines, Hugh gave what seemed superb interviews. He sent up his desire to buy himself 'penis-extension cars' like a Porsche or Jaguar with his new Hollywood earnings, sighing that Elizabeth simply wouldn't allow it.

'She says its uncool at my age.'

He moaned comically about the press intrusions that were now an infuriating part of his and Elizabeth's existence. His social life, he said, had been wiped out as a result.

'If I go out, it's "Hugh has been a naughty boy" or "Who's *that* you're with, Hugh?" ' He talked up a storm about *Nine Months*; about his mutual (and merciless) teasing mateyness with Tom Arnold (who had rapidly been taken up as Hugh's newest best friend on set); confessed – out of the blue – to being 'an old-fashioned English pervert obsessed with ladies' underwear'; and added a new line to his usual description of his and Elizabeth's relationship as mostly a brother-and-sister one:

'Which isn't to say that's not a sexy thing. Because I think the idea of incest is quite titillating.'

How close Hugh comes, time and again, to almost directly quoting Nabakov's Humbert Humbert on the subject of the thrill of the thought of incest!

The intended effect of these new confessions isn't difficult to fathom. Here was the Mark II Hugh Grant: more daring, *naughtier*, a little darker than the old model – but not so naughty as to reveal his old image as a sham. It is, of course, a path trodden by thousands of actors before him; the careful tweaking of public perceptions to create a more fascinating screen persona, while taking great pains not to crack the original mould.

However, in Hugh's case, these larkily off-the-cuff, off-colour comments would prove too little, far too late to ballast him against a sex scandal. His quotes were about to blow up in his face in a spectacularly embarrassing manner.

Even as the copies of *Premiere* and *Vogue* were hitting the news stands with their merrily Hugh-friendly interviews, the world's celebrity press from both sides of the Atlantic was hitting Los Angeles on the scent of very fresh blood indeed.

Elizabeth Hurley had just received two of the most hurtful phone calls of her life. One from her agent – and one, a few seconds later, from Hugh. On 27 June 1995, Hugh wasn't tucked in bed alone at 1.15 a.m. Hugh Grant was lounging, unzipped and thighs splayed, in the front seat of a white BMW receiving the attentive professional services of a Los Angeles street tart.

TWENTY-SIX

'What's goin' on?'
A horrified Hugh to vice cops
on 27 June 1995

'Then on the last night I made my big mistake, and
hit that bad business I told you about. I don't like to
sound judgemental, but it really was a big mistake. I
was surging down Sunset Boulevard: purely on
impulse I hung a left near Scheldt's where I've seen
those sweet little black chicks parading in tiny pastel
shorts . . . Anyway, the upshot is, one way or
another, I'm lying in the front seat of the Boomerang
with my trousers round my knees and copping a
twenty-dollar blowjob . . .'

Martin Amis, Money, 1984

He was just another dumb guy who got unlucky, no
different from hundreds of other similarly unlucky dumb
guys routinely scooped up in the red-light district of
Hollywood's Sunset Strip and he merited no different
treatment. So ran the official line from the Los Angeles
Police Department's Hollywood division after booking
suspect no. 4454813 on 27 June 1995.

But the world might be forgiven for supposing otherwise
when it awoke, on Wednesday, 28 June, to discover
gleefully splashed across newspaper front pages the ashen-
faced police mugshot of the screen star, and of the prostitute with whom he'd been caught in the murky pre-dawn
hours the day before on a Sunset Boulevard sidestreet. And
alongside the full-colour mugshots sat the publication of
Hugh's arrest sheet – offering details about the actor in a
style that at first reads like a publicist's weary response to
a fan magazine questionnaire – 'Height 5-11: Hair Bro:

Eyes Blu: Weight 175: Birthdate 09 09 60'. But side by side with it was information of a strikingly different nature:

Time arr 0115, Time bkd 0229 . . . Location of arrest 7560 Hawthorn Av . . . Charge and code 647 (A)PC . . . Definition LEWD CONDUCT . . . Bail $250'.

What had seemed publicly unthinkable just 24 hours earlier was now cold newsprint fact. And it had, in fact, been confirmed by the ever-helpful Los Angeles Police Department's press office with commendable speed. A fax was received by the London office of *The Times* from the press office a record 33 minutes after Hugh's arrest.

Police stated that Hugh had been under observation by two plain-clothes vice squad officers from the moment he'd entered their patch shortly before 1 a.m. on 27 June. There was only one likely reason for a brand-new, flashily expensive, white BMW to be cruising the sleazy half-mile strip at that hour and two patrolling officers – Terry Bennyworth and Ernest Caldera – intuitively marked the anonymous male driver as a potential suspect. They'd have bet their badges that here was a rich guy looking for paid sex.

Their suspicions were doubly confirmed when Hugh kerb-crawled alongside a 'known prostitute', Divine Brown (born Estelle Marie Thompson on 8 August 1969), on the corner of Courtney and Sunset, the district's most active and intensely policed haunt of heterosexual hookers.

There was an initial wobble of hesitation on Hugh's part, a last split second of sane thinking. Officers Bennyworth and Caldera observed the BMW idling past the streetwalker, then it doubled back and pulled up alongside her. The driver was seen furtively motioning Thompson to climb into the passenger seat, motoring quickly to the quieter, nearby residential street of Hawthorn Avenue and then parking the vehicle in deep shadow between dim streetlights.

The vice cops simply cooled their heels for several minutes (to allow an offence to get under way), then rushed the car, one from each side, first peering through the side windows with their flashlights to observe the expected 'lewd act' in progress and then bawling at the shocked couple to get out. For the next few seconds, procedures went strictly by the book – with a hangdog Hugh quietly replying 'sixty dollars' in answer to the question how much he had paid for the prostitute's services and producing identification.

It was then, Thompson would later reveal, that the arrest – both she and Hugh were now in handcuffs – took a bizarre turn. As she sat in the back of an unmarked police car waiting to be taken in for booking, she noticed the arresting officers calling excitedly to other police nearby and gesturing towards Hugh. There was something definitely out of the ordinary about this suspect, though Thompson was still unaware of the truth. This john's ID wasn't just in his wallet – it was also plastered the length of Sunset Boulevard on huge 20th Century Fox billboards promoting the upcoming summer comedy blockbuster, *Nine Months*.

As every single one of the famously Hollywood-savvy LA cops could have told Hugh that morning, 'Son, your sense of timing needs some *serious* attention.'

Hugh had, of course, long known that his charming, big-budget 'date movie' *Nine Months*, was to open across America in mid-July. For weeks, after all, his entire life had revolved around the results of preview screenings – and his appearance, with Elizabeth expected at his side, at the Hollywood première. He was immersed in recording TV interviews for the major USA networks and was booked to promote the film on America's influential live late-night TV talk shows. He was perfectly aware, too, that Elizabeth was – that same week – launching *her* all-important perfume campaign for Estée Lauder in London with the attendant fanfare of a press conference, personal appearances and interviews. The name of this new scent was, most unhappily as it turned out for Elizabeth, 'Pleasures'.

The Hollywood division's police mugshot of Hugh Grant shows a man wishing with all his heart he was elsewhere. His mouth is a tight drawstring purse. His hair is still visibly flattened by the LA Dodgers baseball cap he wore, according to Ms Thompson, pulled low over his face when they began their encounter – and now, as per police regulations for such photos, absent. He wears a sagging, unbuttoned, unbecoming, striped, short-sleeved shirt and his shoulders are hunched in defeat.

In contrast to the 34-year-old actor, 25-year-old 'Divine Brown', with a prior police record for prostitution, and in a skin-tight scarlet top, has her arms folded defensively over her bare midriff and her chin raised, and the expression on her remarkably pretty face appears to be just fractionally escaping a sneer.

The newspaper reports accompanying the mugshots all carried the actor's statement of confession and contrition, hastily issued by Hugh's publicists: 'Last night I did something completely insane. I have hurt people I love and embarrassed people I work with. For both things I am more sorry than I can say.'

In the hectic hours after the arrest, the Los Angeles police were cheerfully obliging in offering further sound-bites on Hugh's sexual Waterloo. Yes, indeed, Hugh could be jailed for the offence, face a $1,000 fine – or both – and be forced to undergo AIDS education. Yes, this was the standard punishment for the offence – and any prior convictions would, of course, be taken into consideration. No, the film star hadn't proved a difficult arrest: quite the reverse, he'd been 'extremely embarrassed' to be sure but 'very nice and cooperative'.

The trickle of information from LA swelled into a flood of furious commentary and questions. The most obvious – posed by the US chat-show host Jay Leno on the first of Hugh's gulping *mea culpa* TV appearances a fortnight after his arrest – was, 'What the hell were you *thinking*?' The next was, 'What on earth does Elizabeth say?' And so on, through to the most likely impact of the arrest on his career, especially with Hugh's court appearance scheduled for 18 July – just three days after the opening weekend of *Nine Months*.

There were reports of initial disbelief and confusion among 20th Century Fox studio bosses at how a meticulously orchestrated, and reportedly $10 million, promotional campaign for *Nine Months* had apparently been torpedoed by its star – all for the thrill of wearing a mint-flavoured condom for 20 minutes of unclimaxed oral sex with a Hollywood hooker.

Yet as the details unfolded, some of Hugh's friends wondered if the actor had, in a truly bizarre way, been inspired by a book – specifically, Martin Amis's 1984 cult black comedy, *Money*, which is about greed and the pursuit of personal gratification in the film capitals of New York, London and Los Angeles.

A copy of *Money* is on the bookshelves of almost every Brit in Los Angeles involved in the film world. On page 158 of the US Viking edition is a detailed description of the book's fast-living, anti-hero film director on the loose in LA. Riding high on the success of his film being shown that very week in LA – as *Nine Months* was in preview cinemas – the drunken, seedily glamorous character rents a Boomerang car and 'on impulse', while cruising down Sunset Boulevard, where he has been previously captivated by the sight of pretty young black hookers in their micro hotpants, picks one up, turns into a residential street, parks his car and shells out a 'bargain' twenty bucks for a front-seat blow-job. Martin Amis, who appears as 'himself' in his dazzling novel, even has the character refer repeatedly to the hooker incident as a 'bad mistake' and 'bad business', as Hugh would later do on the US talk shows.

The novel's narrator, while exulting in the sordid thrill of the encounter, is also interrupted in mid-session and his first horrified thought is that he's been caught by the vice squad. In fact he is being bawled out by an irate housewife in whose drive he has parked his car. He escapes – revelling over and again in his huge good luck – back to his regular girlfriend, whom he loves to see dressed in 'brothel' underwear.

Was it possible that Hugh Grant, who sometimes complained to journalists that he wasn't sure who he was, couldn't even cheat on Elizabeth without a script?

Hugh's Awfully Enormous Misadventure began the weekend of 24 June when he and his *Nine Months* co-stars, including Tom Arnold and Jeff Goldblum, were wheeled on to face the press in Los Angeles for a grinding round of publicity interviews. These assembly-line events with stars doling out rigidly timed chunks of quotes to dozens of journalists one at a time, hour after hour – in order to furnish each writer with an 'exclusive' chat – are loathed alike by both actors and reporters. Unfortunately film publicists have yet to devise a less humiliating method of giving stars mass exposure to the maximum number of publications.

The *Nine Months* junket at the Beverly Hills Four Seasons Hotel that weekend before the arrest was no exception. Hugh, say journalists present, looked exhausted and white-faced, and was clearly running on empty after enduring a day of trying to transmit his trademark charm and caustic wit in 40 separate interviews, each at four-minute intervals. Hugh also told the *San Francisco Chronicle* that he'd experienced a thoroughly draining Friday night before the press meetings carousing with Tom Arnold.

'I tried to have a fun night with Tom. But I got too drunk too quickly because Tom doesn't drink. People kept buying him bottles of champagne, and I was his drinker of the evening.' The night, noted Hugh, casually, ended at 'a couple of low dives which I can't even remember'.

Monday, 26 June, was Hugh's day off before a major *Nine Months* press conference on Tuesday. He shared a sushi-and-sake restaurant supper with the *Nine Months* director Chris Columbus and the men – buoyed by excellent preview test-screening reports on the film – parted shortly after midnight. Hugh then apparently changed his mind about meeting some 'new' Hollywood friends at a private music recording session, and was slowly cruising on Sunset Boulevard in the small hours of Tuesday when green-eyed Divine, soliciting right under the noses of a vice patrol in a tiny red miniskirt, her cushiony lips painted scarlet, caught his eye . . .

After his arrest, after being freed without having to post the usual $250 bail – and following the famously 'short and tearful' confessional phone call he placed from the police station to Elizabeth at their film production office in London (at about noon British time) – Hugh slunk back to the Four Seasons to face his incredulous co-stars and director, to make exquisitely painful further calls to his parents, and prepare a hasty statement for his publicists. It was of scant comfort to Elizabeth that at least her boyfriend hadn't gone straight from his illicit tryst back to their beloved flat above Sunset Strip.

If there had ever been a moment – from the blood-freezing second the first vice officer flashed his torch through the window and yelled at him to get out of the car – that Hugh imagined he could prevent his misdemeanour becoming public, it was long gone. The Tuesday *Nine Months* press conference at the Four Seasons was abruptly called off. Hugh, a statement insisted, had a stomach complaint which kept him confined to his hotel room. Even as journalists invited to the press conference were frostily gathering up their tape recorders and wondering suspiciously exactly what magnitude of 'stomach' complaint could prevent a new star boosting his first big Hollywood movie, copies of the *Nine Months* promotional poster, showing the actress Julianne Moore whispering into Hugh's ear, were already being merrily faxed between film production offices throughout Los Angeles – all with suitably smutty amendments. '*Nine Months* – to One Year for sex with a Hooker' read the film's 'new' title.

'It was a pure LA moment – par excellence,' crowed one insider mercilessly.

Wednesday, 28 June, found Hugh whisked out of Los Angeles and in hiding at his brother's Manhattan apartment. Across the Atlantic Elizabeth saw her London debut as Estée Lauder's fragrant new cover face collapse hopelessly into farce as she was mobbed for comment on her boyfriend and the hooker. The contrast with the storm of rapturous attention the actress won wearing *that* bombshell Versace dress at Hugh's *Four Weddings* London première just a year earlier could not have been more cruel. Britain's Secretary of State for British Heritage expressed, briefly, his sympathy for Hugh. The British film industry, he added, was unlikely to collapse as a result of this one-off incident.

Elizabeth skulked tearfully at the West London flat of her upper-class protector – the devoted Brocklehurst – while the latter – adding yet another rich pleat to the drama (he's actually a stepcousin of Prince Charles's mistress, Camilla Parker Bowles) – gave out occasional, somewhat batty, bulletins about the state of his ward's emotions. 'Bearing up well . . . terribly crushed' and so forth. Five and a half thousand miles away the sweaty week-long siege of Sunset Boulevard began in earnest with the Los Angeles correspondent of a British tabloid nailing 'wanted' posters to palm trees, offering the elusive Divine $150,000 for her exclusive story.

Not since the hunt for the Great Train Robber Ronnie Biggs in Rio, noted one senior journalist, had so many reporters swarmed over one place with so precious few hard leads. Sunset Boulevard's prostitutes began demanding a minimum of $20 in advance before they would open their mouths to reporters. A number of reporters handed over wads of cash to enterprising pimps claiming to 'represent' Thompson, only to see the pimps, their promises – and the advance payments – melt into the night.

On Thursday, 29 June, Elizabeth braved the London press launch of the new Lauder perfume. Her cosmetics contract, she'd been advised, was not in jeopardy over Hugh's astonishing indiscretion (*though it hasn't exactly been ideal all round has it?* seemed to be the irritated subtext). But Hugh – now back in Los Angeles and preparing to board a private jet for England – could find little genuine cheer in the personal letters and messages of support that had started to arrive from friends and even from, he later claimed, 'famous film stars'; nor even in the kudos of having the personal services of Hollywood's most prominent 'celebrity' lawyer, Howard Weitzman, secured for him.

He was a lawyer whose own star had, in truth, dimmed recently. In 1993, he had spectacularly failed to prove that Kim Basinger had had the right to withdraw from a starring role in the movie *Boxing Helena* two years previously, a failure that left the actress with a staggering $6 million settlement filed against her. The lawyer's reputation as a no-holds-barred fighter on behalf of illustrious clients had also been shaken by his resignation from the O.J. Simpson defence team after just two days. This was despite his having been a friend of Simpson's since the late 1960s.

It was on Thursday that Elizabeth announced to the world, 'I am still bewildered and saddened by recent events and have not been in a fit state to make any decisions about the future. For years I have turned to Hugh for help in difficult times and so now, even though my family and friends have been very kind, I am very much alone.'

Broadly speaking, Elizabeth was spitting furious, hurt beyond consolation and in no mood to offer instant forgiveness, as her mother, Angela, later obliquely confirmed to reporters. With that, the actress fled to the rented farmhouse at West Littleton, near Bath – with an unshakeable cortège of a dozen press motorcycles and four cars in eager pursuit all along the M4 motorway.

Friday, 30 June, at 1.15 a.m. – three days almost to the second since being booked by the Los Angeles vice cops – Hugh, too, drew up at the farmhouse, in a black Mercedes with tinted windows. Later that day, long-lens photos of the couple lunching tensely alone together in the garden flashed round the world.

When a double mattress was delivered to the farmhouse, a reporter's call to the mattress company confirmed that Elizabeth had ordered it the day of Hugh's arrest and had been unusually specific about its destination. 'It is,' she had told a company representative, apparently with studied deliberation, 'for the *spare* room.' (This would later be revealed as a red herring: Elizabeth claims she had simply ordered it for friends expected that weekend.)

Saturday, 1 July. Elizabeth publicly abandoned Hugh to the company of his housekeeper at the farmhouse, seeking solace with Brocklehurst again, this time sweeping off – her bags packed – to his Sudeley Castle estate in Gloucestershire. She permitted photographers a parting glimpse of herself, pale and downcast, in a chic and childish summer frock studded with large plastic ladybirds. The dress was chosen with considerable thought. Now was the time to promote a demure image. To distance herself, in fashion terms, from the remotest association with hookers.

Now was *not* the time to awaken anyone's memory of her cheeky bare-bottomed pose just a few months before for the front cover of the UK's *Sunday Times* magazine. Or of her boyfriend's secret preference for dressing her up in the tightest hotpants and white knee-length boots.

'They wouldn't understand [this outfit] at all in LA,' Elizabeth had joked four years earlier, referring to the boots and hotpants. 'They'd think I was a hooker.'

Now was most certainly not the moment to remind the world of Elizabeth's more explicitly raunchy poses published the previous year in the British magazine for males not yet out of adolescence, *Loaded*.

Neither Elizabeth nor Hugh, it was reported, showed up that Saturday for the London wedding of one of Hugh's most staunchly loyal and oldest friends, his former flatmate and co-comedy writer, Chris Laing. Though the intention may well have been to prevent turning the occasion into a media circus – or into an anarchic out-take from *Four Weddings* – sadly, the timing of Hugh's fall from grace was most hurtful to those closest to him.

Again, on 2 August, he was conspicuous by his absence from the London première of *The Englishman Who Went Up a Hill but Came Down a Mountain*, though this time the actor was candid about the reason for his absence – fear of attracting the wrong type of publicity for the film.

Sunday, 2 July. In Britain, and later America, Hugh's crowning humiliation materialized with a three-page exclusive interview in the shamelessly prurient British tabloid, the *News of the World*, with Estelle Marie Thompson, a.k.a. Tuesday's tart, Divine Brown. In prose that seemed authentically detailed if sounding highly rehearsed, Ms Thompson – once a wannabe actress herself and a mother of three – shared her brief encounter with the screen idol. Her client, she alleged, had demurred at wearing a condom (she had had to insist), called her 'gorgeous' and his 'black sex fantasy,' had been rougher than she liked, and kept his radio tuned to an easy-listening music station during business. (This radio station would later, sleazily, attempt to cash in on its tiny part in the scandal by booking Ms Thompson for a series of advertisements: the idea was rapidly dropped after vociferous complaints about its poor taste.)

She revealed that they might have escaped detection altogether if only he'd coughed up the $40 extra needed for sex in her room, instead of a lewd act in the front seat of his hired car. When asked by a broadly grinning police officer back at the station whether she was the ' "one who was with the movie star . . . Hugh Grant," ' she shot back, 'Who the hell is Hugh Grant?' Now she knew. He was the $60 'john', who was currently reaping her a reported $160,000 in exclusive interview fees, that's who.

And Divine obligingly posed in a scarlet version of Elizabeth's infamous Versace dress for the newspaper's front page, and – on page three – in a miniskirt and thigh-high plastic boots identical to those worn by Julia Roberts in her role as the Cinderella prostitute in *Pretty Woman* to prove how very, very fast she'd caught on.

In the next fortnight, figures as diverse as Newt Gingrich, America's House Speaker, and the celebrated murder trial defendant O.J. Simpson, found themselves caught in the tailspin of the Hugh Grant scandal.

Much closer to home back in the UK, Hugh's parents found themselves under intense, and intensely disliked, siege at their cherished Chiswick home.

The media dragon, which their beautiful, talented and unpredictable younger son seemed to have brought tamely to heel in recent months, was now a fire-and-brimstone-breathing monster.

The Grants' elderly neighbours were badgered mercilessly for quotes. James and Fynvola Grant, who had staunchly guarded their privacy throughout Hugh's meteoric rise, were hounded for comments on the way to 60-year-old James's out-patient hospital appointments.

Hugh's 'lewd act', they read, had transformed their boy into a legitimate target for comparison to every Hollywood rotter and sexual rogue, from Roscoe 'Fatty' Arbuckle (tried, formally acquitted but never forgiven in 1921 for killing a young actress at a party by stabbing ice into her vagina – a crime for which he may have been framed in the first place) and Errol Flynn (ruined in 1942, even though also acquitted – on under-age sex charges), through to Roman Polanski and his still-standing statutory rape charge, Woody Allen and his scandalous attachment to his ex-lover's adopted daughter, and the Brat Pack actor Rob Lowe, who was caught on video enjoying a three-in-a-bed romp, sending his career into a nose-dive. In print, as in his private life, Hugh Grant was keeping some extremely unsavoury company.

Hugh, meanwhile, though already exhausted to the bone before the arrest, was shuttling back and forth – grey-faced and bedevilled by sinus problems – between London, New York and Los Angeles. He was worried sick and genuinely guilty, he told friends, by the strain under which he'd placed his family and Elizabeth. His parents, for their part, ached for his predicament.

His brief attempt at a reconciliation with Elizabeth hadn't worked and the friends the actress 'permitted' to comment about her to the press – Brocklehurst and the journalist William Cash – appeared to be speaking with more hope than certainty that the couple had any genuine long-term future. But now he owed it to Hollywood to make amends. He specifically owed his studio, his *Nine Months* co-stars and his director, Chris Columbus, to turn his disgrace – somehow – into audience-attracting column-inches. He also owed it to Mike Newell, as director of *Four Weddings*, and therefore the architect of Hugh's spectacular rise, and also as the director of the new Hugh Grant film to be released in the USA just one week after *Nine Months*: *An Awfully Big Adventure*.

By the beginning of the second week of July, Hugh appeared to face an impossible task. He'd achieved mega-stardom, his face on magazine covers the world over, his mugshot on T-shirts, his name on everyone's lips (even, reportedly, those of the Princess of Wales). Yet – against all expectations – Hugh was about to deliver the goods.

TWENTY-SEVEN

'You must stir it and stump it,
And blow your own trumpet
Or trust me, you haven't a chance.'

W.S. Gilbert

'I believe that England is ... capable of not seeing
anything but badness in me, for ever and ever. I
believe America is my virgin soil, truly.'

D.H. Lawrence (letter)
after experiencing publishing problems

On Monday, 10 July 1995, queues of fans began throng-
ing as early as 4.30 a.m. outside the NBC television
studios in Burbank, California – where *The Tonight Show*
with Jay Leno is recorded before an audience at
11.30 a.m. for broadcast twelve hours later. The lure of a
live peek at the most gossiped-about actor on the planet
drew pre-dawn rubber-neckers in their panting hundreds
to the studios' parking lots. Some had driven through the
night from neighbouring states. A number sported the
notorious police mugshot T-shirts of Hugh. One woman
doggedly paraded with a placard: 'I would have paid you,
Hugh!' (but told reporters she was, in fact, married and
was simply having a little fun).

A passable Hugh Grant lookalike turned up, spouting
lines from *Four Weddings*, to jostle and crane alongside
TV crews from as far away as Japan and Australia, and all
apparently resigned to a seven-hour vigil as temperatures
rose to a sweaty 92°F.

They were at least rewarded with a brief appearance
from Leno himself – megaphone in hand – begging them
with a broad grin to 'go back to your homes!'

Inside the studio, as Leno's often brilliantly satirical show finally got under way, the ticket-only studio audience shuffled, fidgeted and whispered, desperate for the host's opening routine of gags to give way to the main meat.

For the former stand-up comedian Jay Leno then came one of the sweetest moments of his career. Since taking over the cherished American institution of *The Tonight Show* from Johnny Carson three years earlier, Leno had been locked into a bitter ratings war with his rival chat show king, David Letterman. Their five-nights-a-week shows are screened simultaneously coast to coast. Night after night, Letterman pulled the bigger audience. But there was no doubt which channel America would be tuning into *this* evening.

After 30 minutes of teasing wisecracks, and with the watermelon smile of a show-host who can just feel his ratings heading for the stratosphere, Leno thundered, '*Hugh Grant!*' to a deafening whistlestorm of cheers and foot-stomping as the actor sloped into view – sober-suited, blinking and twitching – from the wings of the studio, and the band struck up a tune later identified as 'Superfly'.

And, for one perfectly pitched moment, it seemed that the chat-show format *could* make high entertainment and hard information one and the same, with Leno's roguishly direct opening shot, 'What the *hell* were you thinking of?'

Hugh side-stepped the salvo so deftly, you barely noticed the footwork. 'Um, well, it's, er, it's, er, it's not easy. The thing is, um, people keep giving me tons of ideas on this one. I keep reading new psychological theories – I was under pressure, over-tired, or I was lonely, or I fell down the stairs when I was a child or whatever. That would be bollocks to hide behind that. I think you know in life pretty much what's a good thing to do and what's a bad thing and I did a bad thing. There you have it.'

The warmly sympathetic applause greeting his words – soon to be echoed by Hugh's friends in private – virtually dictated Leno his next soft lob. Short of risking alienating his star guest by rephrasing the same question ('So you reckoned you could get away with hiring a hooker?'), the genial Leno graciously opened the way for Hugh to stammer through a series of 'the kindness of strangers' themed soundbites.

'The public has, uh, been really fantastic . . . I mean the people who really matter in this case are my girlfriend and family and stuff like that . . . but it's been really touching to me . . . I've received tons of letters from everyone from f-f-famous filmstars I haven't met to incredibly interesting letters from people with problems like epilepsy; then you really realize, you know, my problems aren't so bad.' (The audience took this at face value but Hugh's comment about 'letters from people with problems like epilepsy' recalls a line he spun to his old university newspaper, *The Cherwell*, in 1994, about mainly receiving fan mail from 'people in wheelchairs' adding hastily 'which is, of course, lovely'.)

Leno chummily offered the opinion that Los Angeles 'is an odd town in its way, in that people seem to react . . . with glee when [something bad happens] to someone as successful as yourself. People love to be the first to jump in there – and whatever!'

But Hugh refused, charmingly, to act the victim: 'I didn't really ever think it would become the circus it has become. I see that there's juice in it, and I'm sure if I wasn't the person who had perpetrated this whole thing, I would be enjoying it as much as anyone else. But it's pretty miserable on the other side of the equation. But you know it's not just for me. It's bad when they're jostling your father . . . Sex was never the main topic of conversation in our house, but having said that, it was so touching. People like my father were wonderful, you know. I called him and that's a bad phone call to have to make, but he said, "Look here, old boy, I was in the army; I know about this sort of thing." He was cool, very cool . . .'

And Hugh was good, very good.

But his televised chagrin with Leno wasn't entirely swallowed hook and all by the American viewers – the *New York Post* was far from alone in its subsequent arch poll of readers when it asked, 'Star's sorrow: Was it just an act?' There was little doubt the actor was pulling out all stops to *appear* sincere. As the film essayist Anthony Lane, generously reviewing Hugh's Leno performance in the urbane *New Yorker* magazine, also pointed out, 'Sorrow can be an act and still be genuinely ghastly – even more so, because of the effort required to keep it up.'

Hugh returned time and again, and unprompted, to the side impact of the scandal on Elizabeth: 'I completely understand everyone having a good joke about it. If I'd been a single guy it would be hysterical by now. But it's really not funny when you've got someone like this. Like I've said, I've done an abominable thing. She's been amazing about it . . . She's been very supportive and we're going to try to work it out. Time is of the essence.'

It was all terribly *Brief Encounter*-ish. And it was, of course, terrific TV.

As Hugh relaxed further into his 'ordeal', he bounced off some lovely one-liners. To Leno's swipe at the British tabloids that they 'are far, far worse than the American press', he offered the cool rejoinder, 'They have never been famous for their restraint,' and 'That's been interesting. It's hard to keep your temper, and I've managed to a point, but my father taught me a very interest-ing thing. He doesn't bother. He just says: "Ill-mannered buggers . . ." '

(Interesting, too, is this tendency of turning his family into a gallery of eccentric, comic supporting characters in his private drama, which would have evolved further by Hugh's next TV appearance.)

And by the stage he was permitted by Leno to start promoting *Nine Months* – the reason, of course, he'd been booked on the show – Hugh was sufficiently unbuttoned to let slip the one line that sounded suspiciously rehearsed and timed in advance for laughs. There was the smallest, but unmistakable, subtle signal to the audience that a hilariously unfortunate choice of words was heading their way when Hugh delivered his sexually double-entendre crowd-pleasing line: 'Though I've never been one to, uh, er [gazing ruefully about the studio as if only just –

and most uncharacteristically – aware of his coming verbal blunder] . . . blow my own trumpet, as they say, but it's a very funny film and I want people to see it.'

The West Coast's *Tonight Show* ratings for 10 July were, for the first time ever, double those of the East Coast's *Late Show*. A record 18.5 million tuned in. Hugh's appearance that night also inspired one of the sharpest newspaper cartoon takes on the whole muddied nature of celebrity, crime and public confessions. The *New York Post* of 12 July showed Jay Leno grinningly grilling O.J. Simpson, 'What the hell were you thinking?' with O.J. tearfully admitting, 'I've done an abominable thing', and Judge Lance Ito wiping his eyes. The following day the Hugh Grant circus continued in full swing.

Hugh's court case was held a week earlier than it had been listed, with the actor's A-list celebrity lawyer, Howard Weitzman, and Steve Cochran pleading 'no contest' on his behalf to the charge of lewd conduct in a public place. The plea, read out at the Los Angeles Municipal Court, effectively guaranteed Hugh a clean record if he stuck to the terms of the sentence, paying court costs, and fines to the tune of $1,180, agreeing to two years' unsupervised probation and delivering to the court, by November, a certificate proving he had undergone AIDS counselling.

As the city attorney's office – ever obliging in schooling the British media in the intricacies of lewd-conduct charges – explained, the only special treatment Hugh had merited was the change in court date. This was at the specific and reasonable request of his lawyers to avoid a media frenzy. There was nothing remotely unusual about Hugh waiving his right to appear in court either. It happened all the time. The actor would only be required to undergo a 'few hours' of counselling, and yes, he could do it in the UK. Hugh escaped the stiffest possible penalty for the offence, six months behind bars, because of his hitherto clean record.

Estelle Marie Thompson was not so lucky. When she was sentenced on 6 September – after changing an earlier not-guilty plea to the same quickie no-contest plea, two previous convictions for prostitution in 1993 tripped her up. By violating the terms of probation set for the 1993 offences, the 25-year-old mother was slapped with six months in jail, a $1,350 fine and five days' community service, and was ordered to take AIDS counselling.

Though Thompson didn't waive her right to appear in court, her smart pinstripe suit and her lawyer's claim that she had largely turned around her life since 27 June and had been doing 'charity work' cut little ice with Judge Robert Sandoval. Perhaps he, like the rest of the world, had been following reports of the young woman's non-charity work since her latest arrest.

These included an advertising spot for Brazilian television, promoting a line of lingerie. 'I love men. They're so much fun, so sure of themselves, so unpredictable. And yet – too bad for you – so fickle,' Thompson was shown saying, while riding in a limousine along Sunset Boulevard where she and Hugh had been arrested. 'So if you don't want to lose your man to someone else, if I were you I would wear Valisere.'

There were rumours of a porn movie and the spectacle of Thompson making advertisements for the Los Angeles radio station that had been playing in Hugh's car during their transaction – hastily pulled after a public outcry.

With his sentence, at least, out of the way, on Tuesday, 11 July, Hugh – all smiles – attended the première opening of *Nine Months* with, as widely tipped, Elizabeth – all deliberate scowls in a virginal white minidress – material-izing at his side for the event at Los Angeles' Century City complex. The movie was, of course, now unstoppably generating its own publicity. Preview audiences found themselves being polled by journalists eager to know whether Hugh's antics put them off his *Nine Months* film character as Samuel the child psychiatrist afraid of com-mitment (most said it hadn't). A mirth-provoking trailer for *Nine Months*, showing Hugh's film character in a police mugshot from a clip that had actually been cut from the finished movie itself, was summarily yanked from cinemas. A backup advertising campaign suddenly replaced the posters showing Hugh's co-star Julianne Moore whispering suggestively into the star's ear, which were being wittily defaced from coast to coast. The new posters carried baby pictures of the five leading actors instead. Tom Arnold did the talk-show rounds, loyally sticking up for Hugh and trotting out 'let him who is guiltless cast the first stone' speeches.

A visibly irritated Newt Gingrich, America's House Speaker, whose private life and unhappy marriage were also under intense media scrutiny, was even asked by reporters for *his* Hugh Grant comment. He refused to answer – but exploded at another reporter who asked the Republican politician what sort of underwear he favoured, 'You ought to be *ashamed* of yourself! I think it's *stupid* for you to ask that question!'

It was if the clock had been turned back over 30 years to the prurient furore unleashed in 1963 when a Mrs Eddie Fisher decided to become the second wife of a man who was still encumbered by a first wife, Mr Richard Burton. America had an unstoppable appetite for Hugh Grant and Elizabeth Hurley and was soon gobbling up the latest news from London, which confirmed the fury that lay behind the actress's fish-faced expression at the *Nine Months* première. Police acknowledged that Hugh's Earls Court flat had been broken into while he and Elizabeth were in Los Angeles, and that a dent in the bathroom door was an imprint of the actor's Bafta award for *Four Weddings*, which lay smashed on the floor. A letter of apology Hugh had written to Elizabeth was also found, angrily shredded.

The police did not appear to connect either of these small acts of vandalism with the 'opportunistic' burglary. Here was surely evidence, if any more was needed, of Elizabeth's legendary temper.

Meanwhile, back in America, the actor still had the most accidentally revealing of all his post-scandal television interviews to come – on CNN's *Larry King Live*.

TWENTY-EIGHT

*'This is the excellent foppery of the world, that,
when we are sick in fortune – often the surfeit of our
own behaviour – we make guilty of our own
disasters the sun, the moon, and the stars; as if we
were ... fools by heavenly compulsion ... liars and
adulterers by an enforced obedience of planetary
influence; and all that we are evil in, by a divine
thrusting on: an admirable evasion of whoremaster
man, to lay his goatish disposition to the charge
of a star!'*

*(Advice about not blaming the divine thrusting
of stars for one's goatish behaviour with
whores – Shakespeare,* King Lear, *I.ii. 131.
Familiar to Hugh Grant. Possible useful
inspiration for snappy television quotes.)*

'It was disloyal, shabby and goatish.'

*Hugh Grant to Larry King
on a similar subject, 12 July 1995*

Two days after his Leno show triumph, Hugh went
face-to-face in Los Angeles with CNN's six-nights-a-week
primetime talk-show host, Larry King. High hopes rode on
this interview. In his ten years of *Larry King Live*, broadcast in over 200 countries, the 61-year-old King has grilled
every notable and quotable in politics and entertainment,
among them Gorbachev and Brando, Sinatra and Clinton
and many more.

Though he's a highly erratic interviewer – best when
blithely unembarrassed asking the same hard question
over and over again, worst when clumsily trying to 'bond'
with an interviewee – King's almost non-existent sense of
irony functioned as a wonderful foil for Hugh's strategic

dives into meaningless larkiness. The tough, Brooklyn-raised Larry King – reliably said to earn $2.7 million a year from his talk show alone – of all Hugh's post-scandal interrogators and operating without the distraction of a live audience also came closest to peeling back a corner of the actor's public mask of abashed humility. But viewers who missed the chat-show host's brief explanation that guests appearing on the *second* half of his show, after Hugh Grant, were to be legal experts discussing the O.J. Simpson murder trial, might have been thrown by King's opener to the film star.

'The obvious question Hugh,' he barked. 'What do you think of the Simpson trial?'

After a small silence and a startled chuckle, Hugh – in an open-neck blue shirt in contrast to the formal suit and tie worn for Leno – plunged in, 'Yeah, well, the – you caught me out a bit because, um, the terrible thing is, I'm afraid I was enjoying it, only I didn't really know much about it in England. On my various trips here I started to – you know, you do get caught [up in it] even though it's phenomenally long and boring – you know, I found myself watching it for hours and now I feel dreadful because I know what it's like to be accused.'

King asked Hugh if he'd expected anything like the avalanche of comment he'd dislodged. 'Well, again, I didn't really realize that, before, actually this afternoon when someone finally dared to show me all the clippings . . .'

'You hadn't seen them?' asked King, a strangled note of disbelief in his voice.

Hugh: 'Well, I knew, I was aware of the British press storm but I didn't imagine anything could ever be worse than that. How wrong I was . . . I would rather be famous than notorious, I think . . . I said what I said on Jay Leno and I don't have excuses. I don't having anything more to say except I'm very sorry. I hope in the end people will perhaps let me get on with the rest of things and, especially, my biggest concern has always been, well not my *biggest*' (here Hugh pauses and laughs awkwardly, as if he were waiting for King to guffaw over the 'chance' double entendre of 'biggest'; King remains stonily silent and Hugh hurries on) '. . . but right up there, that people won't let it obscure this film, which is so funny . . .'

King: 'So was there a reverse fortune here in a sense that this will bring more attention to this film?'

Hugh: 'Certainly there were cynics, I think, who said that, and I don't suppose we'll ever know really, but, as I said, the bottom line is the film is already doing fantastic business so that's the main thing.'

King: 'Did they always plan a Wednesday open, a midweek open?'

Hugh: 'I don't know. Pass.'

King: 'The one thing you didn't answer – which is a fair question – is why?'

Hugh: 'Yeah, well, like I keep saying, I would think that would be a very difficult question to answer. Um . . .' Hugh keeps stammering a non-answer of sorts but King overrides him.

King: 'You're a performer, your popularity is growing and this stuns people. Everybody has skeletons in closets but we wonder *why* we do the things we do.'

Hugh: 'Right, yeah. Well I am very bad at that kind of thing.'

King: 'Self-examination?'

Hugh: 'Yeah, I honestly couldn't tell you. You know, as I said on Jay's show, I am prepared to accept some of the things that people have offered one, like stress or pressure or loneliness – and it would be lovely to say that was the reason – but I think that would also be a bit false. I think in the end you have to come clean and say it was disloyal, shabby and goatish.'

King (conspicuously underwhelmed by Hugh's Shakespearian turn of phrase): 'Don't you say *why* did I do this?'

Hugh (visibly growing in confidence): 'I think that's more of an American syndrome. [Then reining back a little] I mean, I really do.'

King: 'Whereas in Britain they would just say "bit of a bad goal"?'

Hugh: 'Well, they might not say that [smiling at King's uncertain lurch into the British vernacular] ... yeah, something like that.'

King (still doggedly offering a variation of the 'why' question): 'But there wouldn't be a lot of self-examination?'

Hugh: 'It's not the same in England. One thing I noticed making *Nine Months* was that every other actor in the cast was in analysis apart from me ...'

King: 'Are you comfortable in Hollywood? [Pause] That came out weird.'

Hugh: 'I was certainly *getting* comfortable. It's become a place – you know perfectly well, I'm sure, it's very nice when you are doing well and absolutely miserable if you're not and I did have stints here before when I was not doing very well and going to auditions when they don't even say "hello, Hugh, how nice to see you".'

King: Oh, you have been out?' (Like many Americans, Larry King seemed to be under the kindly illusion that Hugh was a fresh arrival in Hollywood rather than an *habitué* who had on and off – for years – stayed at his girlfriend's flat within handy hailing distance of the notorious Sunset Strip.)

Hugh (ever so casually): 'Yeah, I've come and done the rounds a couple of times.'

King: 'And been rejected?'

Hugh: 'Pretty summarily. Yeah, you know. You'd go to auditions and there'd be a sign: "actors sit here"; there would be no one even to say, "hello, welcome" and all that, so it's a pretty miserable place, I think, when you're not doing well. But having said that, when things were going well, um, absolutely delightful, if you like sycophancy.'

King: 'Do you think this kind of thing requires help ... and people who care?'

Hugh (appearing, not very convincingly, to misunderstand innocently): 'Er, I've got very good helpers actually. I've been lucky like that. Fabulous agent, fabulous PR, things like that. You *do* need help.'

King: 'That's exterior help. What about interior help?'

Hugh (accepting King's point): 'Oh you mean analysis?'

King: 'Not only analysis, psychology, some kind of ... why we do what we do. We've all done it.' (One trusts that Mr King means seeking professional analytical help, not hookers.)

Hugh: 'No, I don't know. I think I'm old-fashioned like that. In that, perhaps wrongly, I've always thought that if you read enough good books, you know, you're kind of sorted out in life, without having to go too self-centred and internal, which I think is the danger of too much analysis or psychoanalysis.' (It might have been more illuminating to American viewers if Hugh had explained that one of his all-time favourite 'good books,' his 'Bible' he calls it, was *Lolita*.)

King: 'Do you bring what you do, whatever you do in life, to [your acting]?'

Hugh: 'Well, you try to do that, now, especially in leading parts ... the key is to bring out a bit of yourself, otherwise there's too much acting going on.'

King (in truth, obviously not all *that* interested in Hugh's theories on acting): 'Do you resent the tabloids now?'

Hugh: 'Well, uh, I can't pretend they're my absolute best friends. Uh, in England when you've got two hundred long lenses pointed into your house, you can't even move from room to room without being front page. And when they're cruel about – you see, as I said before, I think it's fine to be a bit cruel about me and in fact it feels sort of right to be suffering, but when they have a go at Elizabeth, who is a victim in this, or when they jostle my father, who is not very well and on the way to hospital, it makes you hate them a bit, yeah.'

King (stung to a note of genuine outrage, perhaps mindful of his own recent hospital stay for heart surgery): 'They *bothered* your *father* on the way to *hospital*?'

Hugh: 'Yeah, and to get me to come out of the house, in the country, in England, they at one stage called an ambulance – to the house. They wanted their picture but there might have been someone dying in the street who needed the ambulance I suppose.' (This apparent concern for the hypothetical person dying in the street comes across staggeringly weakly and is oddly reminiscent of Hugh's over-the-top take on his own drink-driving convictions in 1985 and 1986, of which he said, 'It was disgraceful . . . I could have killed a *child*.')

King: 'It's also reported that you and she [clearly meaning Elizabeth, not Divine Brown] have broken up. That's not true. Or is it?'

Hugh: 'Well, of course the vast majority of things are not true. Apparently I lost [her] a contract with Nina Ricci – I've never even *heard* of Nina Ricci.' (This is the equivalent of a Shakespeare scholar claiming ignorance of *Hamlet*. It is highly unlikely that Hugh is unfamiliar with Nina Ricci. The products of this exclusive perfume and clothing house sell at superior outlets worldwide – like Saks Fifth Avenue and Harrods – and rank alongside Pierre Cardin, Christian Dior and YSL. Hugh is a connoisseur *par excellence* of designer names and has long boasted about showering Elizabeth with tight and sexy clothes by Alaia, Chanel and Agnes B, casting himself as a wealthy Richard Gere figure indulging his own Pretty Woman. Before the New York première of *An Englishman Who Went Up a Hill but Came Down a Mountain* in May, Hugh and Elizabeth roamed Fifth Avenue's finest boutiques, picking a Chanel coat for the actress and matching it to two South Sea pearl necklaces – one black, one white – which were lent to her for the evening. Store assistants recalled Hugh hovering over Elizabeth, telling her which designers best suited her.)

King (though clearly innocently unaware that the actor facing him is ridiculously claiming not to have heard of one of the biggest fashion names in the world – Nina Ricci – despite boasting elsewhere about reading *Vogue* from cover to cover every month shrewdly refuses to take the Ricci red herring): 'So you are together?'

Hugh: 'Yeah, we're together. Yeah. We are. As I said before we're trying to make the best of it. I mean I can't say to you, you know, everything is going to be rosy, um, because only time will tell. The wounds are still relatively fresh.'

King: 'Why do you think we are – as Sinatra [a great buddy of King's] once said – why are people so perversely interested in bad things that happen to people who entertain them?'

Hugh (after a half-giggle): 'I don't know – gosh, that's deep again. I know I am and that's terrible, of course.'

King (interview now wandering into the realms of the surreal): 'If it were Jack Lemmon, you'd be saying "Jack!"' (uttered in a tone of mournful reproach).

Hugh: 'Not if it were Jack Lemmon. That would be horrible if it was Jack Lemmon. If it was some rival, yeah, I'd be thoroughly enjoying it. I've never made any pretence about that. Um, and like I said before, I like the O.J. trial . . .'

King: 'So you *would* be reading about this?'

Hugh: 'Oh yeah.'

King: 'That's a frank admission. That's British too, isn't it? In America they'd say, "I hate all of them and never pay attention to them".'

Hugh: 'Right. Well, no, I'm afraid I have – enjoyed previous scandals. I never rang the hotline you could ring in England to listen in to the Princess of Wales talking . . .'

King (eagerly): 'Were you tempted?'

Hugh: 'Of course. I think we all were. But I never did and that's the main thing.'

King: 'Were you bothered by some of the bad reviews?' (Meaning for *Nine Months*, not Thompson's *News of the World* blow-by-blow account of 27 June.)

Hugh: 'In a way we were encouraged that there were a few sniffy ones, because Chris Columbus [the film's director] told me there were a few sniffy ones for *Mrs Doubtfire* and *Home Alone One* and *Two* and all those films took over a hundred and fifty million dollars at the box office so we think it's a good sign.' (By the end of the boom summer season of 1995, *Nine Months* had grossed only just over $60 million – not substantially more than it had cost to make – at the US box office. For a movie to earn serious money, the rule of thumb remains that it needs to take about three times the cost of production. Entertainments analysts widely agreed that, judged on its star cast, budget and high profile, it was a summer 'loser' – especially compared with *Apollo 13* at $153 million, *Die Hard with a Vengeance* at $98 million, *Pocahontas* at $134 million, and the cash cow of them all *Batman Forever*, which raked in $181 million.)

King: 'Are you – Tom Hanks told us that he tries not to be – box office oriented? He realizes that people are going to say how much did it take in but he tries not to . . . Same with you?'

Hugh: 'That's a whole new ball game to me, the box office . . .'

King: 'Because you were appearing in low budget [films] right?'

Hugh: 'Right, where you never particularly thought about that. I don't know what you *were* thinking about – art, I suppose. Now it does enter the equation. It will be difficult in the future – if I have a future – to balance, to balance these two things.'

King (pouncing): 'Good question. *Do* you have a future?'

Hugh: 'Well, um, I don't know. I'm the most pessimistic person to ask in the world. People are being, I must say, very kind.'

King: 'Your career's gone through the roof now, all the attention focused on you. Therefore more people will see your talent. It didn't change your talent did it?'

Hugh: 'Well, um, no I don't suppose it changed anything like that, but I don't know – I always look on the dark side.'

King: 'Well, let's say you didn't know Hugh Grant and you're a citizen of the United States. Would you go and see this movie out of curiosity?'

Hugh: 'Well, yes I would. Yes, we'd have to say so. It's a must.'

King: 'So it's a kind of a plus. There would be some people who think you did this to gain attention –'

Hugh: 'I think there are a few . . .'

King: 'There are better ways to gain attention?'

Hugh (sarcastically): 'You would have thought there would be a few. Yes.'

King: 'What do you do now, career-wise?'

Hugh: 'Well I have a couple of things. I have a development deal with one of the studios, Castle Rock, and there's a thriller in particular that I think I might – non-comedic, yeah, which would be interesting for a change. I've done about five comedies in a row.'

King: 'What's been the reaction to this?'

Hugh: 'Hollywood-wise, if that's what you mean. It's been fantastic. Yeah, the offers are coming in thick and fast. Then, people on the street, absolutely terrific too. As I said on Jay's show, *tons* of letters, fabulous letters. People especially, I think, on this side of the Atlantic have always been so generous to me and up. I think they basically want to see the best in people and that's not always the same with us nasty Brits . . .'

(Here the veteran King reveals just why he has kept his show on the air for ten years – and why, too, the viewer sometimes experiences an urge to throttle him. His next question shows he has no intention of being lamely led up Hugh's garden path about the 'nastiness of Brits'.)

King: 'Has this happened to you before? [Then, unaccountably, before Hugh has time to answer] It's none of our business . . .' (leaving the actor able to respond with a startled laugh).

Hugh: 'No, quite!'

King (recovering well): 'You've never done anything like this before?'

Hugh (not quite so much at ease; you can see him wondering how he didn't see this angle coming): 'No. No.'

King (in full terrier-shaking-a-rat mode): 'Not that you were *arrested* before. That you've never *done* anything like this before?'

Hugh (looking as though he wished King would belt up): 'No. No.'

King: 'It was just that one night, *that* moment?'

Hugh (tightly): 'Correct. Yes.'

King (undeterred): 'And you don't ponder on *why*? It would drive me *nuts*!'

Hugh (giving up trying to fob off questions with two-word answers): 'Well, I'll always ponder on it but there's nothing more I can say. I think it was an atrocious thing to do and disloyal. I can't beat myself up any more than that.'

King: 'Also, everyone imagines you – when you met Elizabeth, that moment, all the men were trying to imagine – what do you say?'

Hugh: 'Well, I mean. I – well – don't, I can't really . . .'

King: 'It must be terr –'

Hugh: 'Yeah, it's up there. [Hugh then wanders into a brief paean of praise for his parents before introducing a new family member] Yeah, my father is great. My mother is great . . . And my grandmother, *extraordinary* –'

King (taking the bait): 'Your grandmother?'

Hugh: 'I mean *incredible*. She just says [affecting a light upper-middle-class drawing-room drawl], "What I tell people, darling, is that you had a few drinks with the boys and got a bit fresh with the girls and leave it at that". She must be in her nineties.'

With one lovely line, Hugh has deftly allied himself with the self-serving 'class' defence of consorting with prostitutes. That it is something a gentleman may indulge in – with discretion, naturally, but without blemish to his character. Screeds have been written about this aspect of the Hugh Grant scandal, majestically invoking the names of Charles II and his mistress, Nell Gwyn, and the Prince Regent (later George V) who attended a Covent Garden flagellation parlour; and wheeling out descriptions of British MPs in the late eighteenth century being pleasured in their coaches by ladies of the night.

All overlook the glaring difference between these fine gentlemen and Hugh. The others lived when convention powerfully dictated that good women did not enjoy sex.

A *real* gentleman didn't have much choice other than the Nells, or the thinly fictionalized Moll Flanderses and their like (the seventeenth- and eighteenth-century, and later Victorian, good-time – if often pox-ridden – girls), if he didn't want either to impose himself repeatedly, beast-like, on his long-suffering wife or to implode with frustration. The position of a movie star in Los Angeles in 1995 is, most would agree, markedly different from that of the seventeenth century's lusty Charles II and his convent-bred wife.

The justification of paid sex as a perverse *noblesse oblige* in late-twentieth-century society is about as convincing as a stockbroker clubbing his cleaning lady to death on the grounds that this commonly happened to serfs in the middle ages.

On 27 June 1995 Hugh *did* have a choice. He could have let himself be used – as a passport to almost-fame – by any number of available party-girl-cum-wannabe actresses from the Los Angeles districts of Bel Air, Beverly Hills and Malibu and the canyons of Benedict, Laurel and Coldwater. Party girls who haunted pick-up joints like the Monkey Bar, the House of Blues – where Thompson, ironically, reportedly later gained admission by boasting that she 'was the one caught with the movie star' – or the Viper Room. But his paranoia about being taken advantage of ruled out this choice. Or he could have used a prostitute and prayed she kept her mouth shut – at least after the encounter. In other words, use someone else for sexual gratification. By adding the delicious little word portrait of his redoubtable granny and her genteel euphemisms for oral sex, Hugh distanced himself from the reality of the act. Hugh's grandmother also sounded remarkably like the real-life Lady Penelope Aitken, who was quoted, in reference to Hugh's predicament, in the *Daily Express* on 10 July: 'Much ado about nothing. All men behave like that given half the chance, it's just human nature.' King, however, did not probe Hugh for further Wildean testimony from doughty family members. But back to the interview . . .

King: 'Do you buy the comparison to Cary Grant?'

Hugh: 'Uh, I've always thought that was a little silly, flattering, of course – but, uh –'

King: 'If Tom Hanks is called kind of a Jimmy Stewart on the basis of – you are quite comfortable with light comedy, handsome, English – play[ing] this kind of role of the guy things happen to?'

Hugh: 'Wearing ladies' underwear.'

King (sensing a send-up rather than a scoop, nevertheless repeating faintly): 'Wearing ladies' underwear?'

Hugh: 'No, I mean, of course. [Cary Grant] is a real icon. I absolutely adore his stuff but I never sat down and thought, "I'm going to model myself on him." Nor did I and nor would I ever put myself even remotely on the same planet.' (An overstatement. Four days before his arrest Hugh had toured Hollywood – in the about-to-be-notorious white BMW – with a reporter from the US magazine *Entertainment Weekly* and had paused outside Cary Grant's old house. 'Quite lovely, no?' he had said of the idol's former residence, adding, 'A bit smaller than expected, though, don't you think?' So much for the iconic Cary Grant's mansion.)

King repeats, in a garbled fashion his question about press intrusion into Hugh's life.

Hugh: 'As a matter of fact, all the British press is pretty much tabloid now. Um, the broadsheets.'

King: '*The Times?*'

Hugh: 'They *all* covered it in just as much detail, and with equal lack of restraint – and venom.'

King: 'Why is that?'

Hugh: 'I don't pretend to be innocent myself. I read.'

King: 'How about the BBC? Are they covering you?'

Hugh: 'Yes, yes, certainly. All the TV channels in England have had cameras in the house as well.'

King: 'You're doing a movie called *Restoration* with Meg Ryan?' (The Restoration comedy film, made in 1994, that finally reunited Hugh with the American director Mike Hoffman and the scriptwriter Rupert Walters, of the student film *Privileged*.)

Hugh (looking annoyed): 'Er. I have *done* that. It's a cameo part and coming out later this year. I had quite a long backlog of things I'd committed to before my life got better. So I had to do it, which is not to say I didn't want to, because it was a very funny script. It's a very nice cameo part. I play this evil, seedy yellow-teethed, beauty-spotted painter in the eighteenth century and I spy for the king.'

King: 'Do you have scenes with Meg?'

Hugh: 'Actually, no.'

King (jovially): 'Unfortunately!'

Rather than agree that it was indeed unfortunate that he failed to shimmer with *Sleepless in Seattle*'s Meg Ryan, Hugh bounces on to film budgets.

Hugh: 'It was very alarming. As you could imagine, I could probably put the budgets of all the seventeen films I made before into this one [*Nine Months*]'.

King (looking as though he wished to fire his researchers and croakingly echoing Hugh's statement with disbelief): 'You've made *seventeen* films?'

Hugh: 'Yeah. I've been plodding along for ages. It's just that in the past I've preferred to make failures, um, and now I thought I'd have a go at films people actually [wanted] to go to see and the novelty ... yes, it is extremely frightening and I was quite intimidated. People kept saying, "Let's talk about the script" and stuff, and I'd say, "me?" '

King: 'Your part as an expectant father, who doesn't want to be an expectant father, it's an old French kind of farce isn't it?' (One trembles again for King's researchers. Somehow the fact that *Nine Months* is an Americanized remake of the recent French movie *Neuf Mois* seems to have been scrambled.)

Hugh (testily): 'Well, it's not an old French farce – it's just [based] on a French film made a year ago.'

King (rapidly reverting to a tried and trusted 'soft' celebrity question): 'What whetted your appetite about doing it?'

Hugh: 'I thought it was funny. It's as simple as that. I'm very fussy about scripts, perhaps because I've been starved of them for so long. Suddenly they've all come along – and I'm almost ridiculously fussy about what I think's good and what is not good and this one made me laugh and I also thought it was fun to be really neurotic for once. In *Four Weddings and a Funeral*, I was relatively this passive character – in this one I'm more neurotic.'

King: 'Is that easier to play?'

Hugh: 'Not necessarily easier. It was just a different strand of my character that Elizabeth in particular was keen people should see. Elizabeth loves the film.'

Hugh then launches into his standard *Nine Months* publicity shtick, claiming that his fellow actor Robin Williams was quite 'mad' and facetiously insisting that Tom Arnold was in love with him.

King (not noticeably charmed by this): 'So that's what you're breaking here tonight? You and Tom?'

Hugh: 'It was just a sex thing. It wasn't a love thing, so there's nothing for his new fiancée to get jealous about.'

King (refusing to prolong such silliness with a single sharp rejoinder): 'Okay. And nothing for your girl to get jealous about?'

Hugh (quietly): 'No, not in this case.'

King (returning after the break and again blindsiding Hugh, by suddenly mentioning the terms of his 'probation'): 'Does that mean you have to do anything, do you –? What is it?'

Hugh (dismissively): 'I don't know. [Howard Weitzman, his lawyer] hasn't mentioned anything like that before. I only know from what I've seen on the news about that.' (Hugh's humility did not extend to acknowledging the criminal nature of inducing a young woman to perform sex acts for money. In this, he was firmly on the side of those who thought the LA police had better things to do than shine torches into the suspiciously parked cars of 'consenting' adults.)

King: 'When do you go back home?'

Hugh: 'Ah, well I have more of these things.'

King: 'You're going to do two others. You're going to do the *Today* show, then Regis and Kathie Lee?'

Hugh: 'Yeah, then David Letterman.'

King (sounding surprised): 'You're going to do David Letterman?'

Hugh: 'Uh, I think so – Leslee?' (He appeals comically for the assistance of Leslee Dart, one of his publicity spokeswomen.)

King: '[David Letterman] was concerned that you had left him out of the sweep.'

Hugh: 'Uh, I want to publicize the film. It's as simple as that. I don't – I never have wanted to talk about this but I realize it would be absurd to pretend it hadn't happened.'

King graciously makes the point that Hugh had been booked for this interview before the scandal blew up and not as a result of it.

Hugh: 'No. I'd hate people to think that I was, in case there are any weirdos who thought that for some reason I wanted to come and bare my soul.'

King: 'Do you feel kind of weird that the lady in question is going to make a lot of money with tabloids talking to her?'

Hugh: 'Um. No – I, I, I think that was bound to happen. I don't, uh, feel any way at all about that. Um. That whole side of it is sort of numb.'

King: 'Numb? Is it weird to be in town? Just to *be* here?'

Hugh: 'Um, well, not particularly, especially because people have been so damn' nice.'

King (referring to calls made to the show by viewers): 'All the callers are supportive. But how's Elizabeth? There's concern for her. She's very popular.'

Hugh: 'Terrifically well. I mean obviously it's been difficult and miserable. We've been together for eight years through thick and thin.'

King: 'Have there been separations ever?'

Hugh: 'No.'

King: 'So even through the thick and the thin, you've never parted?'

Hugh: 'No, no. We've lived on separate continents [Hugh giggles] but we've always been together.'

One of only two calls from the public broadcast on the show is now heard – the other one is lost in a storm of static. The deep South is, apparently staunchly behind Hugh. Angeline from Weaver, Alabama, commends the actor for his 'honesty' and says she can't wait to see *Nine Months*.

King: 'How do you explain it to yourself, that the people are showing such great affection? Is it maybe that this isn't as big a deal as others might think it is?'

Hugh: 'Thank you very much. Angeline was it? It's incredibly nice. I think it *is* a big deal actually. I think it is a big deal. As I told you before, if I was a single person you could argue that it was a –'

King: 'Consenting adults?'

Hugh: 'Right. Although it's obviously – oh I don't want to get into all this; it's not nice for the people who live round there and everything. But as it was, you know, I have a girlfriend and I've caused her an immense amount of pain and it's a bad – and there's a crime there in betrayal.'

King: 'Is there any place you've gone and you've been hooted? Or people have been rude?'

Hugh: 'Um, no. Not really, no. The only place where people have been anything less than incredibly supportive has been in the British papers.'

King: '*Nine Months* opens today. Thank you, Hugh.'

TWENTY-NINE

> '*Depend upon it that if a man talks of his misfortunes there is something in them that is not disagreeable to him; for where there is nothing but pure misery there never is any recourse to the mention of it.*'
>
> Samuel Johnson,
> *a writer hugely admired by Hugh Grant*

Hugh's last stop on his jog round America's television networks came on Wednesday, 19 July, on CBS's live *Late Show with David Letterman* – the most popular, and unpredictable, of celebrity chat slots. As a previous guest of the veteran show host – long before the Sunset scandal – Hugh seemed relaxed and at home from the moment he loped on to the Manhattan sound stage, as the band struck up an arrangement of Bob Dylan's 'Blowin' in the Wind'.

'Hugh, how's your summer been goin'?' was Letterman's laconic opening crack – predictably bringing down the house. Hugh laughed just long enough to signal that he was game for a tease. 'Well, it's been lovely. Um. No. Obviously, obviously it's a bad one. It's a very, very bad one. But I was interested in the introduction we've just heard about the little boy who's coming on later who found a sapphire in a bucket of dirt [a reference to a later guest on the show] and, I'm going to try and live by that metaphor.' This brought a roar of approval from the audience.

Letterman: 'I just want to say one thing. When *this* happened, we had a decision here to make ourselves. We decided well, if we make jokes about your misfortune, likely you wouldn't want to come on the show and we would understand that entirely. But I was thinking to myself, if something like this ever happened to me – and, believe me, it's just a matter of time [huge laughs] – you know I would make jokes about it myself. So I understand how uncomfortable it all might have been and I can't thank you enough for being nice enough to honour your commitment. Thank you, that was very, very, very generous.' (Whistles and applause.)

Hugh: 'You know, it's fine; I mean, I haven't seen you every night but I'm told you've been very restrained and limited yourself to twelve small jokes a night. So, that's marvellous.' (Letterman's best joke had been his typically irreverent Top Ten list of future movie titles for the actor with *Poca-hooker* in the number-one position.)

Letterman: 'Has this just surprised the hell out of you, the way it turned into be something huge?'

Hugh: 'We-ell, a lot of people ... [huge laughs] I was surprised when I came back here because, um, I pay people to lie to me. When I was in England after this, you know, they were all speaking to me on the phone and saying, "Hugh, the story's *dead*. It's dead, there's nothing in the paper, there's nothing on the TV." So it was something of a shock to come back and actually be unable to get out of the car.'

Letterman: 'What is that experience like, when you see people when you travel, when you're in hotels, how are people responding? I mean, based on this reception you got here tonight, good heavens, you're nearly canonized.'

Hugh: 'People have been extraordinarily nice, and of course, the thing is, I'm not really the one who deserves the sympathy. You know, my girlfriend and people like that. [Cheers and claps] Having said that, of course, I'm delighted that people have been nice and specially that they've gone to see the film, that's a huge relief. Because that was a big worry.'

Letterman: 'You know, I was thinking about this this afternoon and I am trying to find some clarity about this situation and what I've come up with, it's something – it's just embarrassment, that's all this is. Nobody likes to be embarrassed, nobody – certainly – likes to embarrass themselves. But truthfully, beyond that, what really do we have here? It's not much.'

Hugh: 'Well, it's nice of you to say that. I think there are two things. There is a crime – uh – which is a personal one, again to my girlfriend, to my family and people like that. The actual deed itself, it just depends on your cultural standpoint, I think ... there are people in Saudi Arabia who would dismember me for this. And then again I was talking to, you know, a French friend of mine the other day, a producer, and she said, 'I 'ear you haf a problem.' I said, 'Yes, I was arrested with a prostitute in Los Angeles.' She said, 'Oh yes [bored voice] ... you know I haf a script to send you ...''

Letterman: 'If you think about it, and I don't even know if ... this is even appropriate to the conversation, but if you take a look at this, we have consenting adults, and putting aside for the time being that it *is* illegal – but nonetheless, consenting adults, it's a misdemeanour right?'

Hugh: 'I believe that's the word, yeah.'

Letterman: 'And then you look at our own president, the most powerful man in the world, who gets sued for sexual harassment – you know, to me, that's a bigger problem.'

Hugh (chuckling): 'Yes. [Applause] But he's a good man, is he? Harvey Weinstein, the great friend, the one who's being so nice to me throughout all this – you've met Harvey Weinstein, head of Miramax films here, who's been a real staunch supporter – he was telling me last night, in fact boring me to death about Bill Clinton, saying he was a good man and so, I don't know what to say about that except I'm sure everything will work out nicely for Bill.'

Letterman (unleashing his trademark cackle): 'I'm sure he will appreciate your support. But aren't you just racked with fatigue at the very topic at this point? I mean, good God, you know ... I would be, I'm getting kinda tired of it now.'

Hugh: 'I am humiliated and I am particularly humiliated by having to do this last week's round of ... it's like those monks in the middle ages who used to crawl from city to city flagellating themselves. I think in the end you just become a laughing-stock.'

Letterman then assures Hugh it will be just 'one of those things you look back on'.

Hugh: 'You sound like Larry King. He's been married about twelve times.' (An exaggeration: Larry King, of CNN, has been married six times, although he claims that, since his first marriage as a teenager 'was never consummated' before being annulled, and because his fourth marriage was a rematch with his second wife, he is technically merely 'four times married'.)

Letterman: 'Listen to what Larry has to say!'

Hugh: 'Then he had a quadruple bypass which sorted him out.' (A rare understatement on Hugh's part, it was a quintuple bypass.)

Letterman: 'Yeah, he's okay now!'

Hugh: 'I'm having one tomorrow.'

Letterman: 'It'll just be an experience in your life and that's all it will have meant.'

Hugh: 'Yes. Right. Exactly. On to the film.' (Huge applause – then a commercial break.)

Letterman asks about acting with his *Nine Months* co-star Tom Arnold.

Hugh (deadpan and opaque): 'He's not well. Um. A fish. We all know that.'

Letterman: 'Did you guys get along?'

Hugh: 'No. Yes. We got on fine. There is a theory that we swapped personalities during the film, which I've always denied up until now, but so many people are saying that this whole thing was his fault and I'm trying to come round to that point of view now. It was Tom Arnold's fault.'

Letterman: 'He should be arrested for anything ... [anyway] the film has all turned out nicely.'

Hugh: 'Yes, it's been a huge success. That's the bonus. That is the sapphire I suppose in the bucket of dirt.'

A clip of *Nine Months* is then screened, showing Tom Arnold apparently molesting Hugh in the process of giving him the kiss of life – to huge applause.

Letterman: 'This summer you have suffered enough.'

Hugh (still joking about having exchanged personalities with Arnold during filming): 'I became a worse person and he's now going to do a Merchant–Ivory film next.'

Commercial break.

Letterman: 'So how will you spend the rest of your summer? Do you have more pleasant things to get on to? You must be tired of doing show after show after show and then dopes like me grilling you about the situation.'

Hugh: 'I think disappearing for a bit, or try anyway.'

Letterman: 'Any further projects to look forward to?'

Hugh: 'Well, a film I did comes out on Friday, a small film called *An Awfully Big Adventure*, which is directed by the same man who made *Four Weddings and a Funeral*. I look forward to that.'

Letterman: 'And I'm going to do my part now. We're not going to do any more jokes about this. We're going to put this to rest as far as I'm concerned [huge applause]. It was terribly nice of you to come under the circumstances and terribly nice of you to be here under any circumstances, always a pleasure to have you. Thank you, Hugh.'

THIRTY

'Last night I dreamt I went to Manderley again. It seemed to me I stood by the iron gate leading to the drive, and for a while I could not enter for the way was barred to me. There was a padlock and a chain upon the gate.'

Opening of Rebecca, *by Daphne du Maurier, quoted in part by Elizabeth Hurley to Barbara Walters, 26 July 1995*

Elizabeth all but upstaged Hugh's serial US TV-show confessionals by agreeing to just one carefully orchestrated appearance. She flew to New York to film an exclusive interview with the queen of kid-glove celebrity interviewing, Barbara Walters.

The session, with Elizabeth highly reminiscent of her idol Audrey Hepburn in a kittenish, fluffy, orange, midriff-baring sweater and tight black pants, was taped in a Manhattan hotel on Wednesday, 26 July. But broadcast was delayed until Barbara Walters's ABC news magazine show, *20/20*, aired the *following* week, on Friday, 4 August, by which time the actress was beyond the immediate clutches of either US or British journalists, having slipped off to South Africa for six weeks to play a junkie stripper avenging her boyfriend's killer in the B-movie *Spear*.

The tremulously maternal Walters – infamous for once tenderly enquiring, on air, of the veteran actress Katharine Hepburn, 'If you were a tree, what sort would you be?' – was, from Elizabeth's point of view, the ideal interrogator. Soft, endlessly solicitous and rarely tempted to tease her subjects, or back them into awkward corners, Walters posed the minimum threat to Elizabeth's new status as an injured innocent.

Indeed, at times the exchange didn't come off as a primetime news interview so much as a tea-shop tête-à-tête between a tongue-tied niece and her slightly distracted maiden aunt. Yet, again, the broadcast's smash ratings confirmed that America's fascination for the couple was still bubbling at the Richard Burton–Elizabeth Taylor level of hysteria. Elizabeth's interview was the second most watched programme in the USA that week, seen by some 20 million viewers.

Walters introduced Elizabeth as the woman who had sparked 'a frenzy of international gossip because of the man she lived with and has loved for eight years ... [and tonight] for the first time she talks about the sexual indiscretion that has made headlines around the world.'

Walters described the actress as being 'understandably very nervous' before their interview. A newsreel clip then showing a beaming and poised Elizabeth being introduced, in New York that spring, by Leonard Lauder, President and CEO of the Estée Lauder companies, as the firm's new 'image for the future'. 'I am really flattered beyond belief to be chosen to be the new, um, face of Estée Lauder,' chirped Elizabeth.

Walters then pointedly informed viewers that, from autumn 1995, Elizabeth's portrait would be used in an advertising campaign for Lauder cosmetics in 100 countries worldwide. 'Millions of images that will make Elizabeth Hurley's face one of the most recognizable of the decade,' she declared firmly. Walters chose not to mention that the actress/model had even made the latest edition of *International Who's Who*, sandwiched between two rather unlikely neighbours: Hurley, Denis, a retired South African ecclesiastic, and Hurley, Michael, an Irish ecumenical theologian and Jesuit priest.

Having thus established Elizabeth's credentials – and mentioned the Versace dress that 'perhaps began her moment of fame' – Walters confided approvingly that Elizabeth had come to the interview alone, without any silly entourage of publicity people.

She then solemnly intoned that, 'Charles Dickens could

have written these lines about Elizabeth Hurley: It was the best of times, it was the worst of times ...' (though mercifully she spared viewers the remainder of the quotation about ages of foolishness, epochs of belief, winters of despair and so forth).

Finally Walters opened her interview with, perhaps, not quite the question the whole world had been waiting to ask Hugh's girl-friend: 'I asked the Estée Lauder people why they chose you and I said, "Were you looking for an all-American image?"; and they said, "No, no, we were looking for" – and I wrote it down – "the sophisticated woman of the twenty-first century".'

Total silence from a blank-faced Elizabeth greeted this statement. Walters hastily prodded her: 'How do you like that?'

'I'll take that on the chin,' replied Elizabeth. 'Um, very nice. I have never felt one jot sophisticated. I can be reduced to feeling like a very scruffy schoolgirl in two seconds flat by most people, but by the time they've done their retouching and their lighting, maybe yes I can look sophisticated. I like that.'

Elizabeth then described her appearance as a rebellious teenager: 'I think my mother would say I looked a perfect fright. She hated it. I had a nosering. I had sixteen earrings. I had white hair, pink hair, blue hair – teenage things. I think any teenager worth their salt has a bit of rebellion in them.'

Walters: 'Something intrigued me. [But evidently not something that Elizabeth had just said] You recently registered in a hotel under an assumed name. The name is Rebecca de Winter. Now I remember the film *Rebecca* by Daphne du Maurier. Rebecca never appeared. She was mysterious, beautiful ... why did you pick that name?'

Elizabeth: 'Rebecca is – you start off thinking she's an angel. And, um, in fact we find out she's an incredibly unpleasant person. Very manipulative ... [then leaping adroitly over the chasm she had just dug for herself] I just love the name, you know – the house is Manderley and the first line of the book is "Last night I dreamt I went to Manderley again".'

Fortunately for Elizabeth, in the light of Hugh's behaviour, Daphne du Maurier had changed her mind over her *original* opening sentence for the novel, which read, 'Well, it is over now, finished and done with . . .'

Elizabeth: 'I dream every night I wake up at Manderley. That's what I want.' (An odd statement, since the novel describes a young bride discovering her husband murdered his sexually unfaithful first wife.)

Walters (visibly slightly puzzled, but working fast to make any sense of this): 'You want to wake up in a beautiful mansion – is that how you see yourself?'

Elizabeth: 'I don't think I do any more, um, I don't know any more.'

Walters (soothingly): 'It's hard now to know what you are . . .?'

Elizabeth (nodding): 'It is, isn't it? And I think I realize as you get older everything does get hazier and hazier. I always assumed that everything falls into place . . . everybody I meet say as they get older they get more and more confused.'

Walters (cosily): 'Tell me about the new film.'

Elizabeth: 'Well, I'm going to South Africa next week with, um, Ice Cube [the rapper]. It's not a typical film to come out of South Africa; it's not about apartheid, it's not about problems within black and white society in South Africa –'

Walters (interrupting a little less cosily, clearly bored with hearing further descriptions of what Elizabeth's new film is not about): 'Does the Estée Lauder company care, at all, what kinds of films you make? Do they worry it might be against the image that you're projecting?'

Elizabeth: 'No. They want me to do anything which would help further myself or my career, you know, and by doing so of course, it's good for the image of the company.'

Walters: 'Were they supportive throughout the last months? Was there ever a question of "don't see Hugh Grant"?'

Elizabeth (crisply): 'Nothing could be further from the

truth. They've been superb, really superb. Um. They've become a family to me now.'

Walters: 'Let's come back to happy days. When you met Hugh Grant you were doing a film together. Was it love at first sight? Did you think he was terrific?'

Elizabeth (warily): 'Um. I think we were astounded by our similarities in some ways. Both physical, we look quite similar, and mainly based on our upbringing, quite frighteningly similar in fact.'

Walters: 'In what way?'

Elizabeth (more confidently): 'Both our fathers were retired army officers, both our mothers schoolteachers, specializing in the piano. Neither of us come from families which have much money; both of us come from families which have a lot of love. Both sets of parents are still together. I mean I've always said, I don't have anyone to blame for anything, I take full responsibility for everything I've ever done because my parents were blameless bringing us up, most unselfish, the best people on earth.'

Walters (clearly a little stunned by this cool guide to how the English fall in love by comparing what points their parents have in common, but heroically hanging on to her original point): 'So is this what attracted you – the two of you had *similar backgrounds*?'

Elizabeth: 'Uh. I remember thinking he looked quite nice in his costume at the time. We got on very well.'

Walters: 'Was it a romance? Is it a romance?'

Elizabeth: 'We – well, you know, present tense is a difficult question to answer.'

Walters: 'To get back – was it a romance?'

Elizabeth: 'I think yes, definitely. I sort of feel he's my family. You know, I think blood is very thick, after seven years in my family, and I felt we'd moved to that stage. Well, you know, you're very, um, at home with each other.'

Walters: 'Did you think of marriage?'

Elizabeth (appearing to consider the question as if for the first time, a remarkable piece of acting): 'No, actually we never did. We started going out when I was twenty-one, when of course you wouldn't begin to think about getting married. And, um, mentally I don't think I've moved on at all from there. I actually find it quite bizarre now when some, I'm sure very well-meaning, people have said to me now [whispering] "*You should just get married*." That's the most bizarre thing I've ever heard in my life ... There has never been a time in my life when I've felt less inclined to get married. So, um, that doesn't go down too well.'

Walters (biting the bullet – but her voice positively soughing with sympathy): 'Was all this a *terrible* surprise?'

Elizabeth (flatly): 'Yes.'

Walters: 'Do you have any idea why? There's been all this psychological "why", "what if?" ... Was it just some, I don't know what, wild, stupid thing?'

Elizabeth (sharply): 'Well, I think that most things you do in life you do because you want to. I always think that to be the bottom line. Yes there's all sorts of psychobabble you can come up with. I think ultimately you want to do something and you do it.'

Walters (the maiden aunt suddenly on the alert): 'How did you hear about it?'

Elizabeth: 'Um, my agent told me.'

Walters: 'Before Hugh talked to you?'

Elizabeth: 'Seconds before.'

Walters: 'Oh God, what did you say? What did you say?'

Elizabeth: 'Well, I think I – I felt like I'd been shot. I ran out thinking, I think I'm in shock.'

Walters: 'There were the pictures of you arguing in the garden, looking very angry. I think some people wondered, "Why on *earth* did you do it in the *garden* with the media photographers?" Or was that on purpose? Was that to show that you were angry?'

Elizabeth: 'No, at that stage the only thing I was angry with was the fact that I had three hundred and fifty paparazzi people with long lenses trained into every single room in my house. You know, it's the hottest day of the year, um, we even had cameras aimed into the bathroom, so curtains had to be drawn. You know, we don't have such thing as air conditioning in England. I wanted to get outside; we weren't arguing at all. I was just thinking, Jesus Christ, I can't even walk to my own greenhouse to water my tomato plants without some jerk at the end of the garden with a camera on me. That's actually what was annoying me.'

Walters: 'And in the middle of it all a mattress was delivered?'

Elizabeth: '*That* was bizarre . . .'

Walters (sensing, finally, a straight answer coming): 'Would you explain that please?'

Elizabeth: 'Yes, the morning before I got my horrible telephone call I invited some people to stay for the weekend. And I needed a bed for our spare bedroom. So I rang and ordered one. And then I went out to lunch and then came back and I of course – everything exploded.'

Walters: 'What are you now? I mean once and for all, Liz, you're going to have to answer it and then I hope you don't have to again, but where is it and where are you with him?' (To be fair to Elizabeth this is not the easiest question to understand.)

Elizabeth: 'Well, I don't know really. I'd like to say that everything's getting easier and easier, falling into place. But it isn't really. I don't know. I mean. I think the deciding thing, I keep saying to myself, is . . . what if instead the telephone call had been – he's been killed in a car crash? That's ten billion times worse.'

Walters: 'In a car crash he would be gone for ever. And there's no embarrassment, there's only sympathy and love left.' (Walters is tantalizingly close to implying that a car crash might have its distinct advantages. At least that's how Elizabeth interprets the statement.)

Elizabeth: 'Yeah – but lost for the rest of my life. So, um, you know, I don't have that. I don't know really. I'm really looking forward to going away to South Africa. I'm there about seven weeks.'

Walters (scenting blood in the water): 'So you won't be seeing him for seven weeks?'

Elizabeth (ever so diffidently): 'Oh I don't know. He may come out for a while. Um, I don't quite know. It's very, very difficult in England. It's actually intolerable to be, you know, on display all the time.'

Walters: 'Is there an explanation? I mean, can you say something when you would say, "Yes, I understand, I can forgive now"?'

Elizabeth (coolly): 'I don't think there's a question of understanding.'

Walters: 'Is it [a question of] forgiving?'

Elizabeth: 'Forgiving . . . forgiveness is a very difficult subject. But that's something that has to be worked out. It would be very easy now to become very hard.'

Walters: 'To say never again? [No answer, she hurries on] You went to the opening of *Nine Months* with Hugh Grant which was, at least to the world, a way of saying, "I still support you". It didn't look like that.'

Elizabeth: 'No, I was as miserable as sin.'

Walters: 'But you went.'

Elizabeth: 'Yeah, I went.'

Walters (through slightly gritted teeth): 'So that's an act of *what*?'

Elizabeth: 'Well I – you know – I don't think you should hit someone when they're down. I've never thought that.'

Walters: 'What did your parents say about all this?'

Elizabeth: 'Well, that's, that's – you know – a tough one. Um. Well I think you know Dad's initial reaction was that he should be horsewhipped – like any good father's [reaction] should be. Um. It's very hard for them of course, you know because they've loved him for a long time but they love me more.'

Walters: 'You're a very honest lady – have you always been like this?'

Elizabeth: 'I'd love to be able to lie. I'd – I – love it. I'm not very good at it. I can't be bothered to think of anything to say which isn't the truth. I've always found it easier just to tell the truth.'

This is in stark contrast to Hugh's own take on the concept of truth: 'I don't believe in truth, I believe in *style*.

I think the truth is a tremendous chimera. Or maybe I don't understand it.' Compare Oscar Wilde's *The Importance of Being Earnest*: 'In matters of grave importance, style, not sincerity, is the vital thing.'

Walters: 'So where do you go from here?'

Elizabeth: 'I don't know, I don't really know to be quite honest. Um. I don't know.'

The interview ends with Walters's co-host saying, a little rhetorically, 'That's honest, she *is* candid. But, you know, the thing I can't get a reading on is what will she ultimately do?' And Walters replied that she didn't really know, either.

CHAPTER

THIRTY-ONE

'Go and live in peace.'
Talk show host to Hugh Grant,
July 1995

Two days later, on Friday 14 July, Hugh approached the climax of his trial by television with an appearance on the New York NBC morning show, *Today*, and – least taxing of all – immersed himself in the warm bubble-bath of forgiveness offered by the veteran Manhattan morning magazine-show hosts, Regis Philbin and Kathie Lee Gifford, on ABC's *Live with Regis and Kathie Lee*.

On both Hugh was on top form, perky, yet rueful, offering his hesitant non-answers to the standard questions about the scandal as if considering them for the first time and revealing little glimpses of his wit – sunshine peeping shyly through clouds rather than the glancing shafts of his pre-scandal life. To *Today*'s Katie Couric, he confessed he was surprised that the media interest had not yet burnt itself out. Hugh also risked implying that it was the media mockery – rather than his own actions – that was the cause of Elizabeth's distress.

'They can go on hounding me as much as they like, but they should damn' well leave her alone. If they could see the real sadness the media attention actually causes her, if they could see her head hang, I think they might ease up on the jokes.' He also sought to undo the damage of his comments about visiting 'low dives' with Tom Arnold and allegations that he was an *habitué* of girlie bars with the statement: 'I've never really pretended to be totally squeaky clean. I'm glad I'm not. But I don't *frequent* topless bars, although my brother did take me once. But that's the only time. Nor have I been to a million Latino bars with Tom Arnold.'

That was an absurdly exaggerated charge that Hugh had never faced. As he had done so often in the past, from the beginning of his Gaveston days, Hugh sought to glamorize his own life, hinting that, well, a chap's mother might very well do more than whistle if she knew the extent of his social activities. It was *Hugh* who had boasted, with a wink, to journalists of tipsily accompanying Tom Arnold to low-life West Coast nightclubs. The revelation wasn't the result of an investigative tabloid witch-hunt. (In the same way – in the heady aftermath of *Four Weddings* – Hugh had disingenuously tipped off a newspaper friend about Madonna pursuing him, and had subsequently expressed enormous astonishment at the fuss this created.) It was also Hugh's air of misleading youthfulness that insulated him from ridicule over his assertion that 'my brother did take me once' to a topless bar, as if he were a wide-eyed lad on exeat from school rather than a sexually cynical male in his mid-thirties.

On *Live with Regis and Kathie Lee* the actor was at his charming best. Kathie Lee, who had expressed her fondness for Hugh in advance, told the studio's West 67th Street audience, 'He's been *repentant*, which is a wonderful biblical word we don't use enough these days!' Hugh trotted out his recollections about auditioning for the role of Tarzan, which of course he did not, and answered questions – amid a blizzard of advertising breaks – about whether he considered being caught with a hooker 'as a blessing' since otherwise his 'life might have gone on a path that ultimately could have been far more damaging', with the response that he hadn't really considered this. He joked, donnishly and with faint echoes of the larky school cricket report of his youth, that the name of his film company – Simian Films, simian meaning 'of or pertaining to apes' – was most appropriate to his recent behaviour.

He also manfully faced the intrusion of enquiries such as 'Do you really hate your hair?' 'Well, we're sort of partners,' Hugh pricelessly quipped.

He claimed that the only reason Tom Arnold stood so close to him for publicity photographs at the *Nine Months* première earlier that week was because Arnold's 'acting career has taken a dive and he does the bodyguard stuff' and referred to the scene in the film in which Arnold gives him mouth-to-mouth resuscitation as one of the 'two bad things that have happened to me this year.'

It was all arch, knowing and playful with Hugh – literally – receiving a benediction from the kindly, sweetly enthusiastic and avuncular Regis Philbin, who, at the end, placed his hand on Hugh's head and announced, 'We wish you well. Go and live in peace!'

This last piece of advice was harder to follow: Hugh's post-show limousine ride – he was flanked by publicists in the car and his driver was an off-duty cop – rapidly turned to farce. Fans and tabloid photographers pursued the limo along Manhattan's Upper West Side. Then uniformed New York cops appeared on the scene and pulled over one of the outraged tabloid photographers, with the result that the whole red-light-jumping affair made the next day's headlines.

THIRTY-TWO

'Would someone please tell me who this guy's press agent is? I mean, have you ever seen so much written about so little?'

The singer Courtney Love, on the media coverage of Hugh's arrest, quoted in Newsday, *August 1995*

When Hugh Grant first heard rumours that a biography about him was being planned – long before the Sunset Strip scandal – he reacted much as he did when we met in a New York lift that snowy Grammy awards day. Hugh flew into a cold rage. During a British radio interview broadcast at the time, Hugh publicly spat out his personal disgust for the London literary agent then tentatively trying to set up the deal. That this was her job, matching book projects to authors, cut no ice whatsoever. Neither did the fact the agent he condemned happened to be an old acquaintance of his. (She endured some sniffy rebukes from one or two Hugh Grant 'camp followers' on the London club scene for a while, but survived otherwise unscathed.)

When the actor further discovered his opposition hadn't halted the project and, later, that I had been commissioned to write the book – again entirely in the wake of the *Four Weddings* euphoria and months in advance of his downfall with Divine Brown – Hugh hit back harder. His publicists informed anyone who asked that my only motivation for writing was naked financial greed. I was, I read in the gleeful gossip column titbits that followed in Britain, the USA and even Australia, shamelessly trying to cream money off his newly famous name.

Without a word being written, war had been declared. From a brief flurry of bombastic phone calls I received from London contacts of Hugh's at my home in New York, I gathered I stood accused of breaking some sort of Oxbridge code of *omertà* about the real Hugh Grant. The Mafia, I even suspected gloomily, could stand to learn a thing or two from Oxford about middle-class clan loyalty. In case there was any lingering doubt about his feelings, Hugh went on to volunteer, in answer to a questionnaire-style interview given to the UK's magazine for the homeless, *The Big Issue*, that I was the person he most disliked in the world. Overnight, he seemed to have cast himself as a seething Frank Sinatra with me in the tell-all role of Kitty Kelly. I don't imagine the magazine's readers were greatly interested in this spat.

Of course, the spectacle of a freshly canonized screen actor angered by the possibility of an unauthorized biography is not unfamiliar. We all have our secrets, our buried bodies. Some actors counter the challenge by racing to put out their own version of events first. Hugh was offered the opportunity by a British publisher to put his name to a lightweight volume, provisionally entitled *How to be a Gentleman* at the time of *Four Weddings* fever. Wisely as it turned out, since it is generally the mark of a gentleman *not* to get arrested by the Los Angeles cops for lewd conduct, he declined.

Other actors make pained pleas about their need for privacy when faced with unwarranted publicity. Or trust they have reached the stage, by the time a full-blown biography is in the works, of having erected sufficiently spy-proof barriers around their inner selves in the shape of high-walled country hideaways, a discreet inner circle of confidants and a phalanx of agents and publicists on permanent sentry duty.

Those barriers were not yet in place around Hugh Grant when I began research. His rise from Hugh Who? to a bankable leading man had been too swift, altogether too unpredictable to render him instantly a Hollywood Untouchable. That was part of the fascination of writing about him. My motivation for writing, for what it's worth, was never money. Hugh's rise to the top ranks of Hollywood, after so many frustrating years of toiling in obscurity, was simply the most sensational British film story of the decade.

Very, very few of us who make a living writing about film and television actors are ever lucky enough to have known a screen idol when he was a mere clay-footed mortal. To observe Hugh further, in the very process of metamorphosing from a British actor into an American sex symbol, to watch the Polaroid of his star persona actually developing, was, well, luck with a cherry on top. This was an irresistible project. And his friends did talk. Many – like me – were unimpressed with the notion that knowing Hugh meant signing an unofficial secrets act. Or that fame was a wand that erased or magically altered the past.

Hugh had no high-walled Bel Air hideaway either. His London base remained his modest flat in Redcliffe Square, Earls Court. The 'luxury' – meaning rather naffly overfurnished and ludicrously expensive – farmhouse, Littleton House, near Bath, that the actor temporarily rented with Elizabeth hardly provided the security of a Hollywood-style estate either. As the world's celebrity photographers discovered with predictable relish in the mad days of late June, 1995, Hugh and Elizabeth had only to wander innocently into the garden to be captured by a hundred telephoto lenses.

Hugh, in any case, had eagerly courted maximum publicity in the months before the scandal. He had to. The image-solidifying performance he delivered in *Four Weddings* had made him a star – and now, or probably never again, was the moment to establish an accompanying star persona in the public eye. Even the American gossip columnists marvelled, a little archly, at just how available Hugh made himself to the media. The privately biography-shy Hugh Grant appeared on the front covers of all the entertainment magazines. Week after week. The new British film superstar was hailed around the world. Hugh was the new 'Cary Grant for the nineties'. (Though whether Hugh rated comparison with the notoriously temperamental, vain and sexually confused Cary Grant revealed in books after his death, or the polished screen idol version his public worshipped was never debated.)

On cover after cover Hugh smiled wistfully in designer linens, frowned broodingly in beige, pulled madcap comic faces, and held forth about his life and his flotilla of 1995 films – *The Englishman Who Went Up a Hill but Came Down a Mountain*, *Restoration*, *An Awfully Big Adventure*, his first US big-budget project, *Nine Months*, and *Sense and Sensibility*, the Jane Austen novel adaptation he had filmed in the spring of 1995, due for its USA release in December – with a beady eye on the 1996 Oscars.

Each magazine carried, mostly, the same playfully flattering interview with minor variations in the anecdotes. The lovely start of the USA's *Premiere* magazine pre-scandal interview by its senior editor Holly Millea is typical: 'Hugh Grant pulls the pin on a charm grenade and hurls. *Whoooosh*. It hits the floor, rolls towards your toes, and *kaboom*! A cloud of upper-class English accent envelops you, fogging all your senses and sensibilities . . .'

The grenade metaphor was an apt one. Here was an actor on a personal campaign of disarmament. Hugh was presenting one side of his off-screen persona to interviewers in fusillades of *bons mots* and self-deprecating quips. Hugh seemed the blessed antithesis of that other youngish, genuinely upper-class British movie star export, Daniel Day-Lewis, whose dislike of publicity had made him a famously inscrutable interview subject.

In captivating contrast, Hugh appeared quotably indiscreet, casually dropping that his nickname for the younger of his two nephews by his brother Jamie and his wife Nicola happened to be 'Pheasant' because, he insisted, the boy – christened William – resembled the bird. He had, he claimed waggishly to another interviewer, amused himself while filming *Sirens* by exchanging schoolboy humour faxes on the subject of haemorrhoids with its director John Duigan.

He made jokes about Elizabeth's 'ratty' temper and his

own violent jealousy of rival actors who were suddenly hyped by the media. He was, confessed Hugh, so envious of Ralph Fiennes after the latter's breakthrough performances in *Schindler's List* and *Quiz Show* that he found himself cursing the actor whenever they met.

Journalists jaded by other Hollywood stars who talked woodenly about their craft and offered only their sincerest admiration for colleagues were enchanted by Hugh's openly declared weakness for expensive hotels, Catholic cheerleaders (his 'double favourite' he explained), sexy female co-stars and the fawning attentions of fans. Yes, even his own mother, Hugh cheerily claimed and apparently in the spirit of agreement, considered acting a form of prostitution.

Favoured journalists – Hugh's new 'best friends', though he is privately absolutely scathing about the intellectual and physical shortcomings of many he meets – were invited for drinks at 'his' London club, the newly opened rival to Groucho's, Soho House, or to admire the freshly painted Kensington offices of his own Hollywood-financed production company, Simian Films.

To the media, particularly the American media, Hugh was the seductive epitome of candour, good humour and feisty charm. His sloping grin and cut-glass accent were a bonus. His sexy girlfriend Elizabeth was further icing on the cake. Even his admissions of an intense fear of failure, of a swift and ignominious return to recording plays for British radio once his Hollywood 'hot streak' was over, served merely to boost his image of take-me-as-you-find-me larky honesty.

Behind the scenes, however, the larky honesty dried up. Hugh still tried to kill the biography, grilling friends over whether or not they had 'squealed' and silencing any official comment about his work, even from sources like the Oxford Film Foundation, which had, of course, started his career with *Privileged* in 1982 and genuinely deserved the credit. This was the real power of his new fame.

Hugh, so notoriously careless with other people's secrets – from letting slip his former best friend Danny

Daggenhurst's cosmetic name change to publicly announcing that he personally sponsors a Pakistani child, which inevitably lead to a frantic tabloid hunt to track down the unfortunate girl – was fiercely defensive when it came to his own.

The truth about Hugh Grant is that he has spent over half his adult life training a naturally highly competitive, arrogant and deeply insecure personality to match his heartbreakingly beautiful looks. Hugh can charm at will. He flexes his charm and automatically notes the impact, much like a bodybuilder pumping a muscle in front of a mirror.

Hugh can focus on one person – an interviewer, a guest at a party, a friend he hasn't called in months – and draw them to him with a murmured confession of indiscretion, a melting gaze and an extravagantly worded apology for his previous inattention. But he can strike like a cobra if he feels slighted – or ignored.

He is almost endlessly fascinated by the effect he has on the people he meets, then suddenly bored stupid, even disgusted, with the whole charade of playing Hugh Grant. Hugh is an intelligent, uniquely self-interested observer of his impact on his fellow creatures. He is, in short, ideal movie-star material. The notorious Hollywood gossip columnist Hedda Hopper once wrote, shrewdly, of Marlon Brando, 'He is a combination of sham, seeing through sham and defying it, yet a bit guilty of sham itself.' So with Hugh.

There is also a large element of double bluff to Hugh's jokey asides to journalists or friends about how much he enjoys the trappings of luxury. In reality he *wants* the world, and old, once bitterly envied and privileged Oxford contemporaries in particular, truly, madly and deeply to envy *him* now. To envy *his* financial success, *his* A-list-status on-set trailers, *his* VIP seats at Versace collections in Europe, *his* fame.

Unfortunately, those who are driven by envy themselves – that potent by-product of arrogance and insecurity that haunts so many talented actors – often wildly overrate it as a motivating trait of everyone else.

* * *

One of Hugh's close friends remarked stiffly to me, immediately after the prostitute scandal, that he expected I was 'relieved' by it. To be truthful, this was hard to deny. Not because I believed it would drive a stake through Hugh's brilliantly poised career, but because it revealed a powerfully defining glimpse of the real Hugh. The act was characteristic, not aberrational. It exposed the private limits to his publicly vaunted loyalty to Elizabeth and his somewhat unoriginal concept of a 'naughty' sexual thrill.

Hugh conspicuously failed to answer Jay Leno's question, 'What the hell were you *thinking*?' I think I can answer it here. Hugh was almost certainly laughing scornfully to himself that night on Sunset Strip: 'If *only* the world could see me now!' Hugh got his wish.

By the winter of 1995, Hugh looked – professionally – to have survived the scandal. Like O.J. Simpson, whose trial Hugh had followed so avidly, this actor too had been found not guilty. Hugh had succeeded in parlaying the publicity into personal star power. He was, the world over, a news gossip item if he so much as sneezed. Even CNN carried solemn reports of Hugh's fourth speeding offence in four years when he was convicted of driving at 98 miles per hour in his black 2.6-litre Mercedes after a day on set in Devon filming.

Now he had his phalanx of publicists to steer him through the next stage of his career: Leslee Dart, a strictly A-list publicist, in New York; and Richard Lovett, one of the hottest, most ambitious of the 'Young Turk' agents and the new president of the Creative Artists Agency (CAA), representing him in Los Angeles.

Both Hugh's post-scandal films were highly respectable vehicles: the period romp, *Restoration* and the adaptation, scripted by Emma Thompson, of Jane Austen's novel *Sense and Sensibility*, directed by the brilliant Taiwanese Ang Lee, who made the international sleeper hit movies *The Wedding Banquet* and *Eat, Drink, Man, Woman*.

Hugh's own production company, Simian Films, announced its first Grant-starring movie, the thriller *Extreme Measures*.

Divine Brown established herself as a semi-famous professional partygoer, wooed by gossip columnists on both coasts of the USA and looking cannier and sleeker with every appearance.

Elizabeth continued to model – in an oddly frumpy campaign – for Estée Lauder, duck questions about her commitment to Hugh, act in B-movies and announce to the world, via her close friend and media confessor William Cash, that she was now considering embracing Catholicism. Apparently, quoth William, because this was what lots of famous people did. The Hugh Grant–Elizabeth Hurley nuptials were not announced. I doubt they ever will be.

Like everyone remotely associated with Hollywood, I am guilty of Hollywood hypocrisy. I wouldn't be writing about people like Hugh if they weren't famous, and they wouldn't be famous if people like me weren't writing about them. So it goes on. Hugh is a star. A big one now. I don't doubt that I could be charmed by Hugh all over again.

Charmed. But not fooled.

INDEX